KV-002-362

Entertaining television

MANCHESTER
1824

Manchester University Press

Entertaining television

The BBC and popular television culture in the 1950s

SU HOLMES

Manchester University Press

Manchester and New York

distributed exclusively in the USA by Palgrave Macmillan

Copyright © Su Holmes 2008

The right of Su Holmes to be identified as the author of this work has been asserted by her in accordance with the Copyright, Designs and Patents Act 1988.

Published by Manchester University Press
Oxford Road, Manchester M13 9NR, UK
and Room 400, 175 Fifth Avenue, New York, NY 10010, USA
www.manchesteruniversitypress.co.uk

Distributed exclusively in the USA by
Palgrave Macmillan, 175 Fifth Avenue, New York,
NY 10010, USA

Distributed exclusively in Canada by
UBC Press, University of British Columbia, 2029 West Mall,
Vancouver, BC, Canada V6T 1Z2

British Library Cataloguing-in-Publication Data
A catalogue record for this book is available from the British Library

Library of Congress Cataloging-in-Publication Data applied for

ISBN   978 0 7190 7791 3   *hardback*

First published 2008

17 16 15 14 13 12 11 10 09 08   10 9 8 7 6 5 4 3 2 1

Typeset in Sabon
by Servis Filmsetting Ltd, Stockport, Cheshire
Printed in Great Britain
by Biddles Ltd, King's Lynn

Contents

This book is dedicated to viewers of British television in the 1950s (particularly, of course, those who were watching the BBC). It is especially dedicated to my parents Jenny and Chris Holmes.

Figures

All images Copyright BBC.

Acknowledgements

I would like to thank the University of Kent and the British Academy for funding the research for this book. Thanks also go to the staff at the BBC Written Archive Centre – especially Els Boonen, who shared my enthusiasm for the project, while wading through my enormous photocopying requests. Friends and colleagues, especially Deborah Jermyn, Andrew Klevan, Nick Rumens and Aylish Wood, offered valuable intellectual and personal support during the writing of this book. Finally, thanks go to Manchester University Press for supporting the spirit of the project, and for publishing *Entertaining Television: The BBC and Popular Television Culture in the 1950s*.

Part of Chapter 2 was previously published as "(Re)visiting *The Grove Family* – 'Neighbours to the Nation' (1954–57): Television History and Approaches to Genre", *New Review of Film and Television*, 4 (3), December 2006, pp. 287–310.

Parts of Chapter 3 were previously published as "The 'Give-Away' Shows – Who is Really Paying?: 'Ordinary' People and the Development of the British Quiz Show (1945–58)", *Journal of British Cinema and Television*, 3 (2), 2006, pp. 284–303, and "But the Question is – is it all Worth Knowing?: Quiz Shows on 1950s British Television", *Media, Culture and Society*, 49 (1), pp. 65–86.

Introduction

In 1955, the Producer of the BBC's fictional serial *The Grove Family* (1954–57) made the following comment about the programme's billing in the *Radio Times*:

> I understand . . . that . . . [the] word "popular" was deleted from our billing. This may be policy, but I thought we were fighting against Commercial [television] and that some of our ideas may be changed. It's a small point, but you may wish to take it up.[1]

He received a scribbled reply from Ronald Waldman, the Head of Light Entertainment, which reads: "I suppose the theory is that it's for the <u>viewers</u> to decide . . . whether the family is popular!! This show proves all!".[2]

The same year, the BBC were discussing the idea of producing a "problem" or "counselling" programme for television. The Head of Talks, Leonard Miall, explained:

> [I] saw and listened to a large number of them when I was in America. They make compelling listening. But it is listening of an eavesdropping variety and it puts the listener or viewer into the position of a spiritual Peeping Tom. I hope we shall not go in for them. I know we would draw an enormous audience if we did.[3]

These examples explicitly address questions of the *popular*, and invoke some of the different meanings associated with this term. For example, in exploring definitions of "popular culture", Raymond Williams notes various possible interpretations, ranging from "inferior kinds of work", culture which is "well liked by the people", "work deliberately setting out to win favour with the people", to culture which is "made by the people" (1983: 237). The first three definitions circle around the BBC examples. In both of the cases above, "popular" television is seen as something largely decided by viewers ("well-liked by the people"), and in this respect, it has a quantitative dimension. In relation to *The Grove*

Family, it is understood that viewers will make the programme popular simply by watching it. This may also be the case with the "problem" programme, but here we see how the popular, not coincidentally equated with America, is explicitly conceived as an "inferior kind of work", and something to be deplored. The idea of attracting an "enormous audience", particularly with programming which might provide questionable pleasures and desires, is seen as undermining the cultural mission of public service. Significantly, both of these exchanges take place in 1955, the year that saw the advent of commercial television in Britain and the end of the BBC's monopoly. This certainly ushered in much political, institutional and cultural debate about the status of "popular" television, and how the BBC was to situate itself in relation to this terrain.

These case studies immediately bring into view the unique and often difficult relationship between public service and the popular, and both programmes are seen as having an uneasy relationship with the BBC's identity. But at the same time, they are nevertheless very much part of its television service. There is no evidence to suggest that the BBC don't want *The Grove Family* to be popular: the exchange simply indicates that they don't wish to shout about it, and thus risk being seen as "deliberately setting out to win favour with the people" (Williams, 1983: 237). While the discussion of the "problem" show might point toward a blanket suppression of the popular, the BBC did in fact produce such a programme and only four months later, *Is This Your Problem?* (1955–57) went on air. These programmes represented negotiations with the popular, and this is what *Entertaining Television* is all about. It explores BBC television's relations with popular programme culture in the 1950s, ranging from the "soap opera", the quiz/game show, the problem show, to television's circulation of celebrity culture. Commercial television (ITV) is clearly integral to the context from which these programmes emerged, but the focus is on the BBC.

The BBC and popular television in the 1950s (*Surely* you mean ITV?)

The BBC has dominated the writing of British television history, and work on ITV has only more recently come to the fore (Holland, 2006, Thumim, 2004). Cathy Johnson and Rob Turnock's illuminating collection *ITV Cultures* opens by explaining that:

> ITV has not been readily understood as a producer of "quality" programming, instead being popularly associated with lowbrow quiz and game shows, light entertainment and action adventure series . . . This is in contrast to the broader tendency to associate those programmes that have received "serious" academic and critical attention with the BBC. (2005: 3)

As Johnson and Turnock note, this also constructs a false opposition between public service and commercial values: ITV was set up as an extension of the public service concept from the start, itself a measure of the degree to which Reithian values "still pervaded broadcasting, and . . . of a more general distrust of unfettered money-making" (Crisell, 2001: 90). But this opposition also has implications for how the BBC is perceived. If ITV has not been taken seriously enough, the BBC is sometimes taken too seriously. For many, the title of this book might appear to be a contradiction in terms. Conventional narratives suggest that some of the genres and topics considered here – soap opera, quiz/game shows or an appetite for "celebrity culture" – were more the province of commercial television. The BBC is not perceived as the producer of "popular" television at all in the 1950s, whether in terms of cultural values or audience ratings.

In discussing perceptions of the BBC versus ITV in the 1950s, Janet Thumim has argued that "each institution was summarised . . . in popular discourse, by epithets thought to characterise their intentions and performance: hence the BBC was 'stuffy', 'paternalist', 'priggish', whilst ITV was 'vulgar', 'brash', 'slick' " (2004: 27). As her use of the past tense implies, Thumim locates this popular discourse as circulating at the time. This claim is not in itself problematic, but it is difficult to separate it from the extent to which "a substantial myth has grown up, based on a picture of the energetic . . . showbiz visionaries [of ITV] elbowing aside the complacent bureaucrats of the BBC" (Black, 1972: 109). Like all myths, this opposition contains elements of truth, but it is also the product of a number of "common sense" assumptions which require revisitation (Johnson and Turnock, 2005: 4).

The discussion so far can be seen as interrogating what Jason Jacobs calls the relationship between the "macro-overview of broadcasting history" and the more local analyses of specific genres or texts (2000: 9). In focusing on the institutional history of the BBC, interventions such as Asa Briggs's *The History of Broadcasting in the United Kingdom* (volumes 1–5) have offered an influential model of such a macro-overview, although the scope of his work did not include an analysis of the programmes themselves. Since the increasing interest in television history in the early 1990s, scholars have attempted to combine these perspectives (e.g. Corner, 1991, Jacobs, 2000, Sydney-Smith, 2002, Thumim, 2002a, 2002b, Thumim, 2004, Holmes, 2005a). But the institutional narratives preceded the archival interest in programme forms, and they are often invoked as a backdrop to contextualise studies of programmes, genres and audiences. This is in many ways a practical necessity, and this book clearly draws on this approach. But more than simply contributing "detail", programme studies also offer the opportunity to complicate or challenge wider institutional narratives.

This is not to homogenise the idea of institutional studies. Such studies vary in their focus and approach, and range across official histories (Briggs, 1965, 1979, 1995, Sendall, 1982), "inside" perspectives offered by television personnel (Thomas, 1977, Wyndham-Goldie, 1977), to studies which, while aiming to document an institutional history, include a greater focus on the programmes themselves, and the social and cultural contexts from which they emerged (Scannell and Cardiff, 1991). The point is not that institutional studies have necessarily fixed the BBC's historical identity in particular ways. Rather, it is important to consider how such evidence is *used* to frame and analyse programme case studies. Despite the increasingly self-reflexive attitude to television historiography which is now exhibited by television historians (see Corner, 2003, Bignell, 2005a, 2005b), the potentially complex relationship at work between institutional and programme histories would benefit from more debate.

Much of the pleasure in researching this book came from the element of *surprise* – whether this emerged from the discovery of policy decisions, representations in scripts and on screen, or from the existing traces of audience reception. Jacobs has usefully emphasised the importance of allowing for "chance and exploration" in one's approach, as "we have to be alive to the contingent opportunities that the archive may hide" (2006: 18). At the same time, it is important to qualify this emphasis on the unexpected. Researching the BBC programmes and genres examined here offered less the experience of sweeping away existing perceptions of BBC television in the 1950s than the sense of looking in two directions at once. As the programmes mentioned at the start of this introduction might hint, case studies could confirm *and* challenge historical assumptions simultaneously. It is precisely this contradictory dialectic which the book aims to capture.

Television studies and television history: connecting past and present

The study of drama once dominated the writing of British television history, particularly that associated with the "Golden Age" of the 1960s. This also reflected the rather masculine, middle-class bias which had structured the development of British television historiography. There are now signs of change, with studies of popular fiction (Sydney-Smith, 2002, Thumim, 2004), current affairs (Holland, 2006), magazine programming (Thumim, 2004), cinema programmes (Holmes, 2005a), cookery shows (Moseley, 2006) and natural history programming

(Wheatley, 2006) all emerging from archival research. Furthermore, one of the earliest interventions in the study of British television programme cultures, *Popular Television in Britain: Studies in Cultural History*, edited by John Corner and published in 1991, actually marked a clear break with the emphasis on "serious" drama some time ago, moving across popular comedy, sport, teenage music programmes and television celebrity. *Popular Television in Britain* also encompassed the BBC *and* ITV, and as its title would suggest, we do not necessarily find in it the polarised construction of the two channels which this introduction has outlined.

Yet the possibilities offered by Corner's book were not always taken up, and if they were, they took some time to take hold in British television historiography. In 2002, and in introducing her *Beyond Dixon of Dock Green: The Early British Police Drama*, Susan Sydney-Smith (2002) still saw fit to comment that the historical emphasis on the single play, as well as the prevailing framework of art and authorship, had left popular fiction, and a far wider spectrum of non-fiction programming, somewhat ignored. This reflects the extent to which, although television studies may have increasingly embraced the popular, it has occupied an uneasy place in the writing of British television *history*. Particularly when compared to the American context, "there has to date been little written about the 'beginnings' of popular generic forms" in Britain (Sydney-Smith, 2002: 2). This idea of "beginnings" is intended to be reflected in the title of this book. *Entertaining Television* not only focuses attention on a particular aspect of the BBC's remit: it also pivots on the sense that the idea of television itself was still being "entertained".

The privileging of drama has not simply lead to a neglect of a wider range of programming: it has also had significant implications for how the *aesthetic* development of British television has been understood. Jacobs observes how "television drama is typically foregrounded, rightly or wrongly, as emblematic of the aesthetic state of the medium as a whole" (Jacobs, cited in Sydney-Smith, 2002: 6). What the close-up meant in debates about 1950s television drama does not necessarily indicate the meanings it carried in relation to other spheres of programming. With regard to television drama, the intimacy of the close-up might have been praised for its affinity with a penetrating "microscope" (Jacobs, 2000: 122), but this same shot positively repulsed critics when it came to television's treatment of famous faces in the 1950s. With respect to programmes such as *This is Your Life* or *Face to Face* (Chapter 5), critics were horrified at the sight of famous people crying on television. In fact, one critic was appalled that the "traditionally introvert British nation appeared to welcome the chance of crying in public, weeping before an audience, or discussing their emotions, religion and sex-life within sight and earshot of 12 million neighbours".[4]

This description may seem familiar to the contemporary viewer – perhaps curiously evocative of talk shows or celebrity Reality TV. If so, this connection is pertinent to the historical intervention this book seeks to make. The fact that the popular has an ambiguous role in British television history reflects on, while also contributing to, a degree of separation between television studies and television history. In his article "Finding data, reading patterns, telling stories: issues in the historiography of television", Corner rightly highlights how a "question of importance" is:

> the way in which historical writing. . . relates to the relevant area of contemporary study. How does television history relate to television studies? What connection does it make with the guiding theories and concepts, what impact does it seek to have not only on non-historical research but also on pedagogy? (2003: 276)

While "television history" and "television studies" are clearly intersecting spheres, there is still a tendency to turn to television history if we want to "know something" about the past. In comparison, contemporary, and often popular, examples are used to explore key concepts and debates which are relevant to television as an object of study. In other words, it is possible to suggest that "television history" could have *more* impact on "non-historical research [and] . . . pedagogy" (ibid) than it currently does. In this regard, the case studies here aim to explicitly contribute to knowledge about the function and construction of television genre (Chapters 1–3), the role of "ordinary" people as performers (Chapters 3, 4 and 5), and conceptual approaches to television fame (Chapter 5).

Entertaining Television also aims to speak to the more contemporary agenda of television studies in other ways, as the comparisons made with Reality TV or the talk show may suggest. To be sure, even to even broach these links is to risk accusations of de-historicisation: television in the 1950s is *very* different, on so many levels, from television today. While we always analyse the past from the perspective of the present, and we cannot operate outside this temporal framework, Corner's discussion of television historiography rightly argues for the need to recognise the "double dangers" of both an "over-distanced approach (the past very much as 'another country') and an undue proximity (the past as . . . 'today with oddities')" (2003: 277). These outer limits also dramatise the contradictory experience of viewing 1950s television – it can seem familiar and unfamiliar, recognisable, but strange. But I want to suggest here that being overly nervous about making connections *across* television history can also be disabling: we can miss opportunities to explore historical links which can be be productive and revealing. In this respect I share Corner's view that an "enriched sense of 'then' produces, in its differences and commonalities combined, a stronger and more imaginative sense of 'now' " (2003: 275).

A number of the programmes examined in this book, particularly those focusing on the televisual display of celebrities and "ordinary" people, were discussed in terms which now seem evocative of the "tabloidisation" debate. Programmes ranging from the highly celebratory *This is Your Life* to the rather more sober remit of *Is this Your Problem?* were regularly referred to as reprehensible forms of "peepshow television", and as inciting the "morbid curiosity" of the 1950s viewer. But while the debate about the tabloidisation of the medium became particularly visible within the political economy of 1980s/1990s television (see Dovey, 2000), its contours are not new (see Shattuc, 1997). Discussions about what constituted *commercially driven* programming, particularly at the level of aesthetics, subject matter and audience address, were prominent in 1950s Britain, not least of all because it witnessed the end of the public service monopoly and the birth of ITV.

Chapter 1 explores in more detail why and how the programmes examined here might be conceptualised as popular. But it is important to state that all were classified by the BBC as outside the purview of "serious programming" (which is "positively intelligent in nature").[5] All occupied a relationship with seriality, many emerged through relations with "America", and all were seen by critics, and sometimes by the BBC, as linked to the Corporation's attempt to compete with ITV. The programmes all garnered large audiences (sometimes spectacularly so), and this contributed to their derided and/or controversial status (Chapters 3–5).

If the programmes discussed in this book can be seen as having an uneasy relationship with public service, this is illuminated by Jerome Bourdon's (2004) article, "Old and new ghosts: public service television and the popular – a history". Bourdon identifies what he calls the six major "ghosts" to dramatise the often difficult relationship between public service television and popular appeal. As he explains:

> Why ghosts? From the start, massive (popular) pleasure was triggered by programmes that did not fit the educative and cultural ideals of public service. As a consequence, the popular has been regularly denied. But, as the manifestations of the popular were too many and too powerful, they were just like ghosts whose existence was denied, but whose presence was strongly felt. Public service television had no choice but to find compromises between its commitment to be primarily an instrument of education or culture and the necessity of adapting itself to the popular. (2004: 284)

Bourdon lists "peepshow" television, parading the "exhibition of suffering" and encouraging voyeurism, as ghost number six (2004: 298). While he suggests that popular factual programming, in the form of talk shows and Reality TV, represents the most recent embodiment of the popular to challenge public service ideals, my discussion above suggests that it is indeed fitting to see this challenge *as a ghost* – with resonant historical precursors in television's early years. In fact, the topics/genres covered in this book fortuitously mirror the "ghosts" that Bourdon sets out, whether taking in game shows, stars, seriality, "numbers" (ratings), "America" or voyeurism (2004: 284). Implicitly or explicitly, the programmes explored operate at the axis of some, or all, of these categories, and in this respect they can be seen to add weight to Bourdon's wider thesis here. In summarising his argument, Liesbet van Zoonen suggests that this history "demonstrates the repetitive failure of public broadcasting in Europe to come to terms with the popular and to develop a constructive incorporation of the popular as part of its mission" (van Zoonen, 2004: 274). Yet while the quotation from Bourdon suggests that "the popular has been regularly denied", it also pivots on the idea of a negotiation *with* the popular which, as *The Grove Family* and the "problem show" have already made clear, is very different to refusal or suppression. If following the logic of the latter route, they wouldn't have existed at all. But a wealth of archival material attests to the fact that they did.

The "beginnings" of generic forms?

In aiming to contribute to knowledge about the beginnings of popular generic, it is necessary to recognise, as Sydney-Smith does, that genres they "do not arrive 'ready-made'" (2002: 5). Yet in discussing popular drama on British television at this time, Thumim has suggested that:

> Within the broad field of popular drama and comedy series [genre] was relatively uncontentious: producers and viewers quickly arrived at a consensus whereby broad differentiations such as comedy, Western, gangster, crime/police were functional descriptors of programme content and address. (2004: 126)

This is quite a substantial claim, particularly when criticism has increasingly foregrounded the discursive, and thus often unstable and contingent, nature of generic categories. Building on previous approaches adopted in film studies (Neale, 1990, Altman, 1999), Jason Mittell's *Genre and Television: From Cop Shows to Cartoons* (2004a) has argued for the value of a discursive approach to television genre. Rather than simply approaching genre as an "inherently textual element", it is important to examine how generic categories are also articulated, activated and produced by a programme's wider intertextual framework. Given that, in researching 1950s television, the programmes themselves sometimes no longer exist, Mittell's approach seems particularly attractive to television history, while it also offers a further methodological and epistemological perspective on the question, how can we "know" a text that has not survived in audiovisual form?

Based on a Foucauldian conception of discourse (frameworks of thinking which take place within wider systems of social and cultural power), Mittell's paradigm points us toward the political function of generic categories. As he expands, we "should focus on the breadth of discursive enunciations around any given instance, mapping out as many articulations of genre as possible and situating them within larger cultural contexts and relations of power" (2004b: 174). The goal, then, is not to arrive at a "proper" definition, but to explore how genres are culturally defined, interpreted and evaluated, and this process should be recognised as far from neutral. For example, the bid to categorise quiz/game shows as "give-away" programmes (the critics), aims to activate very different meanings when compared to the use of the term "audience-participation" programme (the BBC). Furthermore, as Chapter 2 explores in relation to *The Grove Family*, the ambiguous currency of the term "soap opera" in relation to 1950s British television leads to a wider examination of the generic struggle surrounding the programme, and its intersection with discourses of public service, realism, gender and class. In summary, rather than taking their existence for granted, Mittell's emphasis on retrieving a plurality of generic labels leads us toward thinking about how and why generic categories are conferred.

Journeying into the archives: evidence, approach and imagination

The problem of access to programme culture confronts all historical studies of television. Institutionally, technologically and culturally, early television programming was regarded as live and ephemeral, and there is almost a complete absence of audiovisual material from the period before 1955 (Jacobs, 2000: 4). The programmes examined in this book begin in or around this juncture, and the availability of audiovisual material varied considerably between case studies. Only two editions of *The Grove Family* exist, and other programmes, such as *Is This Your Problem?* or the range of BBC quiz and game shows, have not survived in audiovisual form at all. In contrast, many editions of *This is Your Life* have survived, in part because they were perceived as having a certain cultural, if not critical value (documenting the life of a famous person), as well as a long-term institutional value (clips from the programme have often been used in subsequent profiles of film, sport or music stars).

As television historiography has grown, scholars have increasingly turned to written sources to reconstruct programmes from the 1950s, either in conjunction with existing audiovisual sources, or as the primary textual evidence. The BBC Written Archive Centre, aptly described by Sydney-Smith as a "veritable treasure trove" (2002: 15), has been recognised as housing extraordinarily valuable material, ranging across production and policy memos, scripts, press cuttings and Audience Research Reports. While the use of these sources has become increasingly pivotal to the construction of British television history (and thus accepted as a valid method of historical enquiry), the internal evidence from the BBC necessarily offers a very particular perspective on programme culture. With the official written records obviously produced by "the people in charge" (who could in fact be quite remote from the processes of production) (Buscombe, 1980: 77), such evidence might perpetuate conceptions of the BBC's elitist identity, thus conflicting with the project of this book.

But just as the programmes seem to simultaneously confirm and challenge existing conceptions of the BBC's institutional identity, so the experience of using the archival material can be cast as similarly contradictory. The written evidence can offer an exciting, privileged and even *intimate* sense of access which sits alongside, and intersects with, the image of a remote and unfamiliar world. The same contradictory dialectic can be associated with the reconstruction of the programmes themselves. Jacobs formulated the conception of the "ghost text" – the term he uses to describe the reconstruction of programmes which "do not exist in their original audio-visual form but . . . exist as shadows, dispersed and refracted among buried files, bad memories, a flotsam of fragments" (2000: 14). This *does* capture the simultaneous presence yet absence of the programme in question, and when audiovisual material is absent (as is the case, for example, with *Is This Your Problem?*), the parameters of analysis depend as much on imagination as they do on existing traces of evidence. Nevertheless, the idea of a "ghost text" downplays the extent to which access to a programme through the written archives, particularly at the level of "inside" institutional knowledge, can be far *greater* than is often possible with contemporary programme studies. This is a *different kind* of access, certainly, but not necessarily one that is more restrictive.

This may of course be countered by the suggestion that this depends on what you want to find out. Johnson and Turnock argue that although it is possible to construct some understanding of the style, content and form of television programmes from written sources, these are "no replacement for viewing the programmes themselves" (2005: 5). But even when we are talking about the detail of visual style, aesthetics and audience address, this hierarchy between audiovisual and written sources is not unproblematic. Press reception has played a particularly central role in the research for this book, and Thumim describes why such evidence holds a particularly charged fascination for us today:

> [Re]views at this time almost always . . . have a subtext. On the surface might be a discussion of "last night's viewing", but it was invariably a discussion pointing towards an assessment of *the very existence of television*, not yet [itself] taken for granted. (2004: 18; my emphasis)

Press commentary does not represent the responses of the "ordinary" viewer, but it does enables us to tap into some of the (often fleeting) meanings, associations and concerns which circulated around television when it was still seen as "new". If we wanted to explore, for example, the meanings *surrounding* the use of the close-up, the "programmes themselves" can only tell us so much (and I discovered that even the judgement of what is "close" emerges in reception). From this perspective, it is also possible to suggest that the audiovisual record is "not a substitute" for the written resource. This is not to play down the interpretative agency of the researcher, nor to argue that the historical nature of reception makes it impossible for us to draw textual conclusions ourselves. But it does foreground the significance of thinking about how we begin to do this, and the different perspectives which available evidence may offer.

Chapter summaries

Chapter 1 focuses on the institutional context from which the programmes examined in this book emerged. While acknowledging that the concepts of both "public service" and the "popular" are difficult to define, the chapter examines how they were *interpreted* by the BBC, and how their relationship changed over time, moving across the early history of radio and television, up until the advent of ITV. The chapter then sets out how and why the case studies examined in the book might be categorised as "popular".

Chapter 2 explores *The Grove Family* (BBC, 1954–57), which has secured a certain visibility in British television history due to its status as "British television's first soap opera". Precisely because soap opera is often perceived as a highly commercial genre (with its roots in American commercial radio), we are primed to expect that what is now perceived as the BBC's first television soap is likely to be tempered by instruction and education. Adopting a discursive approach to genre (Mittell, 2004a), and drawing on new archival research into the programme, Chapter 2 revisits this categorisation with the aim of reassessing how *The Grove Family* has been categorised and perceived. In exploring the generic clusters through which the programme negotiated its identity (principally documentary, comedy, crime and melodrama), the chapter examines *The Grove Family*'s bid to address a wide audience, particularly one with an expanding class base, while exploring how this address was shaped by its complex investment in realism.

Chapter 3 details how the quiz or game show, or to use the dominant term from the time, the "give-away" show, has been used to map sharp differences between the BBC and ITV in the 1950s, particularly in relation to notions of popular appeal. But it is possible that the impact of *television* on the genre has often been read as simply the impact of ITV. If we are to begin to understand the response to the "give-away" show in the mid-to late 1950s, there is a need to bring the BBC back into the picture, not only in terms of television, but with regard to the previous history of BBC radio. While there were certainly differences in how each channel approached the genre, an examination of the role played by prizes, knowledge and "ordinary" people as performers demonstrates that the comparative relations between BBC and ITV here were more complex than existing accounts imply.

If the quiz/game show can be seen as constructing a utopian space, offering the promise of "wealth without work" and an accelerated image of the affluent society, it also sat alongside a less positive image of life in post-war Britain. In this regard, Chapter 4 focuses on the BBC's "problem" or "private life" programme, *Is This Your Problem?* (1955–57), in which members of the public asked the advice of an expert panel (as represented by a doctor, a university vice chancellor and a member of the clergy). In revisiting the long-standing debates about the relationship between "public service" and "public interest", the chapter examines the programme's ambiguous positioning in between the BBC and the new welfare state. It also explores how the visibility of the subjects – the people with "problems" – emerged from a contradictory framework which balanced the hegemonic discourse of the panel with the disruptive implications of bringing marginalised social subjects into view. Indeed, while respecting the historical specificity of the programme in hand, the chapter argues that it is productive to consider the conceptual affinities between *Is This Your Problem?* and the later television talk show.

Finally, Chapter 5 explores television's relations with fame in the 1950s. Canonical conceptions of television fame have emphasised the qualities of intimacy, familiarity, proximity and ordinariness (Langer, 1981, Ellis, 1992). But a key aim of Chapter 5 is to bring out the different meanings which circulated around television's relations with fame in the 1950s, recognising that television constructs its own "personalities", while it simultaneously circulates personae from other domains. After setting out the institutional and cultural discourses which surrounded television fame, the chapter returns to the case study of *The Grove Family* as an example of television-produced fame. It then moves on to examine what is undoubtedly the most controversial programme examined in this book: *This is Your Life*. The chapter details how this *This is Your Life* became a privileged site for debates about television's renegotiation of the boundaries of public/private, particularly with regard to audiences' cultural access to famous selves.

Notes

1 John Warrington to Ronald Waldman, 19 July 1955. T12/137/4.
2 As above; original emphasis.
3 Leonard Miall to Head of Religious Broadcasting, 24 May 1955. T32/1,777/1.
4 *Sunday Telegraph*, 14 May 1961.
5 Undated memo, "Serious Programmes in Peak Hours", T16/149/2.

1

Public service and the popular: debates and developments

> In its function as an "audience getter" and "audience holder", Light Entertainment must adhere to certain basic principles of production. The producer . . . must consider closely the impact of his opening moments. These, if compulsive, will hold the audience beyond what is known in US television as the "nuts point" – . . . the moment at which the viewer might mutter the fatal words "Aw, nuts!" and switch over to an alternative channel.[1]

This quotation reflects on the BBC's approach to television Light Entertainment by 1960. It envisages BBC programming in highly competitive terms, and it does so by invoking the model of American television. The concept of competition is also expressed in terms of a "commercial" aesthetic – the emphasis on a "compulsive" opening which will ensnare an increasingly promiscuous audience.

But while the emphasis on commerciality is striking, as is the keen readiness to learn lessons from American television, this scenario still confirms conventional historical accounts of how public service broadcasting in Britain, as elsewhere, was reshaped by the advent of competition. Since the shift from the "era of scarcity" in television broadcasting to the era of "availability" (and then "plenty") (Ellis, 2000), a shift which has involved the deregulation of television and multiplication of channels, it has become common in the European context to discuss the increased marketisation of television, and the consequent weakening of a public service framework. Within this process, public service broadcasters are seen as losing their once distinct identity, and becoming more like their commercial rivals. In Britain and elsewhere, 1960 is still clearly early in this process. The Pilkington Committee (report published in 1962) famously contrasted the BBC and ITV, accusing ITV of failing to provide a fair and balanced repertoire of programmes, of screening a preponderance of "trivial" fare, and for failing to realise the social and cultural effects of the medium. In contrast, the BBC, who "know good broadcasting; [because] by and large,

they are providing it" (p. 46), were praised for screening a larger proportion of serious programmes, for displaying a greater level of balance in
programme range and scheduling, and for commanding public trust and
confidence. While there has been some debate as to how the BBC, and
other public service broadcasters, have adapted to competition in the
longer term (Wieten et al, 2000, van Zoonen, 2004), there has also been a
general consensus that the BBC and ITV came to occupy a shared ground
in the 1960s and 1970s. They represented what Paddy Scannell termed a
"cosy duopoly", offering broadly similar programme fare and attracting
a roughly equal share of the audience (1990: 19).

But to posit this as a shift assumes a particular picture of the previous
decade – how the BBC responded to the advent of commercial television
when it first emerged. This response was more complex than is often perceived, but this book does not set out to "prove" that the BBC was simply
changed by ITV (thus essentially demonstrating that the process of "commercialisation" began earlier than is assumed). First, such a perspective
would leave many traditional assumptions about the BBC untouched,
including, for example, those relating to the previous history of radio.
Second, and as the Pilkington Committee also observed in 1962, the
"effect of competition on the BBC's service cannot be known with certainty" (p. 44). To gauge this "effect" would involve comparing "the
[BBC] service as it [is] now . . . with what it would have been if independent television had never existed" (ibid), and this is a practical impossibility. To be sure, changes in the BBC's policies, schedules and output
as the 1950s progressed *can* sometimes be linked directly to the advent
of ITV. But they are often also inseparable from the fact that this period
saw television develop into a mass medium.

Not all of the programmes examined by *Entertaining Television* emerge
from the same department. Many were produced by Light Entertainment,
but others were produced by Talks. But they all fell outside what the BBC
categorised as "serious programming", apparently spanning "News and
Current Affairs, talks and discussions, documentaries, outside broadcasts
of national and other major events (but not sport), certain music, opera
and ballet programmes and other programmes of a positively intelligent
nature".[2] (Drama was not included as the "distinction between serious
and non-serious is too subtle".) Although it proceeded to use the terms
"serious" and "light", the Pilkington Committee acknowledged that
what constitutes each category of programming is difficult to measure –
essentially because they are the product of a subjective point of view
(p. 41).

With regard to the internal discourse of the BBC, it is certainly the case
that these terms were conferred in highly opportunistic and flexible ways.

For example, *The Grove Family* (Chapter 2) was "just entertainment" if "the wisdom of some of the activities of the . . . family" were questioned, but it was defensively linked to a more sober remit ("vitally concerned with standards of conduct, law . . . social problems, and facts and morals"[3]), if a scriptwriter seemed to be flouting the programme's standards of "taste". Certainly, this may offer an alternative perspective on the relationship between popular programming and public service, illustrating Dorothy Hobson's wider argument, in relation to soap opera, that "it is in some of the most popular genres that public service is at its most powerful" (2003: 159). Hobson's point draws attention to the fact that the public values of popular programming are often overlooked, precisely because the public and the popular are seen as a contradiction in terms (van Zoonen, 2004: 277). Yet to map this dichotomy also implies that such categories can be clearly defined: that it is possible for the popular (often equated with entertainment) to be siphoned off from more socially valuable, because instructive, public service material. This opposition has a long history, and as Liesbet van Zoonen explains:

> [P]ublic service broadcasting, generally considered one of the core institutions of the public sphere . . . is firmly rooted in the modernist tradition of Enlightenment, which is distinguished by a belief in rationality, progress and the capacity for people to take control over their own lives. Popular culture, with its roots in folklore and orality, has none of that and has been articulated with leisure and consumption rather than with engagement and citizenship. (2004: 277)

Television is now seen as part of popular culture, and discussions about the status of popular television have often been influenced by wider debates about the popular in media and cultural studies (e.g. Fiske, 1987). But van Zoonen's quote highlights the need to be more specific, and to situate the concept in relation to particular historical, institutional and cultural contexts. When under the reign of public service, television in Britain, and indeed radio before it, was not unambiguously part of popular culture. While van Zoonen refers to its roots in folklore and orality, popular culture is more often identified as emerging after industrialisation and urbanisation (with the term regularly used interchangeably with "mass"/"commercial" culture) (Storey, 2001: 7). BBC radio and television in Britain was (and is) disseminated through a mass apparatus, but historically, the status of the commercial is less clear: the public Corporation of the BBC was set up as a non-profit-making institution.

The next section considers the development of public service, as well as its changing relationship with discourses of the popular, before clarifying how the programmes examined in this book can be positioned in relation to this sphere. The problems involved in defining public service have been widely discussed, and as Scannell has famously observed, despite its apparently common sense use, what public service actually means "can prove elusive" (1990: 11). For this reason it is more appropriate to consider how the concept has been interpreted, which also means examining how it has changed over time.

Entertaining the idea of public service

The BBC began radio transmissions in 1922 as the British Broadcasting Company, but on 1 January 1927 it became the British Broadcasting Corporation, a publicly funded organisation with statutory obligations (Crisell, 2001: 28). While established by a royal charter, the activities of the Corporation were mapped out by a licence and agreement conferred by the government. The BBC was famously obliged to "inform, educate and entertain", and more specifically, to report the proceedings of Parliament, provide political balance, and to broadcast government messages in a national emergency (ibid). The Sykes Committee (1923) argued that the wavebands "should be regarded as a valuable form of public property" (Scannell, 1990: 12), and that for this reason, broadcasting should not become an unrestricted commercial monopoly. Broadcasting in Britain was to be a non-profit making monopoly funded by a licence fee, and "public" in this sense carried a range of different meanings, referring to the notion of broadcasting being accessible to all, broadcasting acting in the common good or interest, and a state-related means of finance and organisation (van Zoonen, Hermes and Brants, 1998: 1).

Although entertainment was part of the public service remit, it has often been seen as "ground-bait" – something used to lure an audience to the "real" task of broadcasting: education (Kumar, 1986: 47). This view, and the wider historical emphasis on elitism, has much to do with Lord John Reith, Director General of the BBC from 1927 to 1938. Reith believed that to use so "great a scientific invention [as radio] for the purpose of 'entertainment' alone" would be a "prostitution of its powers and an insult to the character and intelligence of the people" (quoted in Briggs, 1961: 250), yet we should be wary of simply collapsing this with the reality of programme production and scheduling. As Briggs notes, in the very early years when Reith was pronouncing "pure entertainment", such as "jazz bands and sketches by humorists", as a prostitution of the powers of broadcasting, such culture featured prominently in BBC programming (1961: 251).

The rather vague category of entertainment was often conflated with ideas about that (perceived to be) preferred by the wider majority. As simply "giving the people what they want had never been sound BBC doctrine" (Briggs, 1979: 52), this further foregrounds why the BBC's relationship with majority tastes was uneasy. The term "popular" was not always used, although it is clear that the idea of majority tastes often stood in for it. But the extent to which these tastes were to be regulated and restrained did not simply express an innate dislike of the popular: it pointed to the significance of the BBC's mixed programming policy. Given that each listener was intended to be enriched by exposure to the *full* range of programming, the idea of a free market approach, in which audience demand would dictate broadcast output, was seen as a threatening force (and the idea that marketisation fosters homogenisation still has a currency in debates about the value of public service television today) (see Dahlgren, 2000: 26).

Public service broadcasting has traditionally grounded its arguments in questions of cultural value (MacCabe, 1986), so the charge of elitism was to some degree inevitable. The idea of "something for everyone" meant that people received much of what they did *not* want (Crisell, 2001: 33), while the aim to provide the "best" of everything was clearly, like definitions of the serious or light, based on highly subjective criteria rooted in discourses of class. It is often stressed, however, that BBC radio underwent a degree of popularisation in the mid- to late 1930s, a process then accelerated by the Second World War (Scannell and Cardiff, 1981). It was the recognition of a more diverse audience at the level of class, an "acceptance of an audience with different tastes and needs" (1981: 75), which gave rise to the restructuring of the BBC's post-war radio service in 1946. This manifested itself in the cultural streaming of the Home, Light and Third programmes (with the Third Programme representing the somewhat "highbrow" approach). This move was controversial within the BBC because it could be interpreted in different ways. It could be seen as the BBC's most vehement and organised attempt to improve the nation's taste, with the intention being to "lead the listener up the cultural scale" (Sinfield, 1989: 51). But it could also be interpreted as a rejection of the mixed programming policy which had provided the core infrastructure of Reith's conception of public service (Briggs, 1979: 76).

As Rob Turnock points out, however, this structure is significant in challenging the myth that the idea of competition emerged *with* ITV. There was already internal competition between programmes within the BBC, as well as competition between the BBC and the commercial radio station, Radio Luxembourg. Later on, there was competition between BBC radio and BBC television, and producers and schedulers were encouraged to heed this fact (Turnock, forthcoming). Furthermore, even if the concept of key competitive programmes would become more important with the advent of ITV, BBC radio, in the form of the Light Programme in particular, had long since conceptualised output in terms of "popular" or "castle" features which were designed to compete with Radio Luxembourg (Briggs, 1979: 52).

Here comes television – a "surfeit of entertainment shows"?

Television was to develop within this restructured context. Historians have argued that television was largely a post-war phenomenon, not only in Britain, but in other national contexts. Although the BBC Television Service began broadcasting on 2 November 1936, it was only received within a 40–100 mile radius of Alexandra Palace, and in about 400 households (Crisell, 2001: 77). Available to predominantly affluent viewers, the Television Service did not get a chance to develop before it was closed down for the war in 1939, reopening in 1946. Television's development in Britain, whether in terms of its institutional or aesthetic growth, or its social dissemination, was slow at this time, particularly when compared to the American example. This was in part due to the economic circumstances of post-war austerity, as the manufacture of non-essential items, including televisions, was restricted, as were the materials required to broaden the BBC's area of transmission (Stokes, 1999: 32–33). But the BBC's institutional attitude toward television has also been seen as a factor here. In 1937 the BBC calculated that one hour of television would cost twelve times as much to produce as the costliest hour of radio. The service thus resumed in 1946 "not so much with the expectation that it would develop as that it would need to be curbed" (Crisell, 2001: 80).

This raises questions about how television found its place within the BBC's post-war institutional context. Briggs argues that there was a strong "Light Programme influence" on television from the start (1979: 990), but this may reflect a residual antipathy for the medium as much as an assessment of the output itself. With the BBC Television Service representing the sole channel of a monopoly broadcaster, television could be perceived as offering a renewed opportunity to explore the Reithian principles of public service, particularly the policy of mixed programming, which some felt had been diluted by radio's cultural pyramid (Crisell, 2001: 79). Yet it has now become conventional in British television historiography to emphasise the BBC's wider disinterest in television. Often acknowledged here is the fact that Sir William Haley, the BBC's first post-war Director General, conceptualised television as the "natural extension of sound" (Briggs, 1979: 4), with the implication that the medium was be assimilated into existing institutional, and apparently, aesthetic structures. Sir George Barnes, chosen by Haley as the first Director of Television, was known to have shared Haley's view. He wanted television to remain under the same control as radio, as "on its own . . . television would encourage passivity and present a surfeit of entertainment shows" (Briggs, 1979: 6). This seems to assume that, unless carefully restrained and regulated, television might "naturally" embrace an identity as an unlicensed "pleasure machine" (Dahlgren, 2000: 31).

But it is worth sounding a note of caution here. The argument regarding institutional attitudes toward television has been collapsed with aesthetic concerns – the idea that the BBC were not very adept at thinking in "visual" terms, and were more comfortable dealing with the sound-based medium of radio (Wyndham-Goldie, 1977: 18–19). For one, this argument conflates the views of those at the forefront of the BBC's public discourse with the attitudes of writers, producers and directors, and it also denies the diversity of attitudes to television within the Corporation. While Haley may have been talking about television as the "natural extension" of sound, the documents shuttling between Programme Controllers, Heads of Department, writers, producers, directors and actors, were frequently pondering the new specificities, possibilities and challenges of television, and the wider issue of going "visual". In 1951, the Head of Television Light Entertainment, Ronald Waldman, was excitedly instructing producers to think in terms of the "standards of 'pure television' which we have set ourselves to achieve and maintain".[4] Certainly, this was the point at which television is seen to have increasingly resented "its radio ancestry" (Briggs, 1979: 7), and this in itself raises a key point. The emphasis on a period of "Radio-Vision" has been allowed to encompass the early development of BBC television right up until the advent of ITV. With regard to the case studies in this book, there *is* often a palpable anxiety about the visual possibilities of television, something aptly described by Thumim as the recognition that images "could not always be contained by the narrative structures within which they were located" (2004: 20). But rather than simply evidence of a particular set of institutional attitudes within the BBC, this also reflects personnel encountering, exploring and shaping the new aesthetic and social possibilities of television on a wider scale.

It was in the early 1950s that television began to see a more rapid expansion within the BBC. It was represented by its own department in 1950, and in 1952, Sir Ian Jacob succeeded Haley as Director General, and he was keen to push forward with television's development (Briggs, 1979: 9). It was also Jacob who was to oversee the BBC's shift from an institution dealing primary with radio, to one dealing primarily with television. This included the subsequent emergence of commercial television, which began broadcasting in the London area on 22 September 1955.

Here comes ITV!

In 1949 the Beveridge Committee recommended the continuation of the BBC's monopoly, but as the 1950s progressed, the Conservative government saw fit to reopen the monopoly debate, and pressure grew for an alternative service. Advocates of commercial television cited several reasons why the BBC's monopoly of television broadcasting should end. As acknowledged, some felt that the development of television in Britain had been held back by the BBC's institutional attitude toward television, and its apparently enforced subservience to radio. Crisell has outlined how other challenges emerged from the socio-political climate, and he cites a renewal of the process of democratisation that had been gathering pace before the war – the campaign to "let the people decide for themselves" (2001: 77). In this respect, the supporters of ITV cannily conflated the concepts of the "people" and the popular. This was most visibly seen by the pro-ITV group the Popular Television Association (PTA). As backed by set manufacturers, the advertising industry and Tory MPs, the PTA vigorously campaigned for the democratic possibility of "People's Television" (Sydney-Smith, 2002: 92). Others argued that when the Corporation reorganised its radio service into the Home, Light and Third structure, this had already marked a change in which responsibility for engaging with broadcast culture shifted from broadcaster to audience (Kumar, 1986: 55). From this perspective, the BBC itself had introduced an element of "democratic" choice where broadcasting was concerned, and ITV would merely accelerate this framework.

A further impetus behind the case for a second television channel was economic (Crisell, 2001). The newly arrived Conservative office of 1951 promoted the concept of rising affluence, famously encapsulated by the Conservative Prime Minister Harold Macmillan's declaration that "most of our people have never had it so good". The extent to which affluence was invoked as a "central economic, as well as ideological theme of the times" (Hill, 1986: 9) is explored in different ways throughout this book, as are the corresponding debates about the erosion of class boundaries. In the context of full employment, a rise in average earnings, and the growth in personal consumption and home ownership, key to the Conservative social imagery in the 1950s were families enjoying "the good things in life" (Laing, 1986: 12). The social dissemination of television was itself invoked as a key symbol of this context, or as the Conservative candidate for Bristol put it in 1955: "You do not queue for food and sweets. You can see more television aerials and cars – signs of prosperity" (Laing, 1986: 10). The combination of new techniques of mass production with newly available forms of credit produced an expanding consumer market. This in turn fostered a corresponding demand for advertising outlets, and it was seen that television could play a valuable role in this respect.

It is now difficult to fully comprehend the concerns that circulated around the introduction of advertising to British television. With the spectre of Americanisation looming large, many believed that "sponsored" broadcasting, a term used interchangeably with "Plug TV", would become a reality in Britain. Even after the Television Act (1954) announced the decision to implement spot advertising in "natural breaks", there remained a great deal of confusion over the matter, and a concern that advertisers would control programme content (Sendall, 1982: 98). The system which emerged was something of a compromise between those who wanted to end the BBC's monopoly, and those who "feared the worse excesses of American television" (Crisell, 2001: 86). This idea of a *regulated commercial* channel speaks more widely to the institutional framework which governed ITV's emergence.

The Independent Television Authority, which was to supervise the regional programme contractors, was a public body, occupying a role not dissimilar to the BBC's board of governors (Crisell, 2001: 90). Furthermore, it was a measure of the prevailing strength of a public service ethos that ITV was actually set up as an extension of this concept. The new channel still had to conform to a public service remit, with a duty to educate and inform as well as to entertain, and it was to operate under certain statutory obligations (which stipulated, for example, the inclusion of a news service and a proportion of religious programming). In this respect, it was actually not that different to the BBC (Turnock, forthcoming). It is of course possible to suggest that perceptions of difference are relative: British viewers had only known the BBC, and the viewer letters solicited by the press and magazines discuss differences between the channels at the level of programme balance, presentational address, or even "technical excellence".[5] But there was also a fair emphasis on similarity. As one (clearly disgruntled) viewer put it: "ITA, far from being the virile challenger we hoped for, is but a pale copy of the BBC in everything except its plugging . . . the whole set-up fairly reeks of broadcasting house".[6] The emphasis on difference has shaped the polarised constructions of BBC and ITV, at least when it comes to the 1950s. This perspective plays up conflict between individualised and oppositional institutions, and while this may have made for a more dramatic, as well as manageable, historical narrative, difference did not completely define how the co-existence of the two channels was first experienced.

"How do we interpret the competition?"

Eighteen months before commercial television began, the BBC's Board of Management enquired, "How do we interpret the competition?"[7] In certain histories, the dominant emphasis has been on the BBC's complacency, and its refusal to acknowledge the reality of competition. Black comments that "the BBC continued to prepare its schedule as though the competitor did not exist" (1972: 134), while Sendall describes how the ITV companies "awaited the BBC's counter-blow, and were puzzled when it did not arrive" (1982: 112). But the BBC was well aware from the start that, while their revenue did not depend on the size of the audience for each programme, the licence fee could not be justified if the number of BBC viewers substantially declined. As such, the position described by Black and Sendall would have been impossible to adopt in practice. By mid-1955 press reports were eagerly enquiring "Commercial TV: how will the BBC meet the new intruder?",[8] to which Sir George Barnes flatly insisted, "we shall compete".[9] This was an attitude taken up, and accelerated, by his successor, Sir Ian Jacob, and Jacob had little doubt that the BBC would need to compete for audiences (Briggs, 1995: 13).

The period 1954–55 had seen a significant increase in the financial resources allotted to television within the BBC. But with the advent of ITV, the BBC planned to produce twenty more programmes a week, while extending weekly transmissions from 36 to 49 hours (to mirror the schedule of ITV). The internal BBC publication, *The Competitor*, was first produced in February 1955, and it constantly monitored the programming and scheduling plans of the commercial contractors. This interest continued and intensified once the new channel went on air, although it is evident that exactly what to *do* with this information was still a matter for debate. Consider the following memo from the Producer of *The Grove Family*, John Warrington, to Ronald Waldman, the Head of Light Entertainment, in December 1955:

> Commercial television is transferring its top weekday show – . . . "Double Your Money" – to Wednesday night. I have been officially told that this is an effort to break the Wednesday night "Grove Family" hold on the viewing public. . . . Our viewing figures have proved that Wednesday night is [a night when] . . . the BBC holds complete monopoly. Added to this, [the writer of *The Grove Family*] Michael Pertwee lunched with an advertiser

who was paying for a Wednesday spot [at this time] and [he] received no
response at all . . . Other advertisers are refusing to take time on
Commercial [television when the programme is screened]. . . . If we are
really to battle with them, would it not be a good idea to transfer "The
Grove Family" to, say, Friday night? We would be using the Groves as a
pawn to upset the competition . . . I gather . . . that C.P.Tel is all in favour
of such tactics.[10]

In this instance, Waldman justifiably replies that this move would actually look like "a confession of weakness".[11] This response might well be
seen to confirm the argument that the BBC adopted a rather complacent
attitude, but it is worth noting the circumstances surrounding this particular case study: the BBC perceives that there is no need to change tack
because they are "on top". The memo above also indicates that the ITV
programme companies and the advertisers were highly interested in the
BBC's scheduling plans too.

It is possible to observe a shift in the BBC's institutional discourse surrounding the "competitor" in this period. In 1954, and before commercial television began, George Barnes was talking about how far "castle
programmes" for the "big battalions" should be sacrificed for programmes with more minority appeal, and there was also a renewed
emphasis on how "intelligent minority programmes" should try and
garner the widest public.[12] Only two years later in 1956, the debate was
about the degree to which *minority* programmes should be sacrificed for
"peak" or "castle" programmes, and there was an emphasis on how all
productions must consider their relationship "with mass appeal".[13]
Programmes should also fit a prearranged length and schedule pattern,
and at the level of audience address, they must "be compulsive . . . in
fact . . . immediately compulsive. There is no time for the slow development of a series on the air. It must succeed quickly or die".[14] Alongside
such comments, and in fact often within the same memo, it was certainly
still possible to discern the perennial argument that competition will
mean sacrificing "much that is of real value".[15] Yet it is possible to
observe the changing, or at least multiple, meanings associated with this
term "value" during the 1950s. By mid- to late decade, the Corporation's
description of programmes as valuable not only referred to their apparently "intrinsic" value (returning to the polarity constructed between
serious and light fare), but their role within a competitive broadcasting
ecology. For example, *This is Your Life* is "one of [the BBC's] . . . most
valuable properties" *because* it was a show that, at the level of audience
ratings, "ITV could not touch",[16] and *The Grove Family* was conceived
in similar terms.[17]

"We've got most viewers – BBC and ITV say": ratings discourse

It is often observed that ITV ushered in a greater emphasis on the inter-related strategies of seriality and fixed point scheduling – strategies which had not been wholly embraced by the BBC. As Bourdon reminds us, broadcasting was not intended to be used habitually: as a "formative experience, it was supposed to be about the disruption of regular daily life" (2004: 290). For ITV, fixed point scheduling was not simply about building and sustaining audiences: on an economic level, it was also crucial for advertisers to better target or predict audiences for particular programmes (Turnock, forthcoming). The BBC had long since engaged in audience research in radio and television, yet while the BBC's approach measured audience size, it was primarily set up to gauge quali-tative response (as measured by an "appreciation index"). But as Turnock observes, once ITV was on air, "viewers were . . . placed within the new economy of commercially organised broadcasting", and "adver-tisers and market researchers not only needed to know what audiences were viewing, but *when*" (Turnock, forthcoming). The BBC could not exist outside this framework, and as an example of viewing figures oper-ating as a form of "commodified knowledge", the BBC even sold some of its own audience research to the ITV contractors (ibid).

Once ITV began, the term "popular", especially in the press, was yoked explicitly to a quantitative index. Headings in the press which listed "Most Popular TV Programmes"[18] meant the most viewed. As Sendall observes: "Like it or not, the British newspaper readers were forced to live with weekly, sometimes daily, publicity about ratings. The appetite of the press for publishing the so-called 'top ten' . . . proved insatiable" (1982: 135). But Sendall's use of the term publicity is important. Given the argument, as developed by Ien Ang (1991), that television ratings produce a "fictive picture" of the audience, the func-tion of which (to sell audiences to advertisers) is more important than its accuracy, this evidence seems to demand a more self-reflexive and scep-tical gaze than it has so far received.

It is claimed that by February 1957, the BBC's own audience research indicated a 70%/30% split in ITV's favour (Sendall, 1982: 135), but the years 1955 and 1956 reveal a more unpredictable struggle between the channels. In November 1955, the BBC's *Ask Pickles* was top in the Nielson ratings, closely followed by ITV's *I Love Lucy, Sunday Night at the London Palladium* (ATV, 1955–67, 1973–74), the BBC's *The Grove Family*, ITV's *Showtime* and the BBC's *Amateur Boxing*.[19] The BBC's *What's My Line?, This is Your Life* and *Sportsview* made frequent appearances in the "Top Ten", as did ITV's *Take Your Pick, Double Your*

Money and *Dragnet*. It is also notable that the ratings discourse did impact upon the BBC's conception and promotion of its programmes. The introduction to this book opened with a discussion of how the word "popular" was deleted from *The Grove Family*'s billing in the *Radio Times*. Yet one year later in 1956, *What's My Line?* is regularly listed in the *Radio Times* as "TV's most popular panel game", positively trumpeting its claim to a large audience share.

But to read through the constant stream of press reports from the time is to follow a constantly changing narrative which seems uncertain of its own direction. Consider, for example, the headlines running from September 1955 to March 1956: "5 to 1 for the BBC in the ITV area", "ITV viewing lead over BBC is lessening", "We've got most viewers – BBC and ITV say", "Viewers prefer BBC shows", "BBC and ITV in viewers dispute", "ITV Triumph – [by] two million!", " 'We lead, say BBC: No you don't' say ITV", "ITV on top, admits BBC", ending on "ITV down: 'Midlands TV fans did not like *Hamlet*' " – especially when it was scheduled against the BBC's panel game, *What's My Line?*[20] On one level, the ever-changing nature of this story was the product of the different methods of audience research, as well as the different organisations involved in producing the data (the BBC's Audience Research Department, the private enterprise of the Gallup Poll, the US-controlled Nielson Ratings, and the Television Audience Measurement system (TAM)) (Sendall, 1982: 133). Figures were also complicated by the availability of ITV. It was initially restricted to the London area, and even then, only 33% of viewers had sets which could receive the new channel (Crisell, 2001: 87). Methods of calculation were also far from comparable. The Nielson Ratings aimed to measure the number of sets switched on, as calculated by information garnered from electronic recorders attached to a sample of sets. (If a programme was viewed for more than 5 minutes, it was counted.) In comparison, the BBC used personal interviews and the technique of aided recall, asking the panel about programmes they had seen the previous day (Silvey, 1974). But the different systems of measurement only in part contextualise the constantly twisting contours of the ratings narrative. If ratings produce discursive constructions of "the audience" (Ang, 1991), the ratings narrative functioned as a key site of battle between the channels. It was an attempt to claim control at a discursive level, and before the watchful gaze of critics and viewers. This also explains why the BBC, who needed viewers but did not need statistical data to give to advertisers, were just as keen to participate in this narrative as ITV.

The emphasis on ratings, and ITV winning the ratings war, has played an important role in shaping constructions of BBC and ITV television culture in the 1950s. It is implicitly or explicitly used as evidence to show how ITV provided a "lively counter to the stuffiness of the BBC" (Stokes, 1999: 34), addressing the working-class audience in ways they found more appealing. In fact, Sendall goes further, suggesting that "The needs and interests of the new audience were quite different from the needs and interests of the audience for which the BBC had been catering" (1982: 329). Yet this statement, and particularly the extent to which it draws upon discourses of class, pivots on a number of problematic assumptions about the social dissemination of television in Britain at this time. As the economist Chris Hand (2003) has argued, the idea that commercial television drove the adoption of television in lower income households has become something of an "urban myth", and his overall argument is that it is more appropriate to suggest that ITV encouraged, rather than motored, this shift. In addition to this it should be noted that the class contours of the television audience were already seen to be shifting earlier in the decade, as acknowledged by the BBC, the press and fan publications such as *TV Mirror*. In the early 1950s a budget set cost £50 against an average weekly wage of only £7 (Corner, 1991: 2). But BBC Audience Research noted in an internal survey in 1952 that while the possession of a set was "still highly correlated with income . . . well over half of the sets in use May [1952] were to be found in the homes of the working class".[21]

In terms of the BBC, there were in fact multiple dialogues going on about class – a layering of strategies, conversations and attitudes which finds expression in different ways. For example, across the period of roughly 1953–58, there seemed to be a concerted attempt by producers to engage with what was explicitly recognised as the expanding class audience for television. This had real consequences at the level of programme production, shaping characterisation, narrative, set construction (*The Grove Family*), the selection of guests (*This is Your Life*), the regulation of prizes (the quiz/game show) and the mediation of social issues (*Is This Your Problem?*). It may well be the case that the BBC did not always get it "right" (although we don't know that ITV did either), but this is rather different to an image of the Corporation merrily producing programmes in an ivory tower, with scant regard for who was actually watching them.

Popular television in this book: difficulties and debates

This chapter has so far traced how public service broadcasting was interpreted by the BBC, how this concept changed over time, and how the BBC responded to the challenge of commercial television. This has simultaneously indicated something of the changing status of the popular within this context – a context from which the case studies examined in this book emerged. But there is a need to say more about how the case studies might be categorised as popular.

The lesser priority given to a quantitative index ("receipts" or ratings) has historically played an important role in marking out the specificity of public service broadcasting's relations with the popular. But with respect to the BBC, the luxury of existing within the "brute force of monopoly" (Briggs, 1979) was reshaped by the advent of commercial television, and the system was now defined by a commercial, as well as a public service ethos. BBC programmes aiming for mass appeal were not brought into being by the advent of ITV, but they did take on an enhanced significance. The case studies examined in this book were explicitly conceived as aiming for a mass appeal and this was often marked – at the level of class – across their conception and construction. Furthermore, within the ratings narrative of the time, the programmes were understood to attract large audiences, even when the output of *both* channels was taken into consideration. Yet it is also clear that the competition from ITV depleted the audience for BBC programmes, including the case studies examined here (most notably *The Grove Family*). From this perspective, while it is useful to retain as one criterion, it is fortuitous that a quantitative index is rarely on its *own* a satisfactory marker of the popular. Not only is numerical evidence relative (how many viewers = popular?), but as Tony Bennett has observed, the notion of "well-liked by many people" permits "hardly any exclusions" from the category (1980: 21).

If a quantitative definition is retained as one form of criteria, a further commonality can be found in the concept of seriality. With the exception of *The Grove Family*, which was in any case described as a "family serial", the programmes examined here were all the product of programme formats: templates which provided a combination of standard-isation and difference (Scannell and Cardiff, 1991: 377). As Crisell observes, routinised and formatted programming is not an inherent sign of popularisation, but in taking on the characteristics of a mass-produced culture, it often carried these associations where entertainment output was concerned (ibid).

Related to this, a further factor in approaching the currency of the popular here is to be found in the concept of "America". Given that "to take up a position about popular culture is . . . often to take up a posi-tion about Americanisation" (Strinati, 1992: 76), it comes as no sur-prise that the relations between British and American television helped to shape many of the case studies explored in this book. The post-war period is more widely recognised as a time when fears about the

Americanisation of British life and culture were particularly apparent. Britain's status as a declining world power and its substantial War Debt created a dependency on American finance for post-war reconstruction. This fostered (or accelerated) the feeling that British values, histories and forms of culture were under threat. Dick Hebdige has argued that fears about America in the post-war period were shaped by concerns about the "levelling down" process (1988: 47), and as Dominic Strinati expands, "ideas about America being more populist and democratic fed into concern about increasing working-class affluence and conspicuous consumption" (1992: 66). But concerns about Americanisation also had a much longer history in Britain. From the earliest days of radio, existing historical work has stressed the BBC's suspicions of American culture and its bid to assist in the British defence of its "encroaching" influence (e.g. Barnard, 1989). Yet less has been said about BBC television in the 1940s and 1950s, largely because debates about Americanisation have more often focused on ITV. Not only did ITV introduce commercially funded television to Britain, but it was criticised for using a greater number of US imports (although these were tightly regulated by the ITA) (see Sendall, 1982). The BBC imported fewer American programmes than ITV, but they still *adapted* a surprisingly large number of American formats.

Valeria Camporesi explains how:

> In its publications, [the BBC] . . . maintained consistently that its programmes were truly British. And in its productions, it pursued, where it could, different programmes in different styles with American radio playing the role of the imperfect model. Since the 1930s, American models were attentively studied, partially adopted and in greater part translated to suit British ears. (1993: 182)

Rather than a blanket emphasis on Americanisation, this foregrounds the processes of adaptation, resistance and rejection. To be sure, the BBC's emphasis on the need to adapt and translate American broadcast culture often reflected British constructions of a "mythical America" (Hebdige, 1988: 74), and this discourse usually exaggerated the differences which could ultimately be found in programmes themselves (Chapter 5).

Popular television: making judgements

This does, however, indicate how categorisations of the popular are conferred culturally, shaped by the intentions of the classifier and the particular context under discussion. If constructions of the popular are discursive, they can also be seen as mobile and contingent – changing over time (Storey, 2001: 7). As Stuart Hall expands, cultural forms labelled as "high", "low", or "popular", move up and down the "cultural escalator" as their cultural value is depleted or enhanced (1998: 448). This seems important from a historical point of view: programmes from the 1950s do not necessarily look "popular" to us in the same way as television programmes might do today. Refracted through a sense of difference, distance and strangeness, they can look "quaint or clunky" (Johnson, 2006), while the province of the popular conjures up notions of the familiar and the everyday. In fact, Hall's point about the "cultural escalator" here can be illustrated by the fate of *The Grove Family*: in contrast to the BBC's original intentions, it is now seen as anything *but* popular, and is fixed by modern critics and scholars as being rather staid and didactic. In this respect, when it comes to tapping into the popular identity of programmes from the past, traces of reception are crucial.

Some of the programmes discussed in this book, such as *The Grove Family* or *The Charlie Chester Show* (1951–60), were already established by the time ITV emerged, but all the case studies were all invoked by the press, and often by the BBC, as weapons in the new competitive war. Critics, and sometimes viewers, often went further, positioning them as key examples of *commercial* programming and regrettable evidence of what the advent of competition might mean for British television at the level of standards, cultural values and "taste". This was often expressed in terms of aesthetics, implicitly bringing into view what might be conceived as early debates about "popular aesthetics".

This term is now most associated with Pierre Bourdieu (1986), although it has been taken up and investigated by scholars in different ways (see Bird, 2003, Hills, 2005). Bourdieu's work in *Distinction* is well known, and in examining the hierarchical positioning of popular culture and high culture, Bourdieu explores how distinctions are defined and maintained by discourses of class, as expressed through the learned and acquired cultural capital of "taste". In his conception of a "popular aesthetic" which includes, but is not specific to, the medium of television, Bourdieu identifies an emphasis on content over form, the absence of formal experimentation, and an emphasis on popular participation (1986: 32–34). While important in foregrounding the link between textual aesthetics and discourses of taste, this evidently offers a very broad set of criteria. Furthermore, although aiming to critique social hierarchies, Bourdieu's conception of a "popular aesthetic" is rather dismissive in itself (see also Bird, 2003: 124). In any case, while it may account for some of the often class-based responses to the programmes dealt with here, there is a need to reclaim the idea of "formal experimentation" which Bourdieu excludes from the category of the popular. If this term is used in its widest sense (rather than to imply the pursuit of

the radical or the "avant-garde"), the 1950s is more broadly a time characterised by formal and aesthetic "experimentation" in television, precisely because the language of the medium is self-consciously being
explored. It became clear when researching the different programmes
examined in this book, that this exploration also included debate about
what we might term "popular aesthetics".

In her chapter "A Popular Aesthetic: Exploring Taste Through Viewer
Ethnography", S. Elizabeth Bird aims to wrest the concept of a "popular
aesthetic" away from the text itself in order to think about how audiences make aesthetic judgements about the programmes they watch
(2003: 123). Bird emphasises how popular television has more often been
analysed in terms of its sociological and ideological implications (2003:
118), and she situates this as part of the tendency to evacuate questions
of aesthetic value from the study of popular culture. As she observes, this
has paradoxically had the effect of replicating the logic of Bourdieu's
hierarchy: the popular is seen as subordinating form to function, and the
text is analysed in terms of "what it 'does' for the consumer" (2003:
124). Furthermore, it erects a problematic boundary between critics and
viewers: critics are seen as producing discourses of judgement and taste,
while audiences enjoy their "popular" pleasures (even if they are producing negotiated or "resistant" readings) (2003: 122–123).

This separation emerged as unsustainable in the context of this book.
Audience responses were clearly in part shaped *by* critical discourses, but
it is clear that viewers were making their own aesthetic judgements from
an early stage. (Although the book gives more space to the analysis of
press discourse than viewer response, this is largely due to the availability of existing evidence.) Precisely because it involves judgement, the
exploration of "popular aesthetics" emerged from the *circulation* of programmes as they moved between the BBC, the press critics and television
viewers, whether we point to the question of how to image prizes in the
quiz show, the concern over encouraging a voyeuristic "freak" show in
the problem programme, or the concern over an exploitative aesthetic in
This is Your Life (how ethical was it to show a weeping celebrity?).
Certain themes do recur here – the currency of the sensational, for
example – but these discourses emerge less from a taxonomy of textual
traits than from how these programmes were debated, worried over and
viewed.

At the level of academic analysis, there is a question as to whether
analysing this reception is also a deferment of judgement. Despite the
increasing call for questions of evaluation, particularly at an aesthetic
level, to be integrated into the study of popular television (Jacobs, 2001,
Bird, 2003, Geraghty, 2003), Catherine Johnson (2006) has discussed

how this has largely been explored in relation to contemporary programming. As she observes, there remains an "anxiety about the place of
aesthetic evaluation" in television historiography, in part because of the
"historical 'difficulties' " involved in making judgements about television
from a long time past. One way of approaching this is indeed to consider
the evaluative context in which the programme originally circulated, as
provided by production notes, audience figures and responses, and newspaper reviews. But Johnson goes on to suggest that, while valuable, this
will "not necessarily challenge the evaluative assumptions we (or our
students) might make of . . . old television. It sets up a different set of
evaluative criteria that safely belong to a different period and are there-
fore . . . open to be read as no longer of any relevance". She suggests that
it is more productive to ask, "[How] did this programme use the
resources available to it to construct its meanings within its broader
context of production? And is it successful in this?"

Johnson's timely intervention raises some important points about television historiography, particularly in terms of how historians not only
read and interpret, but also necessarily evaluate, their evidence. At the
same time, and particularly in the context of this book, this argument
raises a number of points or questions. First, the evaluative criteria in
operation at the time of a programme's original circulation are not
necessarily very far removed from these applied now: one of my aims is
to show that what worried commentators in the 1950s prefigures a
number of debates surrounding television today. Second, it has been
argued that judgements about quality and value do not arrive "from
independent assessments, but from referential ones built on comparisons with the surrounding flow of television" (van Zoonen, 2004: 279,
see also Wheatley, 2004). Making judgements about how successful a
programme was in using the resources at the time demands knowledge
of its surrounding programme culture, but such evidence is not always
available or accessible.

Clearly, in choosing to include them in a book about popular television, I have inevitably made judgements about the programmes examined here. We also necessarily make judgements about programmes while
viewing them – even when this seems "difficult" because they are
from the past. For example, while I don't share Thumim's surprise, as
expressed after viewing an extant edition of *The Grove Family*, that the
serial "was able to attract . . . a devoted following" at all in the mid-
1950s (2004: 160), I do suspect that the writing may have been weak
within the context of the time. Similarly, although my only access to it
has been via scripts, I share the view, which was actually also voiced by
a critic in 1955, that *Is This Your Problem?* exhibits something of a

"schizophrenia of tone".[22] In more colloquial terms, it doesn't seem to "hang together well" as a text, with the melodramatic introductions of the host conflicting with the formal discourse of the expert panel. But in the context of this book, this is precisely what makes the programme of great value.

The contradictions of *Is This Your Problem?* emerge from the programme's bid to negotiate its popular appeal – to engage with "opposing groups, classes and values" (Turner, 1996: 178). Bird would no doubt cast this as the "replacement of aesthetic standards by political and social ones" (2003: 118), and I certainly make no apology for my interest in questions of social/cultural power. But it is difficult to see how these fields are mutually exclusive. The social significance of these programmes was often explored – whether implicitly or explicitly – through questions of aesthetic evaluation. This certainly returns us to a primary interest in the criteria which circulated at the time, and it is true that I have little interest in making claims for the programmes as "good" or "bad" television. But this book *is* interested in whether they were seen as such, and this represents a framework which is appropriate to the critical aims of this study; *Entertaining Television* argues that the programmes need to be taken seriously, in that they provide crucial insights into the institutional, cultural and aesthetic development of British television at this time. But at the same time, it also pulls in the opposite direction to the long history of work which has aimed to rehabilitate the value of the popular: a core intention is to demonstrate how BBC television was actually more "trashy" and populist than conventional accounts would have us believe.

The conception of *Is This Your Problem?* above concurs with ways of approaching the popular which are most identified with British cultural studies (and which are seen as counterposed to issues of aesthetic evaluation) (Bird, 2003). A neo-Gramscian approach to understanding the politics of popular culture foregrounds it as a site of negotiation between institutions and their audiences (see Gramsci, 1998, Storey, 2001: 10–12), positioning it as a terrain of struggle in which "dominant, subordinate and oppositional . . . values . . . are 'mixed' in different permutations", even if dominant values ultimately prevail (Bennett, 1998: 221). This approach rose to prominence in television, media and cultural studies in the 1980s, and the strength of its legacy is suggested by the fact that it is of course now hardly radical to assert that ideological production occurs under contradictory pressures. But given perceptions of the relationship between the BBC and the expanding mass audience for television in the 1950s, it seems worth revisiting this argument. It was often in the attempt to address the interests of an expanding audience, particularly in terms of class, that the programmes emerge as dynamic and frequently contradictory cultural objects. While it remains important to consider the specificity of the relations between public service television and the popular, there is nothing about the model above which means it cannot be applied to this sphere. In fact, it is only *because* of the historical tendency to separate these concepts that such an application can be cast as novel in the first place.

"Shall we join the ladies?": gendering the popular

This approach has not only been extended to class. The closest comparison to this book in terms of generic scope is Marsha F. Cassidy's American study *What Women Watched: Daytime Television in the 1950s* (2005), and this link foregrounds the gendered, as well as national, inflections to the popular. Cassidy's book examines popular fiction, the game show, the domestic magazine programme and the phenomenon of television celebrity. Albeit on a smaller scale, British television in the 1950s also offered programmes aimed at women during the day (Leman, 1987, Thumim, 2004). In looking across both channels, Thumim argues that the 1950s was in fact a special, because "tentatively 'open' ", moment in television's experimental address toward women, a time when "the meaning of television (as with woman) was under construction" (2004: 175).[23] By 1960, "virtually no special programming for women remained . . . in the schedule" (2004: 83), and in 1964, the BBC's Women's Programme Unit was disbanded (with its personnel moved into a new Family Programmes Unit).

The programmes explored in this book occupy a complex relationship with the issues Thumim outlines. They are all screened as part of the prime-time schedule, and were understood by the BBC to be aiming for a general appeal. As Thumim points out, women's support was *generally* "assumed to be crucial in embedding habits of viewing into domestic routines" (2004: 25), and this can apply to both channels, as well as to the prime-time schedule. Once ITV began, it had an *economic* impetus to target women within the evening, as well as daytime schedule: they were recognised as the main purchasers of the products advertised in the commercial breaks. To simply take one example, Associated Rediffusion's *Shall we Join the Ladies?*, screened on a Thursday evening at 10 p.m., invites viewers "to join our guest celebrity in a feminine half hour which the men too will enjoy".[24] But this aim to explicitly target women within the wider audience for the evening schedule seemed less marked on the BBC. In 1954 at least it is still openly stated that the "intention is to develop women's programmes more . . . but we are not anxious to put such programmes into evening peak times".[25]

The BBC's anxiety about the "proper" location for women's pro-grammes may support the argument that "questions concerning women and the troublesome concept of 'the feminine' are . . . significant in the . . . tensions marking television's development" (Thumim, 2004: 11). This extends beyond the more specific questions of genre or audience address, to take in questions of reception, or conceptions of the television technology itself. As Lynn Spigel (1992), William Boddy (2004) and Thumim (2004) have explored, television viewing has historically been positioned as a passive, and thus femininising or "emasculating" activity. This conception draws its strength from long-standing constructions of popular culture as feminine, and from gender-inflected associations of passivity (Huyssen, 1986, Petro, 1986). But in relation to the 1950s, Spigel has explored how gendered concerns were often articulated at a spatial level, whether in terms of situating the television technology in the domestic sphere, or with respect to a "series of confusions about the spaces that television brought into the home" (1992: 115). This often pivoted on concerns about television's movement between apparently "public and private worlds" (Spigel, 1992: 109), and given the centrality of the public/private dichotomy in the historical structuring of gender relations, it is no surprise that questions of gender are evident here.

Some of the programmes examined in this book figured prominently as negative examples of television's intrusion into the "private" realm. Conceptions of what is "public" are always premised on what is seen as "private", and this distinction, which can variously be explored as eco-nomic, institutional, spatial and cultural, has different meanings across a range of theoretical and disciplinary contexts (Dahlgren, 1995). Yet the fact that public service has more often been approached in terms of its "publicness" – indeed the term "public" is enshrined in its title – fore-grounds the gendering of the concept, and the fact that public service has not easily encompassed the personal and the "private" (Branston, 1998: 55). Rather than simply figuring television within debates about the decline of the public sphere (Habermas, 1984, see Chapter 4 of this book), the book as a whole adopts the widely acknowledged view that, in relation to the spheres of public/private, television does "not so much perform the function of regulating access to either domain, as to ensure the constant reproduction of both domains" (Kress, 1986: 397). Television was making newly visible, and often bringing into being, a range of images, experiences and identities that people had hitherto not encountered. With respect to the case studies examined here, the debate is often about *publicness versus privacy* as mapped onto *visibility versus invisibility* (Thompson, 1990: 240). In relation to British television in the 1950s, scholars have more often foregrounded the medium's ability to connect the viewer to public space, referencing the significance of the outside broadcast in promoting the possibilities of the new medium, or they have explored television's growing centrality in the sphere of current affairs (Thumim, 2004, Holland, 2006). But if television consolidated the positioning of the twentieth-century spectator as "witness" (Ellis, 2000), this also involved the medium's incursions into the apparently "private" domain – where debates about the popular were worked through. The following chapters aim to offer an insight into this journey.

Notes

1 "Notes on the Future of Light Entertainment", 1960. T16/91/2.
2 "Serious Programmes in Peak Hours", undated memo. T16/149/2.
3 John Warrington to Assistant Head of Copyright, 19 May 1954. T12/137/1.
4 Ronald Waldman, "Light Entertainment Policy", 6 April 1951. T16/91/1.
5 "Your view of BBC versus ITA", 9 October 1956, ITC press cuttings (hereafter indicated as ITC). These are now stored on CD-Rom at the BFI.
6 As above.
7 "Agenda for Board of Management", 11 July 1953. T16/48.
8 *Bristol Evening Post*, 30 July 1955 (ITC).
9 *The Star*, 14 July 1955 (ITC).
10 John Warrington to Ronald Waldman, 6 December 1955. T16/91/2.
11 The programme was in fact later screened on a Friday, although it is not possible to say that the scheduling plans of ITV prompted this shift.
12 George Barnes, untitled memo, 19 October 1954. T16/149/1.
13 Ronald Waldman to Ian Jacobs, 19 November 1956. T16/149/2.
14 As above.
15 Ronald Waldman to Ian Jacobs, 19 November 1956. T16/149/2.
16 Kenneth to ENCA, undated memo. T16/590.
17 In more recent decades, industrial, regulatory and policy debate about the value of public service programming has circled around the concept of "quality" (see Brunsdon, 1997, Wheatley, 2004). Given that the currency of this term – where broadcasting is concerned at least – primarily emerged in the era of deregulation, it is not often used by the BBC in the 1950s.
18 *Financial Times*, 7 November 1955 (ITC).
19 As above.
20 All headlines taken from ITC press cuttings, section "Ratings".
21 "1952 Viewer Survey", folder R9/4.
22 *Truth*, 12 September 1955.
23 Although there is not space to consider the content of this programming in detail here, Thumim notes that while it often reflected the responsibilities allocated to women within a patriarchal society, there were also more serious attempts to "use the opportunity afforded by broadcast television to

consider cultural and political events and ideas in relation to female experience – with the conscious aim of *broadening* that experience" (Thumim,
2004: 61; original emphasis) (see in particular pp. 57–65).
24 *TV Times*, 12 January 1956, p. 29.
25 *TV Mirror*, 9 January 1954, p. 6.

2

"Neighbours to the Nation": "Soap Opera", the BBC and (Re)visiting *The Grove Family* (1954–57)

The Grove Family (hereafter *TGF*) has secured a certain visibility in British television history by virtue of its status as British television's "first soap opera". Despite the fact that only two editions of *TGF* have survived in audiovisual form, its contours are often described with extraordinary certainty. For example, Andy Medhurst has explained how:

> The world the Groves live in is very safe, it's very secure, it's very smug, and it's very cosy. People get on. There's the odd nosey neighbour but nothing really disrupts the social fabric . . . Nice girls go out with boys but don't go too far . . . [It offered] a nice, safe, secure, cosy unit.[1]

Particular emphasis has also been placed on its overt public service intentions, in so far as viewers "were made acutely aware of the need to purchase a TV licence . . . or to protect themselves from burglaries" (Evans, 1995: 232–233).

TGF undoubtedly represents the least controversial example of popular television explored in this book. But it is also clear that the "common sense" assumptions about BBC television from this time ("stuffy", "paternalist", elitist) (Thumim, 2004: 27) have influenced – even clouded – how the programme has been perceived. Furthermore, because soap opera is often perceived to be an intrinsically commercial genre (originally designed by US soap manufacturers to sell products to women in the home), this generic framework primes us to *expect* that what is now perceived as the BBC's "first television soap" is likely to be tempered, even spoiled, by instruction and education. In short, before we have even met the Groves, there is the overriding expectation that they might not be much "fun". But the Groves were described by the British press as "neighbours to the nation", and despite the popular image of the period as ushering in more privatised modes of living, an existence behind twitching curtains as "sitting on the step was not done"

(Hopkins, 1963: 326), it seems rude to make judgements about the neighbours without at least going round for a visit. Given that firm assumptions have already been made about *TGF*, this is more appropriately conceived as an act of "re-visitation".

In discussing the continuous serial, Christine Geraghty describes "a whole which can never be entirely consumed or played out" (1991: 5), and she indicates how soaps are difficult to write about because of the conceptual and methodological difficulty involved in stopping the "flow". In discussing *Coronation Street* (ITV, 1960–), Marion Jordan also draws attention to the problem of episode selection, in that there "are obvious difficulties in treating as homogenous a programme which has gone on the air more than 2,000 times" (1981: 27). With historical research, the task is not so much stopping the flow as trying to get it going again. In terms of *TGF*, this is ultimately impossible. But existing audiovisual material, and especially the vast quantity of written material (including *TGF* scripts), enables a version of this "flow" to be partially reconstructed.

In problematising how the programme has been categorised and perceived, the aim here is not to decide whether *TGF* is or isn't a television soap opera, not least because this implies a fixed and pre-existent category against which it might be measured. Rather, this chapter suggests that it is productive to consider the generic *struggle* around the development of *TGF*. That is not to deny that it often seems productive to approach the programme *through* the theoretical, critical or historical frameworks which have been used to analyse British soap opera. But there is a difference between asserting that *TGF* is/was a "soap opera", and exploring whether it relates to soap opera as critical category. *TGF* often seems to speak to this scholarship, while its relations with the category of soap opera emerge as unruly and multifaceted. This generic tension represented an ongoing struggle in my own approach to the programme, and it seemed that to close this down, or to iron it out, was to do a disservice to the complexity of *TGF* itself.

Sounding out "soap"? BBC radio and the domestic serial

The BBC's engagement with the idea of the family serial begins with radio, and it is here that any assessment of genre should begin. Even before we confront the pejorative connotations of the term soap opera, seriality carries associations of commerciality and popularisation (see Chapter 1). The 1930s had seen a limited amount of serialised fiction appear on BBC radio, but Michele Hilmes (2007) has argued that we can really talk about "soap" on BBC radio from 1941, and she focuses attention on the serial *Front Line Family*. A propaganda vehicle intended to encourage the American entry into the Second World War, *Front Line Family* (hereafter *FLF*) was chiefly aimed at women, and it began on the BBC's North American service in 1941. As Hilmes explores, the development and circulation of *FLF* shows how perceptions of "quality" and public service were highly gendered (and in the context of war, linked with discourses on national identity), and her analysis demonstrates how a popular and apparently "feminine" form challenged both the production practices and the ideological values of the BBC (2007: 2). With the Robinson family as the narrative focus, *FLF* focused on a British family during wartime, and the idea of a serial in a regular slot five to six days a week was quite a departure from BBC practices (Hilmes, 2007: 10). *FLF* proved to be so popular with British audiences abroad that it was added to the BBC's Light Programme after the war (1946), scheduled in the afternoon, with the new name of *The Robinson Family*. After the war the Drama Department established a division to handle serial production, and the success of other serial fictions, particularly *Dick Barton* (1946–51), *Mrs Dale's Diary* (1948–69) and *The Archers* (1950–), "would make radio serials part of everyday, BBC, and British life" (Hilmes, 2007: 18).

But the institutional specificity of the BBC shaped the development of the British serial in particular ways. In 1944, Rudolph Arnheim noted with some approval that *FLF*'s emphasis on a London family living in the Blitz was "not presented as melodrama of high-strung passion, tears . . . and overdrawn suspense . . . The plot is focused on the psychological, social and economics effects of the blitz . . . certainly this is miles away from the aromatic scent of soap flakes" (Arnheim, 1944: 83–84, cited in Hilmes, 2007: 11). According to Hilmes, this demonstrates how an implicitly masculinised British realism was elevated above a feminised, American, penchant for melodrama. This argument draws on the accepted idea that soap opera is often aimed at a female audience, and these associations emerge from the American context. Developing out of serialised fiction in women's pages of American newspapers in the 1920s, the domestic serial drama became popular on radio in the 1930s. Sponsored by large American soap manufacturers such as Proctor and Gamble, the soap opera was intended to function as a commercial vehicle which would stimulate the purchase of household goods. As Robert Allen's historical study outlines, by 1941 nearly 90% of all advertiser-sponsored daytime programming was represented by serials (1988: 19), and by the early 1950s the form began its expansion on US television. The long-running serial *The Guiding Light* (1937–) transferred from radio to television in 1952, and between 1951 and 1959 as many as thirty-five new television soaps were born (Allen, 1988: 126).

This marks a considerable growth when compared to the rise of serial fiction on British television, and it immediately foregrounds the different institutional basis of British broadcasting. In the 1930s, the BBC was obviously not aiming to sell products to women in the home. In fact, there was little mention of women as a specific, designated audience at all (Hilmes, 2007: 7). Although the post Second World War period sees an expanded space for women's programming on BBC radio, Hilmes suggests that the subsequent serials, *Dick Barton*, *Mrs Dale's Diary* and *The Archers*, were constructed as public service antidotes to the perceived feminine excesses of *FLF*. The label "soap opera" lacked a clear currency in Britain at this time, and if the BBC serials were referred to as "soaps", it was only in a distanced sense, and in a way that expressed an unease about the cultural value of this term. As the Producer of *The Archers* urged in 1952, "Call it 'soap' as the Americans do, or the modern counterpart of the folk tale".[2] As Christine Gledhill observes, the BBC's radio serials were appealing to a "particular national formation in [their] . . . claim to realism", and this is supported by "Granada's [later] refusal to locate . . . *Coronation Street* in the soap opera category" (1992: 117). Scholars found a "perfect fit" between *Coronation Street*'s formal and thematic characteristics and those of British social realism' (ibid).

Although the American serials also claimed to be "true to life" and "realistic" (Gledhill, 1992: 117), the fact that the British programmes foregrounded a greater investment in realism is not in dispute. But the issue of gendered address is more complex. The focus on the adventures of Special Agent *Dick Barton*, referred to in the *Radio Times* as a thriller serial (Briggs, 1979: 61), may well play out the idea of masculinisation, but this seems more questionable where *Mrs Dale's Diary* (hereafter *MDD*) is concerned. The BBC did envisage that *MDD*, which began in 1948 on the Light Programme, would "strive to achieve a realism which is specifically withheld from its American counterparts",[3] but it was fundamentally conceived as a women's programme from the very start. It was originally envisaged as "a dramatised gossip session for women",[4] and was scheduled at 4:00–4:15p.m., a time when women were imagined to be taking a break from their home-making duties. With Ellis Powell playing Mrs Dale, the programme focused on Mrs Dale's life as a middle-class doctor's wife in "Kenton", Middlesex, and it followed the everyday happenings in her family and circle of friends. The programme had a wide appeal to women from all social classes, but from 1952, the issue of class in *MDD* is discussed with some vigour, both in the popular press and behind the scenes at the BBC.[5] Comment from both press critics and readers debated whether "Mrs Dale's daily . . . adventures have become too aloof for the average woman listener", and the discussion explicitly raised the question of "the validity of the family as representative members of their class".[6] This represented a healthy questioning of whether BBC radio offered an inclusive class address, while it also reflected on the role that popular fiction played in constructing an image of "reality" (an issue later central to the BBC's conception of *TGF*). But while this debate usefully problematised the idea that "woman" was a homogenous concept, the sense that the address of *MDD* was *gendered* was never in any doubt.

The Archers, still running on BBC radio today, was also initially scheduled during the day at 11:45a.m., directly following the repeat of *Mrs Dale's Diary*. But when it moved from the Midlands Home Service to the Light Programme in 1951, it was scheduled at 6:15p.m., significantly prompting a shift in how its audience address was conceptualised. Its producers explained how the programme originally catered to "the housewife audience . . . but it is quite likely we shall have to modify our approach when we get a family audience in the evening".[7] As one Audience Research Report recorded in 1954, it was indeed seen as "cleverly written in order to give nearly everyone 'a look in'".[8] While the content of *The Archers* might better illustrate Hilmes's argument about masculinisation, *The Archers* also indicates how the domestic serial was conceived as a *flexible* form which could adapt its address to different scheduled slots. This flexibility is not irrelevant where US television is concerned, but it is particularly important in approaching the British context. With fewer channels and the slower development of daytime programming, the demand for cheap, regular programmes has historically been more limited in Britain (Geraghty, 1991). The most visible programmes conceived as soap operas have been offered in primetime, and while they have certainly been studied in terms of their address toward women (Ang, 1985, Geraghty, 1991, Gledhill, 1992, Hobson, 2003), they have simultaneously negotiated a broader audience address. In this sense, it may be problematic to describe British soaps as a "masculinisation" of the form. As Geraghty (2005) has observed, American soap opera is often privileged as the dominant touchstone for the genre. Even if the term itself originated in America, the various national negotiations of serial drama have their own histories and influences (see also Gledhill, 1992). When it came to *TGF*, not only was the term soap opera almost absent, but there was little evidence to suggest that it was seen as a "women's" programme at all. It is partly for this reason that this chapter does not begin with an explicit discussion of gender in *TGF*, or more specifically, the relationship between gender, narrative and audience address. While consolidating the historical hegemony of American definitions of soap opera, this simultaneously runs a risk of closing off other routes of analysis.

Figure 1 The members of *The Grove Family*

TGF first appeared at 7:40p.m., on Friday 9 April 1954. Screened on a weekly basis, it was intended to address a family audience. The Groves were a lower-middle-class family living in the Southern suburb of Hendon (Figure 1). They occupied a double-fronted house in a quiet suburban road, and Dad's building yard was attached at the back. In an early press release, Mr Grove was described as "a jobbing builder earning around £16 per week, a pleasant bloke with a dry sense of humour",[9] and the characteristics of other family members were also circulated. The aim here was to suggest an "ordinary" family who were likeable but flawed, whether at the level of character traits (Jack is "one of the boys who thinks he's very sharp and clever"), or educational achievements (Lennie is "very bright", but Daphne has "trouble under the Education Act [1944] – she can't pass exams").[10] *TGF* was careful to include a cross-generational focus and the BBC explained how they were "aiming to appeal to each age group".[11] The family was comprised of Dad (Bob Grove, played by Edward Evans), Mum (Gladys Grove/Ruth Dunning), crotchety Grandmother "Granny Grove" (Nancy Roberts), son Jack (23) (Peter Bryant), daughter Pat (21) (initially Sheila Sweet, later Carole Mowlam), and the two younger children, Daphne (13) (Margaret Downs) and Lennie (11) (Christopher Beeny).

TGF's most significant television precursor was the children's family serial, *The Appleyards* (BBC, 1952–57), which was shown on a fortnightly basis in runs of six editions at a time. Both programmes aimed to project to viewers a mirror image of their own family lives (Laing, 1986: 182), and when *TV Mirror* asked the Producer of *TGF*, John Warrington, "Who are the Groves?", he replied "They are YOU: the millions of people nightly who turn on their TV sets".[12] This idea of reflection appears to have been taken as given by the critics at the time, and referring to both programmes in 1954, the *Evening News* explains how

"They say that viewers love television 'families' to be 'just like them-selves', doing ordinary . . . things . . . in the routine of life".[13] The fact that these assumptions seem to appear "ready-made" suggests how radio is an important precursor here, particularly in terms of setting up expec-tations about characters and stories reflecting the qualities of intimacy, ordinariness and domesticity. At the same time, generalisations about the aesthetic and cultural "qualities" of broadcasting risk effacing the speci-ficity of what the BBC was aiming to do with both television and *TGF* at this time.

While every care had been taken to make the Dale family of *MDD* everyday and "ordinary" (and many listeners praised them as such),[14] they had also been denounced as offering an "idealised picture of a family without vices".[15] It can't reasonably be claimed that the Groves were any less idealised, but the BBC placed an emphasis on a shift in class back-ground, with the aim of "reflecting" an image of families who were now increasingly buying television sets. The Producer did not simply speak of this relationship between the Groves and the viewers on an abstract level, however: it was explicitly understood in terms of class. Warrington routinely emphasised the need for "more careful observation of the income groups around whom the series is based, and to whom we wish to appeal".[16] Particularly given perceptions of the BBC's class elitism, the sincere aim to provide what the Corporation saw as a carefully inclusive class address is clear (and unlike the rest of the family, Mrs Grove was notably from the North country so as to "broaden the appeal").[17]

The Groves were clearly different, for example, from the Lyons family, as seen in the BBC's comedy *Life with the Lyons* (BBC TV 1955–56, AR 1957–60). Initially a radio show, *Life with the Lyons* appeared simulta-neously on BBC radio and television in 1955, although in 1957 the Lyons defected to ITV, where they remained for the rest of their run. Played by a real-life family, the Lyons were supposedly an American family resident in the UK, although the children had distinctly middle-class, British accents. With their relatively luxurious suburban home, as well as home-help in the form of Scottish maid Aggie, the Lyons are clearly quite affluent.

But lest the Groves are seen as simply ushering in a more democratised form of class representation, it is important to note the existence of *The Huggetts*, launched on BBC radio a year before the Groves first appeared. Emerging from the post-war British film series *Holiday Camp* (1947), *Here Come the Huggetts* (1948), *The Huggetts Abroad* (1949) and *Vote for Huggett* (1949) (all directed by Ken Annakin and starring Jack Warner and Kathleen Harrison), the radio comedy *Meet the Huggetts* began on the BBC's Light Programme in 1953.[18] While drawing on representations of class from wartime British cinema, Sydney-Smith argues that the Huggetts can be seen as anticipating the British soap opera family, and she emphasises their portrayal of "ordinariness and respectability, decent working-class values" (2002: 46).

The Groves were importantly lower-middle and not working class. Yet while there was perhaps the desire that the charges of class elitism lodged at *MDD* should not be repeated, *TGF* can be read less as a radical class break with any precursors, than an attempt to address the expanding contours of the television audience at this time. 1954 is before the advent of ITV, but it is also a time when the rapid class expansion of the audience is taken as given – as discussed by the BBC, the press or fan publications such as *TV Mirror*. As outlined in Chapter 1, the BBC understood as early as 1952 that the television audience was increasingly including a significant proportion of working-class viewers. *TGF* did not so much aim to reflect this fact, as it sought to offer representations which accounted for the changing class contours of the audience on a wider scale. In this respect, lower-middle class is both specific (the BBC became obsessed with getting it exactly "right") and non-specific (it sits somewhere in the middle, offering something which hopefully appeals to all). This idea of a successive negotiation of class identity, with *TGF* aiming to be more "ordinary" and real than *MDD*, and *Coronation Street* making a class break with the Groves (Cooke, 2003: 33), illustrates how perceptions of class, as well as realism, change over time, and how realism is negotiated on a sliding scale in relation to previous texts in the field. At the same time, whether it is actually appropriate to situate the *TGF* in relation to *Coronation Street* at all is pursued on different levels throughout this chapter.

The fidelity of *TGF*'s class representation was routinely praised at the time by critics and viewers alike (see also Thumim, 2004), and following the first edition, the press spoke of how "All viewers know people like Mr and Mrs Grove – pleasant, hard-working folk proud of their independence gained through years of denial and saving".[19] According to BBC Audience Research, viewers would routinely remark that it was a "very true picture of family life with its ups and downs"[20] or would comment how it offered a "homely, natural and true-to-life series".[21] But this begs the question as to what was framed in this very "true-to-life" picture of post-war family existence. Unlike the single plays or drama-documentaries of the 1960s, which were controversial precisely because of disputes surrounding their construction of reality (Geraghty, 1991: 33), Thumim (2004) convincingly argues that popular drama in the 1950s was the drama of reassurance. In this regard, the BBC's aims for the programme are set out in what might be termed a manifesto for the Groves' existence:

> The family is everybody's next-door neighbour. We have tried to make people understand the family is the key and the centre of all social life . . . The home itself centres around Mum and she in return helps Dad – not immediately in his business, but by providing him with a happy and comfortable home. Whenever troubles happen to the children . . . they can always be brought back to the family for help and guidance . . . Indeed, tolerance and understanding are perhaps keywords to the Groves' existence . . . We never allow credit, everything is to be paid for in cash, and obviously good manners, courtesy, honesty, etc.[22]

Integral to the process of post-war reconstruction was the aim to consolidate family life. But intersecting with a long heritage of debates in media, television and cultural studies about how any claim to the real is shaped by discourses of power (Fiske and Hartley, 1978), this memo already hints at the political nature of the programme's image. It begins with what appears as a statement of fact – "The family is everybody's next-door neighbour" – and then proceeds to set out a very particular version of what these neighbours are like, whether at the level of social values, gender organisation or class aspirations. There is also something of a slippage between the idea of the family operating as a reflecting mirror, and the BBC's role in engineering and constructing the image this mirror portrays ("We have tried to make", "We never allow").

But while this description of the programme appears to confirm prevailing perceptions of the family's consensual world, it was apparently written during the very early stages of production. As such, it sets out a static framework which does not necessarily encapsulate how *TGF* was actually brought to life across scripts, programmes, the popular press and viewer discussions. A wider analysis brings out how *TGF* was also interested in exploring *changing* class and gender ideals, particularly as these were shaped by generational differences. It was precisely within the bid to *negotiate* an image of reality, and one which might appeal to a wide audience, that a more complex range of perspectives on family life is entertained.

Narrative: definitions and directions

Although its identity as a serial is not straightforward, *TGF* does speak to the rise of seriality in television from the mid-1950s. BBC television had already been adapting serial forms from radio, and these provided a regular identity for certain scheduled slots – such as the Saturday evening serial drama which offered thrillers, detective serials or literary adaptations (Jacobs, 2000: 110). The success of the six-part *Quatermass Experiment* in 1953 demonstrated the popularity of serial production, as well as its cost-effective nature, and in 1954 the BBC screened its first filmed serials, including the independently produced *Fabian of the Yard* (ibid). Jacobs connects the subsequent expansion of seriality to a range of different factors, including the increase in telerecording and the rise of the filmed series, the routinisation of the production process, and the advent of a second channel. As transmission hours extended and the audience grew, other dramatic forms appeared, and Thumim describes these as the series, the serial and the sitcom, each of which had precursors in radio and print media (2004: 7).

The first discussion of *TGF* begins in 1953 when the Head of Light Entertainment, Ronald Waldman, suggests that the BBC develop a "good family serial". Waldman explains how "an experienced film comedy writer", Michael Pertwee (brother of the actor Jon Pertwee):

> wants to have a go at creating a Television "Archers" or "Dale" family which will run throughout the year . . . [He] suggests that there should not be *any continuity of story* other than family link and perhaps the progress of romance etc, so that viewers can always come in late on it and pick up the threads.[23]

Michael Pertwee's conception of the narrative structure here is confirmed when the programme begins, and he discusses the programme in the *Radio Times*. In inviting the audience to "Meet the Groves" he explains how: "If we are to entertain, and not irritate, a changing public once a week for a minimum of thirteen weeks we have to treat this as a series rather than a serial".[24] We see the assumption that the viewer will *not* watch every week, and that there is no narrative incentive to convince them to do so. This plays to conceptions of the BBC's uneasy relations with the serial form – in part emerging from the perception that routine and habitual listening or viewing would encourage passivity (Bourdon, 2004: 290). In relation to *The Archers* and *MDD*, concern had indeed been expressed about the encouragement of a "drug-like fascination",[25] although such comments were in fact more likely to come from listener descriptions than BBC personnel.

In comparison, ITV picked up the idea of a daily filmed serial quickly. In February 1956 ATV began *One Family*, a "day-to-day serial of the lives of the Armstrong family" set in their big home called "The Old Vicarage at Mossbank, a fictional suburb of London".[26] Screened for 15 minutes on weekdays at 4:45p.m., *One Family* seemed to suggest an address to women and/or children. Prior to this, one of the first programmes launched by ATV was a daily serial for women. Beginning on 23 September 1955 at 10:45a.m., ATV's *Sixpenny Corner* promised a serial "telling the life, love and tribulations" of the newly married Bill and Sally Norton at their garage in the country town of Springwood.[27] More so than *One Family*, the billing for the programme indicates a continuous narrative structure interrupted by cliff-hangers. By May 1956, *Sixpenny Corner* was moved to the evening slot of 7:00p.m., and this suggests a clear recognition of its lucrative role in building an audience. In 1957 ATV's *Emergency Ward Ten* (1957–67) began as a twice weekly half-hour serial, combining an emphasis on how hospitals work with a regular core of fictional characters (doctors and nurses) (Laing, 1986: 182). In fact, given that it begins in 1957, *Emergency Ward Ten* is building its audience at the very same time that *TGF* is exiting the scene.

Lez Cooke sees this as symptomatic of a lack of competitive ethos at the BBC, as well as indicative of the Corporation's residual disdain for a popular serial drama (2003: 19). This perspective downplays the extent to which the programme *was* recognised by the BBC as a key competitive weapon where ITV was concerned. With an estimated audience of 10 million viewers by early 1955,[28] *TGF* was viewed as a valuable BBC property. In 1956 the Producer proudly announced that Friday evening was known as "Grove night as well as bath night".[29] This recognises *TGF*'s competitive importance, while it also indicates a desire to suture the programme into weekly viewing habits and routines. But what does *not* seem present in the early stages, as Pertwee's introductory article in the *Radio Times* suggests, is a clear desire to build an audience by using a continuous narrative structure, although it is worth noting that ITV was yet to emerge at this time. Indeed, by 1956–58, the significance of the serial is more readily recognised in the BBC's scheduling plans, with such comments as "it is the regular series which keeps them [and] . . . that means a pattern".[30]

But there were other factors which contributed to *TGF*'s less continuous narrative structure. As screenwriters for film, the Pertwees were presumably more used to crafting discrete narratives than thinking in terms of the ongoing rhythms of a serial. The decision to schedule the programme on a weekly basis may also have shaped its narrative structure. In terms of available studio space, cost and general production resources, the BBC had balked at the idea of the programme going out two to three times per week. Although at £250 per edition *TGF* was a cheap form of drama output, it was still more expensive than the radio serials (the original estimation for *The Archers* was £55 per episode). Unlike the radio serials, which were recorded up to one month in advance of transmission, *TGF* was broadcast live, and the actors already rehearsed Monday to Friday for the one weekly edition. Furthermore, unlike the radio serials, there could be no reading from scripts.[31] From the BBC's perspective, a daily programme would have been an impossibility, and although this did not preclude the use of a continuous narrative, it may have made it less desirable. Lastly, *TGF* was not on viewers' screens continuously, and the files often mention it as returning for a "new series". In this sense *TGF* was different to the continuous diegetic worlds of *MDD* or *The Archers*, and was not intended to offer a continuous narrative experience.

At the same time, Pertwee's description of the narrative structure as having no continuity does demand clarification. As the original description of *TGF* by Waldman (above) suggests, the progression of romance in the programme formed an ongoing narrative chain, and this was chiefly associated with the lives of the older children, Pat and Jack. In addition to this, several episodes were explicitly announced as two-parters, such as "One for the Road" in 1955, or "Fear" in 1957. There were also clusters of narratives which played out over a number of episodes, sitting somewhere in between clear continuity and the construction of discrete narrative units. These aspects of continuity also become more apparent as the programme progresses, and thus once ITV is on air, although the Producer had certainly asked for "more continuity" before this time.[32] What is meant by a continuous narrative is open to interpretation. Serialisation as a concept referred to repeatable and familiar settings and not simply narrative structures, something which home-produced, domestic drama was particularly well situated to provide (Thumim, 2004: 144). Medhurst has suggested that *TGF* represented the "first time the nation had been gripped by the on-going story of a television family. If that's the definition of a soap, then . . . it was the first [one]".[33] If the idea of an "on-going story" is very loosely defined, then this might in part explain its prevailing classification as a "soap".

What's in a name? *The Grove Family* and genre

As established, however, the term soap opera was not in common use in Britain at this time, and when *Coronation Street* began in 1960, it was referred to as a "drama series" or even a "drama-documentary" (Cooke, 2003: 81). But when it comes to *TGF*, there is more than the issue of generic terminology at stake – simply substituting the word "serial" for the word "soap", as has since happened with *The Archers* or *Coronation Street*. While *TGF* was most frequently assigned the label of a "family serial" it clearly departed, *despite* its status as a television "Archers" or "Dales", from both its radio precursors and television successors. As critics such as Rick Altman (1999) and Olaf Hoerschelmann (2006) have emphasised, it can be problematic to imply a division between "historical" genres and subsequently conferred "theoretical" categories. This ignores how theoretical genres are always also historical, while it also neatly positions the current genre critic "out of the loop", implying that they function as an objective observer "rather than player, in the genre game" (Altman, 1999: 28). Given that this chapter examines how the critical work on soap opera *can* be productive in analysing *TGF*, it does not intend to perpetuate this duality. But it is mindful of the fact that academic work on soap opera, in the British context at least, often *begins* with the narrative model offered by *Coronation Street* – a programme which emerged *after TGF* had been taken off air.

This chapter does not aim to resolve the question as to whether *TGF* should be categorised as a soap, not least of all because, as Jason Mittell outlines, the aim of a discursive approach to genre should not be to ascertain what genres "really mean", or to pinpoint which texts fit where (2004b: 174). Rather, we should "focus on the breadth of discursive enunciations around any given instance, mapping out as many articulations of genre as possible and situating them within larger cultural contexts and relations of power" (ibid). The notion of power is returned to below, but this idea of genre as a *process* (see also Neale, 1990), as well the emphasis on exploring written traces of the programme's circulation, seems particularly attractive in relation to television from the 1950s given that audiovisual material can be scarce. Another way of casting Mittell's point is to ask, "in what genres [was a programme seen to] . . . participate?" (Hoerschelmann, 2006: 26). "[I]ndicators of genre participation" can be found in the multiple sites, ranging across the programme itself, newspaper reviews, production documents, publicity and audience reception (ibid).

The idea of multiple articulations of genre, and a struggle between them, is most explicitly dramatised in the often fraught relationship between the main scriptwriters, Michael and Roland Pertwee, and the BBC. Although other scriptwriters were used as the programme progressed, the Pertwees were the primary writers, and these working practices again reflect the programme's different narrative structure. The BBC files on *MDD* and *The Archers* are filled with the minutes of group meetings which planned future narrative arcs. In contrast, the files on *TGF* play out a rather closed dialogue between the Pertwees and the Producer, John Warrington. Michael Pertwee would go on to have a long career writing for television, but *TGF* appeared to be his first venture into the new medium, and the Pertwees represented a curious choice when we consider what the BBC were aiming for. According to the Producer, the writers must display "a feeling for television and the family".[34] Writers with experience of working on the radio serials were brought in to contribute to *TGF* from time to time, but the prominence of the Pertwees indicates how, while the BBC were increasingly investing in script units and training resources for television scriptwriters, there was not as yet a ready pool of serial writers upon which television could draw. Rather than the BBC plumping for writers with experience of radio, they apparently decided to privilege the skill of writing for the *screen*. Michael and his father Roland had extensive experience in writing for British films. Roland had a long list of credits, including work on the popular Gainsborough costume film melodramas in the 1940s. Michael had largely worked on British comedies and thrillers – influences which may in part explain the various generic frameworks through which *TGF* moved.

The Groves do . . . documentary

The Pertwees were recognised as the authors of the family, but it was the BBC that had "brought them to life".[35] This process was not without its struggles and tensions. In the dialogue which ensued, it was precisely the politics of *TGF*, and its aesthetic, generic and cultural contours, which were at stake. Although this could be perceived as a personal, idiosyncratic dialogue between the writers and the Producer of a particular programme, it raises broader issues about approaches to television genre within television historiography.

A key goal from the BBC's point of view was to offer an image of a real family, not a family played by actors and actresses, and it was suggested that the viewer should discover the Groves as they "would [if] a new family moved next door".[36] This surely conflicted with the family's rather self-reflexive name, as "Grove" referred the audience to the programme's creation at Lime Grove Studios. Nevertheless, the strength of the programme's claim to the real is suggested by the fact that one of the generic descriptors which floated around *TGF* was "documentary". Certainly, many of the outside sequences in *TGF*, which are filmed inserts, do have what we would now associate with a realist, and even documentary, aesthetic, although this link is complicated by the fact that the term documentary had a very loose usage in these early years, taking in outside broadcasts, illustrated talks and "anything more or less non-fictional" (Scannell, 1979: 101). But the label of documentary appeared to have most currency in relation to what has since been mocked as the didactic address of *TGF*. With regard to the much cited (but atypical) episode

"Prevention and Cure", which deals with burglary and home security, some viewers felt it was a "clever blend of entertainment and instruction", while others resented:

> their favourite serial being used in this way. "Entertainment should be entertainment, not just a lot of propaganda" declared a housewife. Viewers in this group found the detailed explanations of the safety devices etc, very boring and complained that the whole programme was too much like a documentary.[37]

It is true that the first sequence in this episode appears to be driven by the desire to illustrate and educate rather than dramatise. The episode begins with Dad and Jack in the study receiving a visit from the police, who are handing out advice to the neighbourhood on home security following a spate of burglaries. Mr Grove explains how he will be glad of the advice, although he doesn't "think there's much to tempt a crook here". This sets up the narrative context for what is to follow (a crook will be "tempted"), but the rest of the sequence is not motivated by the imparting of narrative information. The policeman illustrates how naive Mr Grove's perception of his home security is, and when Mr Grove talks of Gran's "nest egg under the bed", the policeman asks: "Why doesn't she deposit it in a bank, or in a simple wall safe, like this?" The camera then cuts to a close-up of a brochure with the image and text of an advert clearly visible: "Wall Safes: For Protection in the Home". The policeman launches into a discussion of window fastenings, and as the camera moves in to focus on the locks in his hands, he regales the viewer with detailed information about cost, mechanisms and fittings ("Bore two holes, one above the other, and then fit in the screw"). In terms of the programme's positioning at the intersection of different generic discourses, it is clear here that, as the viewers' complaints suggest, an association with "documentary" was not always an occasion for praise. The term is also used to *criticise* both *TGF* and *The Appleyards* when they are seen as "too ordinary . . . more a documentary about the chores of life and [less] of an entertainment programme".[38] Despite the fact that the term documentary lacked a distinct status, it is still used to mark out the appropriate (and inappropriate) material for fictional programming, which is here aligned firmly with entertainment.

Stop laughing please: the Groves are *no* joke!

When it came to the negotiations between the BBC and the writers, a more controversial generic framework was comedy. It is clear that *TGF* was more naturalistic than *Life with the Lyons*, which bears the generic markers *of* a comedy. In the extant edition of *Life with the Lyons*, we hear audience laughter and applause at appropriate moments throughout, and as the opening titles come up, a male voice-over announces the performative entrance of the characters ("Ben Lyons!", "Bebe Daniels Lyon"!) as they emerge into the proscenium-arch performance space. Organised around set-piece gags, as well as forms of direct address to the viewer, the relationship with Variety/music hall, as well as American sitcoms, is clear to see (see also Thumim, 2004: 160–163). *Life with the Lyons* makes for a very different generic viewing experience than *TGF*, but comedy still represented an important, if contested, narrative strand.

In 1954 the Producer bluntly outlined in correspondence with the Head of Light Entertainment how:

> [The Pertwees] have little knowledge or understanding of our own particular family. They have constantly used them as figures upon which they pin plots irrespective of character development. We have carefully developed this family so that they are now very real. As you know, much re-writing and story alignment has been done by me.[39]

The problem here was exacerbated when the programme was reduced from 20 minutes to 13.5 minutes (although at other times it was 30 minutes long), and the Producer reiterated that character development was becoming impossible. There are a "few episodes like last Friday's where it is a simple little joke – in other words, Friday's was in sketch form".[40] A series of comic events, with the emphasis on immediate effect rather than narrative development, is suggested by some of the synopses, especially for the earlier episodes. As the plan for episode 8, transmitted on 27 May 1954, outlines:

> Lennie breaks Frank Turner's cold frame with pebble from his catapult. Later brought home by policeman who, in demonstrating how dangerous a catapult can be, broke Dad's window . . . Turner . . . . Demonstrate[s] high trajectory stuff and pebble breaks window in [car] . . . . From there the episode degenerates into general smashing.[41]

Other synopses beg even closer comparisons with comedy, or to be more specific, farce, and Michael Pertwee's experience in writing film farces seems notable here. The episode "Dramatic Licences" (no longer extant in its original form) has been referenced as an example of the programme's tendency to give moral lessons to its viewers, as it involves a visit from the television detector van (Evans, 1995). But when we examine the wider narrative context, the episode is something of a *tour de force* in farcical events, pivoting on an ongoing chain of comic confusions. The Groves have a dog called Rusty at this time, and a series of confusions ensues over the issue of a licence for the television and a licence for the dog. Rusty gets lost and in the midst of the chaos, the Groves can't find their television licence. The postman then gets mistaken for the television licensing official, and further mix-ups and misheard conversations ensue. Lennie later recalls that the TV licence is kept in the back of the set, but the police are already bringing a new licence round, and ring to say they have also found Rusty the dog. As the synopsis explains:

> It is then realised that the dog has not got a licence. Dad and the children go to the police station, but all is well, when it is realised that the dog won't be six months old until the following day. [This] . . . says Lennie, calls for a party for the dog.[42]

In begging a comparison with the restoration of the status quo at the end of a sitcom episode, this highlights how it is less narrative content, or even structure, which distinguished *TGF* from *Life with the Lyons*. It is more the case that, while *TGF* "participates" in the genre of comedy, it is not understood to be its dominant generic frame, particularly when it comes to performance styles, the construction of mise en scène, and the address to the television viewer.

While uncovering these competing generic frames may begin to question the confident labelling of *TGF* as a soap, they might also be seen as leading us *toward* it. British soap opera has historically pivoted on a combination of aesthetic influences, particularly realism, melodrama and light entertainment (see Geraghty, 1991). Comic narratives are common in British soaps, and they are often used to balance a more dramatic storyline within a particular episode. When *Coronation Street* began 1960 it was sometimes categorised as a "television comedy",[43] and the significance of comedy as part of the family serial was already established by *The Archers*. Another way of viewing *TGF*'s generic hybridity is of course to recognise the category of soap opera as necessarily hybrid in itself. With its interweaving of realism, comedy and (as discussed below) crime and melodrama, *TGF* might actually be said to dramatise this hybridity in more explicit form. Comedy, in what the BBC saw as the appropriate measure, was intended to speak to the family appeal of the programme, and many viewers appreciated this address. Audience Research recorded in 1956 that as "this was a spot that the whole family could enjoy, care should be taken to keep it in a lighter vein, with no major tragedies or unpleasant experiences".[44] With the return of a new series of *TGF* in

1956, certain viewers explained how: "We are so sorry this . . . series has started off with so much trouble for the Groves and hope things will be brighter soon", while it was also suggested that "a little light relief is needed . . . so far there have been too many depressing family troubles".[45]

These comments point to the difficulty of homogenising the narrative focus, as well as the dramatic tone, of the programme. In addition to the comic escapades, other episodes revolved around Daphne winning a poster competition and becoming a contestant on a panel game on BBC television, Mum and Pat deciding to go on slimming pills, Mum and Dad reminiscing about their youth (complete with flashbacks) while a storm rages outside, the family going on a seaside holiday, the Groves helping to deliver a neighbour's baby on New Year's Eve, Jack getting involved with the "wrong crowd" and a drink driving scare, the younger children uncovering a robbery plot involving a bogus Father Christmas, and the romantic entanglements of Pat and Jack.[46] With the programme ranging across domestic squabbles, holiday fun, death, violent crime and romance, this suggests why the BBC are concerned that, drawing on a realist conception of psychologically complex characters, the family illustrate development, and are not simply figures animated by sketches and skits. The BBC were not dismissive of light domestic comedy in itself – as we have seen, they were also producing it. Comedy, as the viewer comments attest, also complemented the BBC's *own* conception of the programme as a wholesome family serial. But what the BBC saw as the programme's over-use of this genre was related to the perception that it threatened its aesthetic and social claim to the real. After all, how could the public take the Groves seriously as next-door neighbours, proffering the ideal of "the family [as] . . . the key and the centre of all social life", if they were not seen as credible in the first place?

"Put a chain on the door because fear is here": the Groves do crime and horror!

Comedy was not the only generic frame through which *TGF* negotiated its identity. Although the popular conception of the Groves suggests that their world is "very safe [and] very secure . . . Nothing really disrupts the social fabric",[47] this demands qualification. While for the most part the family was represented as secure, both ideologically and literally, it is difficult to over-emphasise the ever-present threat of crime. This might again lead us to a connection with soap opera, given that in a more recent discussion of *EastEnders*, Hobson observes how "an ongoing atmosphere of the threat of crime is part of the unspoken ambience of the series" (2003: 134). Hobson's description might just as easily be of *TGF*, although its interest in this sphere largely operated at the level of every-day, mundane crime. While invariably on the "right" side of the law, it was not unusual to find the family helping the police with their enquires, such as when Mr Grove was casting his eye over a line-up to identify a robber, the family were foiling a plan to kidnap young Lennie, or when they found themselves the victims of attempted burglary.

Collectively, these narratives perhaps offer a sense of unrest, suggest-ing that there are forces of disruption lurking beneath the double-fronted suburban house of lower-middle-class life. But they also resist easy his-torical contextualisation, containing, for example, no clear references to the post-war "war on crime" or the juvenile delinquents which populated television documentary or current affairs. As Sydney-Smith's *Beyond Dixon of Dock Green: Early British Police Series* describes, it was ini-tially in the hybrid form of the story-documentary that crime was explored, with programmes such as *Telecrimes* (1946), *The Murder Rap* (1947) and *War on Crime* (1950) reconstructing studio enactments of true crimes (2002: 70). But while both the story-documentary and crime fiction would foreground their public service function (educating, informing, reassuring), there was always the question of appropriate audience address, and related to this, discourses of taste. With respect to the earlier story-documentaries and their penchant for serious crime: "What constituted a . . . diet of crime and violence was found by viewers to be somewhat 'lurid'" (Sydney-Smith, 2002: 66), and correspondence in the *Radio Times* complained that it was unsuitable for a family audi-ence. This relationship between ideological values, scheduling and genre was also negotiated by *TGF*.

The emphasis was largely on petty crime, with aspects of useful advice on crime prevention incorporated for good measure. But this was not always the case, whether we refer to the death by drink-driving accident, or the night when "Fear" came to *TGF*. "Fear" was a two-part story written by the Pertwees which ran in February 1957. Reflecting back on the programme's ambiguous investment in narrative continuity, "Fear" had a rather uneasy relationship with the ideology of the extant 1956 edition, "Prevention and Cure". In "Prevention and Cure" the policeman explains how intruders or burglars "generally pick on a darkened house anytime", and he advises Mr Grove to "Put a chain on the door, and then you can tell your wife if she's ever alone, never to take callers for granted". But these measures don't seem to be at all reliable in "Fear" a few months later when what the scripts refer to as "two escaped crimi-nal lunatics" break into the house and threaten its inhabitants. The sense of threat and fear here is heightened by the fact that the Groves have recently left their family home and moved into a maisonette flat. This was the result of grave financial difficulties after Jack made a bad business deal on his father's behalf. The publicity surrounding the move details how the family have joined the hosts of "flat-dwellers" with strangers living around them. In fact, the Victorian flats represent an "ugly sight", a "decaying monster", which the Groves must revitalise with their "real family atmosphere".[48] This eerie, and almost gothic, context seems pertinent when we examine how "Fear" unfolds.

Dad and Jack are occupied at the Builders and Allied Trades Social Evening, and with the younger children in bed (and Pat having moved out), Mum thinks she hears something in the flat above. Gran tells her not to imagine things, and sits listening to the radio:

> Announcer: With the close of that [dance] number it only remains to say Toodle-loo from the Silly Billies.
> [Howling wind is heard from outside]
> Voice [on radio]: This is the third episode from the *Murders of the Rue Morgue* and your reader tonight will be Boris Schlager.
> [Gran switches off the radio and leans back in her chair]
> Mum [enters]: Gran, don't be startled. We've . . . got some visitors.[49]

Readings of literary crime, mystery and even ghost stories were popular on BBC radio, and the series *Appointment with Fear* was broadcast on the Light Programme between 1946 and 1955 (Wheatley, 2002: 172). But the setting of the scene above, particularly the reference to the openly contrived "Silly Billies", also indicates a flight from verisimilitude. Indeed, in previous times, the BBC would not even allow Mr Grove to listen to the cricket on the radio if the game was out of season. The move from the music to Schlager's reading also plays out an explicit shift in genre and tone, self-reflexively mirroring events in the programme's diegetic world. Mum and Gran know from radio news coverage that the criminals, Tony and Will, killed a prison warden on their escape. To add to the terror, they are immediately informed by Will that: "We're certified see? So it don't matter what we do. They can't do nothing to us". Mrs Grove warns Will and Tony that her "quick-tempered" husband will be back soon, and after Will produces what is described in the script as a "meat axe", she aims to placate them, rather predictably given her entrenched domestic role, with a quick "snack". They all listen to the news coverage about the escape on the radio, and Mrs Grove offers a pretence of calm and normality when a policeman happens to call at the door to warn the family of the escape ("with those two criminals at large you can't be too careful"). The first instalment ends as the policeman walks away, leaving the family trapped with dangerous – and apparently insane – criminals inside.

This edition of *TGF* attracted an immediate response from viewers and press critics. The *Daily Telegraph* reported "Protests over Grove Family", and described how the BBC switchboard was "jammed with calls" protesting about the content of the episode.[50] A letter to the paper from one viewer, a Mr Richard Wear from Weybridge, Surrey, vividly recalls the escapees:

> dominating the home. One, ape-like and convincing, fondled and almost slavered over a butcher's cleaver, threatening mother and grandmother . . . The viewer was deliberately left in suspense until the second episode, which we are now awaiting . . . Children are watching [and] up until now it could be regarded as harmless entertainment . . . Suddenly, without the usual trailer warning nervous viewers, the bed-time child and innocent parent are faced with "Fear". [This represented a] . . . particular play on fear and insecurity as the programme offers a home so easily identified with [our] . . . own. Surely this second episode should be cancelled with an apology and firm promise by the BBC that it is not its intention to enter the "horror comics" market as the answer to competition.[51]

There is a distaste for what is seen as the "commercial" nature of the episode, not only in terms of its use of the cliff-hanger, but its exploitation of "lurid" sensationalism – more akin, the viewer asserts, to "cheap" horror fiction than crime.

It was also this event which prompted what appears to be the only description of *TGF* as a soap opera within the existing BBC evidence from the time. Greatly displeased by the controversy surrounding the family serial, the Controller of Television Programmes, Kenneth Adam, insisted:

> I think there is no doubt whatsoever that a rather bad mistake was made by suddenly introducing into the last episode . . . incidents of violence and terror which in my mind are quite foreign to the . . . romantic atmosphere of soap opera . . . Without abandoning continuity altogether, it is necessary for these two criminal lunatics to be got out of the house where they were left at the end of last week's episode.[52]

Live transmission offered flexibility here, enabling the BBC to make immediate changes to the narrative for Part 2 of "Fear". But the fact that Adam did not work closely with the programme is suggested by his description of its "romantic atmosphere". Even allowing for differences of historical interpretation, as well as the the romantic entanglements of Jack or Pat (discussed below), this description doesn't seem to capture the tone of the programme at all. It suggests a clear gendered address, an address toward women, which is not overtly evident. Yet in terms of the fluid, malleable nature of generic definitions, brought into being at the level of discourse, this seems to be precisely the point. Adam constructs the idea of a "soft", romantic and implicitly feminine programme, to shore up his claim that "Fear" was utterly *in*appropriate.

In contrast to the use of comedy, a key problem here is that straying into the generic territory of horror or crime undermines the promise of a family serial, a term which indicates a moral and ideological terrain, as well as a form of scheduled address. This foregrounds how conceptions of television genre are inextricably related to scheduling practices (Mittell, 2004a, Ellis, 2000), and in relation to *TGF*, we can see this framework in process. There was also the concern that unlike the use of everyday crime, the exceptional events of "Fear" threatened the pro- gramme's realism and its claim to act as a "reflecting" mirror. As Mr Wear's complaint implies, the idea of cultivating proximity between audi- ence and screen clearly backfires here, as the episode undermines per- ceptions of the safety of the domestic sphere.

The idea of genre as a discursive struggle is clear here, and *TGF* was negotiating a space for itself in between the often conflicting demands of the BBC, the scriptwriters and its audience. The programme juggled this moving canvas in complex ways, "strategically activating and denying" aspects of genre as suited to the context in hand (Mittell, 2004a: 198). As Mittell's paradigm suggests, negotiating generic categories is a process shaped by discourses of power. In relation to *TGF*, generic categories are activated and denied in ways which are shaped by the programme's investment in the real (and its associated ideological meanings), as well as wider discourses of taste and cultural value.

"High-strung passion and tears" (but not too much): measuring melodrama

Issues of cultural value are also relevant in assessing the role played by melo- drama. As argued above, for the most part, the idea of a "romantic atmos- phere" does not capture the address of *TGF*. But it is important to recognise that it did have a presence. This was further evidence of the programme's bid to offer something for everyone – in this case, perhaps, the women in the audience. Melodrama is better defined as a mode of expression rather than a genre, and with an emphasis on the privileging of emotional response emerging from interpersonal relationships (Allen, 1988, Mittell, 2004a: 174), soap opera has often been studied as a form of television melodrama, especially in the American context (Gledhill, 1987, 1992, Modleski, 1987). As this chapter has observed, the currency of melodrama, especially in terms of its identity as a commercial, "mass" and feminised culture, has sur- faced as a point of tension in the development of British serial drama (Hilmes, 2007). In her book, *Watching Dallas: Soap Opera and the*

Melodramatic Imagination, Ien Ang also notes early British examples as
non-melodramatic examples of the genre (1985: 87).

If melodrama can be discussed at the level of narrative content,
performance style and techniques of aesthetic construction, we can
immediately sense the different tone of a sequence in which Pat goes on
a picnic with her boyfriend, Ronald (particularly when compared to the
comedy episodes). The script details how:

> The camera starts on a close-up shot of Ronald's left hand taking a coffee
> cup out of Pat's hand. The camera then pulls back as she sets the cup aside,
> then turns as [Ronald] . . . takes her in his arms and kisses her. Pat then
> pulls back and says "you're not to, you mustn't".[53]

Raising issues about the programme's construction of femininity which
are pursued later in this chapter, the possibility of a romantic tone is elsewhere curtailed by the programme's competing forms of generic address.
For example, the story in which Pat receives three marriage proposals in
one day is literally dealt with like farce, and much like the edition
"Dramatic Licences", it is structured around comedic confusions and
misunderstandings.

Rudolph Arnheim approved of the fact that the BBC's radio serial
Front Line Family avoided the "melodrama of high-strung passion,
tears . . . and overdrawn suspense" characteristic of the American soap
(Arnheim, 1944: 83–84, cited in Hilmes, 2007: 11), and it is true that
TGF did not seem eager to venture into this territory. Arnheim's description invokes popular definitions of melodrama, in which it is seen as
pivoting on stock characters, far-fetched *and* predictable narrative
moments, as well as over-wrought acting (Geraghty, 2006: 224). In comparison, writing in film and television studies has explored the term's
notoriously long history, and its multiple uses and meanings. Film studies
in particular developed more complex definitions of melodrama, suggesting that, when compared to realist drama, it offered a different mode
of aesthetic expression and world view (see Gledhill, 1987).

But while potentially productive on an analytical level, it is important to retain a sense of the term's historical currency in relation to
TGF in the 1950s. What did the term mean to the BBC? References to
"melodrama" occasionally crop up in the file memos, and they invoke
some of the dismissive, and popular, definitions mentioned above. For
example, when the Groves were accidentally involved in a bank robbery,
Pertwee felt it would be more apt if a neighbour, rather than a Grove,
was shot in the event. To have a Grove injured would be too far-
fetched, "and [thus] put us more in the melodrama class".[54] Here, melodrama is understood as a schematic plot device which might also involve

"the discovery of hidden relationships, fatal coincidences, missed meet-ings, and lost chances" (Gledhill, 1992: 108), and which Gledhill posi-tions as marking out "powerful underlying forces" in the melodramatic world.

The term also skirts around the BBC's emphasis on the need for natu-ralistic acting – acting which should not announce itself *as* a performance at all. The programme's emphasis on restraint is equally suggested by its infrequent use of the close-up, and while melodrama might demand "the welling up of music, the exchange of glances, a slamming of the door" (Geraghty, 1991: 31), many of the programme's narrative strands, from lost dogs to farcical misunderstandings, would have made such an aes-thetic highly inappropriate. While melodrama embraces music to carry climactic moments, *TGF* avoided non-diegetic music altogether – some-thing also evident in subsequent British soap operas.

The preference for restraint is fascinatingly played out in the final edition of the programme, "Under Way", written by Mitchell Warren rather than the Pertwees. In this edition, the family rent out a bunga-low at the seaside. The first part of the episode involves the last-minute preparations for the holiday, including squabbles over transport, squeez-ing clothes into suitcases, and the trouble of hooking up a trailer to Jack's car. Although Jack and girlfriend Jane are travelling by car with the luggage, the rest of the family take the train. The sequences inside the train carriage, complete with a hubbub of discussion about the swap-ping of seats, are realistic in simulating the rhythm and movement of the journey, and the squabbles are convincingly presented through over-lapping dialogue. The exterior shots, as seen in the footage of the Groves arriving at the station, and then the night-time shots of them walking along the beach,[55] again have something of a documentary quality.

As "Under Way" progresses it appears to dramatise how realism was conceived as the prevailing framework, policing and restraining compet-ing forms of aesthetic address.[56] The family are sitting in deckchairs on the beach, or in this sequence, against a studio backdrop, and the scene cuts between this location and filmed inserts of the action out at sea. Lennie and Jack are going out in a sailing boat, and the family wave them off with excitement. But Gran had already commented before they left home that the boys might "drown themselves", and Mum anxiously enquires as they set sail: "Do you think they'll be all right Bob?" We are thus well prepared for the observation that the "wind is whipping up", and we cut to wardens in the sailing club, peering out to sea through their binoculars as all other boats hastily make for the shore. The scene then cuts between the wardens in the tower and long shots of the boat out at sea. As the weather worsens the boat flips over, and the warden decides that he had "better get a helicopter out – looks like one of them has been knocked unconscious". We cut between what now appear to be quite adventurous aerial shots from the helicopter in the sky, and a close-up of Gran's anxious expression on the shore. Her hands are cupping her face, and her is mouth open, while her eyes are wide with fear. The scene then cuts back to the helicopter, again from the perspective of an aerial shot, and the sound of its loud, rhythmic motor dominates the sequence, blocking out any sound from the panic below. A Royal Navy rescuer is wound down by rope and the unconscious Jack is slowly winched up to safety. At this point, the scene cuts to a medium shot of Mum and Dad in the tense silence of the warden's tower. With the camera positioned behind them, we witness a fleeting moment in which Mum leans on Dad with her eyes closed and her hand lifted to her brow. She then utters the words "thank god" as Jack is hauled into the helicopter. The scene ends with a moral lesson from the (surely rather uncompassionate) warden as he interjects: "I'd thank the Royal Navy and the tax payers. [It] cost[s] a lot of money to get that helicopter out you know. Sailing is a wonderful sport, but you *do* need to know something about it".

This sequence of events represented the finale to *TGF* as a whole – it was the last ever episode – and it was intended to excite the audience. But there is simultaneously a sense of unease about exploiting these possibilities. Whether with regard to aesthetic construction or performance styles, the scene could hardly be described as sensational, and there is a nervousness about celebrating what Geraghty has elsewhere called the "aesthetic pleasures of its telling" (2006: 224). Aside from the realist visual aesthetic of the air-rescue sequences (which could be mistaken for a documentary on the Air Sea Rescue), it is the sound which is most notable, with the deafening noise of the helicopter taking the place of any dramatic music. At the same time, with Gran's reactive gestures and Mum's archetypal fainting pose, the deafening noise of the helicopter also *demands* the use of facial expressions and gestures to show what cannot be expressed in dialogue, and the scene calls upon the women to provide the appropriate emotional responses here. In melodrama, of course, the human body "provides a rich vocabulary of gesture", subordinating verbal discourse to "an expressive language of the visible" (Gledhill, 1992: 108). But these reactions are very brief, flashing up like momentary glimmers in the context of an otherwise restrained, realist framework. Mum's climactic expression of relief ("thank god!"), is also quickly curtailed by the rational, didactic comment from the male warden.

The viewer responses to this episode reflect its use of competing aesthetics, and the cultural values with which they are associated. Some viewers praised the realism of the episode, commenting how "it caught the harassed atmosphere of the 'befores' [of packing] as well as the laziness in the deck chair on the beach".[57] But others felt that it then became too "far-fetched" and unbelievable at the level of script and narrative (the rescue). As Steve Neale explains, melodrama can offer narrative events which seem "unmotivated (or undermotivated) from a realist point of view. There is an excess of effect over cause, of the extraordinary over the ordinary" (Neale, 1986: 7, cited in Geraghty, 1991: 30). There is hardly an "excess of effect" here, but this rescue represented one of several occasions when the programme was seen as privileging, somewhat problematically, "the extraordinary over the ordinary" (with bank robberies, kidnap plots and escaped criminal lunatics juxtaposed with mundane domestic squabbles, the Groves were not short of an eventful life). Given that *TGF* could also be criticised as too depressing and humdrum, more a "documentary about the chores of life" than an entertaining fiction,[58] it is difficult not to be reminded of the paradoxical critique levelled at British soap opera: that both too *much* and too *little* happens within its diegetic worlds.

The analysis of the sequence perpetuates the notion that realism and melodrama are somehow opposed. In challenging this perspective, work on British soap opera has drawn attention to the complex co-existence of realism and melodrama (Geraghty, 1991). British soaps have historically combined a claim to the fidelity of class representation, an emphasis on a naturalistic mise en scène and a narrative interest in topical ("real") issues, with a taste for sensational plotting and moments of highly melodramatic performance. But this co-existence seems uneasy and self-conscious in the sequence from *TGF*, and there is perhaps indeed an underlying anxiety about straying into modes of expression, performance and narrative which were most readily associated with melodramatic "feminine" fiction. But whether this should be positioned as a form of "masculinisation" remains a complex question. This argument still relies upon the invocation of American soap opera as the dominant (only) generic source, and the wider validity of this argument of course also depends on whether *TGF* is positioned as a "soap opera" at all.

"What's another word for social climber?" Consuming class

Despite the prevailing perception that it offered a cosy and consensual world, *TGF* was a form of popular fiction aiming to address a range of audience interests. As such, it does not seem surprising that it should bear the marks of a changing cultural environment and competing forms of discursive address – particularly at the level of class and gender. *TGF* seems interested in the idea of changing class boundaries, and it regularly dramatised a negotiation between the old and the new. This was often expressed at a generational level, with the older children representing the possibilities of changing values and aspirations, particularly as these are expressed through consumption. As noted in Chapter 1, a key theme of the time, particularly in the context of the Conservative social imagery of an affluent society, is the idea of changing class identities and boundaries. Laing describes how, supporting the dominant Conservative image "of the satisfied affluent worker and his family lay a considerable weight of detailed social description suggesting the progressive disappearance of the working class" (1986: 13). The Groves are imagined to be lower-middle rather than working class, perhaps aiming to provide a point of identification for class cultures on either "side". But the notion of a certain indeterminacy – being in the middle – also provided an opportunity to play out questions of mobility.

One of the most intriguing explorations of class and consumerism surfaced around the set of *TGF* – a visual property which had not been required by the radio serials. The living-room set was most frequently used for interior sequences. The family dinner table was situated to the left of the room next to the front door, and in the extant edition "Under Way", the camera tracks right to reveal armchairs, a sideboard and a television set. A picture of youngest daughter Daphne can be seen on the mantelpiece, but the overall effect of the room is quite dark, and it is difficult to make out individual objects. The armchairs are "comfy" looking and large, and sport a floral pattern on a pale background. The wallpaper is also floral, with large roses picked out on a darker background. But as Hopkins reminds us in his social history of the decade, busy wallpaper, particularly of the floral variety, was *out*, as were heavy armchairs with puffed cushions and sagging sides (1963: 343). The emphasis was now on the home space as "a design for living", minimalistic in its "uncluttered", "smooth" and "efficient" contours (ibid). In the immediate post-war years, consumers could only purchase utility furniture, but this soon changed. In 1951 the Festival of Britain showcased the vanguard of changing furniture styles, as well as new textiles and appliances, with influences displayed from America, Italy, Scandinavia and beyond. By the mid-1950s, this furniture made the transition to mass production and prices dropped – with G-Plan furniture the most popular example of this trend.[59]

This context seems relevant when we consider the refurbishment of the Grove home after a fire in 1956. The new set was explicitly described as "contemporary style", and the press took a keen interest in the change, reporting how the Council of Industrial Design, set up in 1944 by the government to promote the improvement of design in the British industry, had supplied the furniture. The furniture was referred to as "Swedish-style", and the new set sported contrasting walls, a black and white tweed sofa, "scientific armchairs", a bamboo coal-scuttle and a modern radio.[60] (The television was evidently still "new" enough to fit in with this landscape.) It is not entirely clear why the decision to alter the set was taken, but it was not well received by the press, nor by key BBC personnel working on the programme. The *News Chronicle* noted that while it might be good business for the modern furniture manufacturers, the new set risks "a rather horrid uniformity of style in hundreds of homes up and down the country . . . Fashion largely dictates what clothes we wear: let's keep it from ruling our homes too ruthlessly."[61] The *News Chronicle*'s distaste for uniformity and homogeneity can be seen to feed off a wider perspective, now most associated with Richard Hoggart's book *The Uses of Literacy*, which argued that traditional working-class culture was under threat from the new mass consumerism of the 1950s. While the Groves are not imagined to be working class, it does seem significant that, as part of his wider distaste for the "demand for conformity", contemporary style furniture is singled out for negative comment in Hoggart's book (1958: 158). Hoggart was also critical of what he saw as the advertiser-peddled values of " 'going one better', 'getting on' . . . 'out-doing all others' ", which were being sold to all classes of consumers (1958: 145).

A similar view, although perhaps one emerging from a different perspective, underlies the internal responses to the set change within the BBC. As the Producer explains, everything the family did now appeared "unreal or false".

> The design is negative. No warmth, unlived in and unloved. In fact, not the home of a pleasant, middle-aged lower middle-class suburban family with four-children and a . . . grandmother. The best description given to me so far is [that it looks like] "a young newly-married civil service clerk trying to be Mayfair on £8 per week".[62]

The idea for the new set had been taken from *House and Garden* magazine, and Warrington insisted that it was "wrong" for the family, as well as the audience, given that:

> Although I know it was bad taste, the first set had a distinct suburban character . . . Frankly, the new set is colourless and completely without any character whatsoever. Certain changes must be made:
>
> i) Pallid wallpaper must be changed to a distinct strong pattern
> ii) Stained dark – chairs and table

iii) We must find many more "ordinary" props, calendars to hang on walls, books, ashtrays and bits and pieces.[63]

The justification behind these discussions, at least on a surface level, is again that the image of lower-middle-class life must appear "true", "real" and "ordinary". But in the memo, we also gain a momentary glimpse, as the reference to "bad taste" suggests, of how the contours of this image are being *actively* drawn.

The set was duly returned to its original form, and the experimentation was later explained as having been prompted by the children. On a broader level, this expressed the view that the younger generation were embracing their role as members of a new mass society – a society which expresses identity through consumption. Just as the new design of the Grove home had been found in *Homes and Gardens*, so Jack and Pat are seen to aspire to ideals constructed by modern media images. Jack is studying modern decoration at technical college, and he reflects on the interior of his dad's office by complaining that:

> Jack: We never get beyond a lick of distemper – white or cream paint inside and out . . . You've only got to look at the magazines to see what's being done in the way of interior decoration. I saw one colour picture of a room with dark green walls and a ceiling of blood-red crimson.
> Dad: With a blonde film star sprawling in the middle of it, I suppose.
> Jack: As a matter of fact there was, but it goes to show the trend of modern thought and I don't like the idea that Grove and Son are twenty years behind the times.[64]

While Jack's aspirations are loosely linked to his career expertise, Pat's modern ideals are predictably expressed in terms of personal consumption. In one edition, Pat and Mum sit examining fashion spreads in magazines:

> Mum: Now I call *that* a pretty house-coat.
> Pat: Show?
> [Mum exhibits the paper]
> Pat: A bit ordinary.
> Mum: Well, I'm an ordinary woman and I like my clothes to match.
> Pat: [flicking over the page] I say! This royal pastel mutation mink is something else![65]

Just as the Groves' furniture is changed back to its original, "homely" state, so these modern ideas are treated with some suspicion by the programme. Indeed, they are presented as faintly ridiculous, and Mum and Dad are set up as the voice of reason. In this regard, Mum and Dad validate a particular generational and class point of view, protecting what is seen as the emphasis on "ordinary" (lower-middle-class) ideals.

There may have been a concern here, as mapped across BBC quiz/game shows (Chapter 3) as well as *TGF*, that the promotion of consumer culture "engenders a sense of cultural fragmentation and promotes class conflict" (Turnock, forthcoming), particularly when public service was built upon the ideal of social unity. It is certainly notable that, although motivated by different attitudes and concerns, Hoggart, the BBC, as well as the Pertwees, all come to the conclusion that people are better off reining in their affluent aspirations and remaining as they are. But while this view has a currency as a preferred perspective across the programme, we should be wary of saying, as Medhurst does, that *TGF* simply instructs the Groves and their viewers to "stay in [their] . . . place".[66] The programme was aiming to provide a range of identification points for different classes, generations and attitudes in such a way that makes firm generalisations problematic.

"Gone all domestic" (and getting out): the contradictions of Pat Grove

The fact that *TGF* wants to explore and entertain change, even if it is ultimately wary of its possibilities, is also demonstrated by its representation of gender, or more specifically, femininity. Thumim argues that *TGF* and *Dixon of Dock Green* (BBC, 1955–79) endorsed a conservative patriarchal model of the family, with the women marginalised and their activities "secondary to the plot construction" (2004: 106) (something which might further question *TGF*'s categorisation as a soap). While *TGF* endorsed a patriarchal family structure, the women were not secondary to plot construction, and the narrative point of view varied depending on the storyline in hand. Nevertheless, the cultural historian Elizabeth Wilson comments in *The Lime Grove Story* that Mrs Grove appears "completely sunk in domesticity", and we see a scene re-enacted from a script in which Mrs Grove insists: "I enjoy housework. I wouldn't want to give it up if Bob earned twice as much. Good gracious – what *would* I do all day?" While some viewers observed that "Mrs Grove . . . had a perpetual worried look and . . . she should go out and have some fun occasionally",[67] the verisimilitude of the family set-up was often praised.

But this is not the whole story, as while Mrs Grove may be "sunk in domesticity", eldest daughter Pat is still aiming to "swim". When the programme first begins Pat is 21, and her biography details how she was not "brilliant" at school, went to secretarial college, and then got a job as a secretary. She dislikes this job and throughout the run of the series, she finds it hard to settle, trying a job in a department store, moving on to work in the local library and then becoming a hotel receptionist.[68] This reflected the long-standing pattern of girls engaging in paid work between school and marriage, and precisely because it was perceived as a "stop-gap", it was often seen as less important than the work done by men. But there are differing views on the extent to which changes in post-war education reshaped the field here. While the Education Act (1944) had enabled universal free education for the young adolescent, Wilson argues that it offered a vision of education which aimed to educate girls for their role as future wives and mothers (1980: 33). John Newsom's *The Education of Girls* (1948) has been seen as a touchstone in this respect, advocating domestic training for all young women, aside from a tiny minority of "academic" girls. Others paint a different view, suggesting that wider educational discourses called attention to issues of equality in education, encouraging girls at least to consider "the positive and self-fulfilling possibility of a career in their adult life" (Thumim, 2002b: 214).

The idea of a contradictory context seems fitting when we confront the representations under consideration here. Pat follows in the path of Mrs Dale's daughter Gwen Dale (played by Joan Newell) in BBC radio's *MMD*, and it is interesting that Gwen's options are set out more openly than John Newsom's ideals in *The Education of Girls*. As the editorial policy explains:

> Gwen Dale . . . is at 19 approaching the time when she will decide whether to pursue a professional career, marry and devote herself to domesticity, or attempt to combine a career and married life. From time to time these questions exercise her mind considerably. She is often irked by the restrictions of family life . . . [but she also] finds the idea of leaving home unthinkable.[69]

This framework is itself problematic in presenting these options as an open, and personal, choice, but the description is nevertheless useful in suggesting how a young woman's aspirations might have been viewed in the early 1950s. But although Gwen is fascinatingly described in one script meeting as temporarily developing a "feminist anti-man outlook", it is also later revealed that she isn't very career-minded after all. In fact, she settles for what *she* sees as a rather uninteresting secretarial job. In comparison with Gwen, Pat does not find leaving home "unthinkable", and the move to her new flat later in the programme signals her economic independence, which older brother Jack does not in fact achieve. But Pat seems even more unsure than Gwen Dale as to which route she might pursue: she is not constructed as career-minded, but she regularly baulks at the idea of marital domesticity.

In the existing audiovisual material, Pat bobs about happily, helping Mum in the home and preparing the sandwiches for the holiday trip. But when it comes to Pat's character, and the actress who first played her, written sources leave different traces. Pat may be expected to help with domestic duties, but the scripts gradually reveal that she is far from successful in this sphere. In one edition called "Convalescence", in which Mum is banned from doing housework after an operation, Pat takes on her mother's role. With Pat standing in the kitchen peeling potatoes, a potential suitor, Arthur Turner, turns up:

Arthur: Look at you. Gone all domestic!
Pat: Someone had to run the house while Mum was in hospital.
Arthur: How do you like the job?
Pat: How would *you* like coping for a family of five?
Arthur: Daresay it would be a bit of a bind. Though doing it for two would-n't be quite so bad eh?[70]

Pat explains how she won't be going back to her job at the library even when Mrs Grove is well, and Arthur is quick to intervene by raising the idea of marriage, insisting that she "needn't [look for a job] – if [she] . . . cares to say the word". Although Pat genuinely likes Arthur, she doesn't care to "say the word", and the conversation ends with her chastising him for using an "as if you owned me tone". The notion that Pat has "gone all domestic" suggests that she is trying out the role, and her rel-atively disastrous culinary attempts become something of a running joke in the family as a whole. These disasters, however, seem to emerge as much from a lack of desire to undertake the role, as to reflect Pat's innately poor domestic abilities. In a later edition when Arthur makes a formal proposal of marriage, Pat admits that she gets:

sort of panicky about settling down . . . It's such a big step and so final . . . It seems as if I lead you on. You're so good to me and I take it all and then when you ask me to marry you all I can say is . . .[71]

On one level, this is presented as an example of immature, female inde-cision, and the script says that Mum "looks on smilingly" as Pat dries her tears. But particularly given Pat's uneasy fit with a domestic role, just what she is "panicky" about is left tantalisingly unclear.

Certainly, Pat's narrative function is largely defined by her status as a future wife, and she introduces a stream of potential suitors – and thus nar-rative possibilities – into the family's life. As her own reference to leading Arthur on implies, this was negotiated quite carefully at the level of Pat's sexual identity. The family passed judgement on Jack's relationships, but the issue here was class conflict (girlfriend Beryl is too "posh"). The concern sur-rounding Pat's partnerships related to the policing of her sexuality. When Pat meets an actor called Ronald on the seaside pier, Dad cautions: "making yourself a bit cheap, aren't you? . . . Watch your step, that's all." In a programme which sees itself as being concerned with what the Producer described "standards of conduct [and] . . . morals",[72] it is not surprising that it is made clear that Pat doesn't go "too" far. As noted earlier in the chapter, the story in which Pat receives three marriage proposals in one day is dealt with like farce, and this generic frame is usefully activated to deal with the potentially difficult question of sexual morals here (*three* partners?). When Mr Grove is asked for Pat's hand in marriage by the third suitor, ex-GI Ed Wilson, the episode ends on the invitation to laugh at his confused exasperation: "Look, I don't know whether you're crazy, I'm crazy or Pat's crazy. But you're the third in the last half hour and that's more than I can stand". Pat's indecision provides the context for the entire narrative here, and one possible interpretation is in fact that she doesn't seem so "crazy" at all.

As discussed in Chapter 5 on the subject of television fame, the actress Sheila Sweet who first played Pat leaves *TGF* in 1956. In terms of the extratextual circulation of the programme, she was the only member of the cast to consistently resist the bid to collapse her own identity with her on-screen counterpart (particularly at the level of gender and class). When *TGF* returns for a new series in October 1956, Sweet has been replaced by a new actress, Carole Mowlam. But more than a change of actress, a minor irritation for the BBC and its viewers, this can be read as speaking to the programme's contradictory negotiation of femininity. The programme itself is contradictory in so far as Pat is hesitant about following the path laid out by Mrs Grove – a character who now seems to be untouched by what is understood as the conflict and uncertainty over women's place in the post-war world. But Pat's character is perhaps not untouched by this dilemma, and the discursive struggle between actress and role amplifies the uncertainty expressed by the text itself.

Conclusion – goodbye Groves . . . ?: "A wedding and, ultimately, babies are wanted"

Rather than fetishising *TGF*'s dispensation of social advice and its role in "social engineering" (Thumim, 2004: 146), this chapter has examined the programme from a more varied perspective, exploring its conception across a range of institutional, textual and cultural sites. *TGF*'s clearest relationship with public service emerges from its bid to provide "something for everyone", and it was through this effort that it negotiated its popular appeal. Issues of genre are central here, and in moving away from a textualist approach to television genre, a discursive approach (Mittell, 2004a) may offer particularly exciting possibilities for television history. *TGF*'s practices of generic negotiation *were* shaped by its textual form, but this was only part of the story: practices of categorisation here

were brought into being by the discussion and circulation of the programme as it intersected with debates about writing for television
(medium specificity), television scheduling and regulation, and the BBC's
projection of social values. Without this wider framework, we are left
with the atypical audiovisual evidence of "Prevention and Cure", and the
prevailing conception of *TGF* as a not very appealing "soap". The point
of this approach is not to enable us to decide whether *TGF* is or isn't a
television soap opera, although it is inevitable that readers will make
judgements of their own. The examination of the programme might be
seen as questioning this label as clumsy, ahistorical and retrospective, *or*
it might locate its roots more firmly within this genealogy, contributing
to an understanding of the influences which make up this category today.
There is undoubtedly, and often maddeningly, much of the programme
that seems to anticipate the later development of British soap opera,
although it is also the case that the application of other conceptual frameworks would yield different results.

TGF was transmitted for the last time on the 28 June 1957. It is not
entirely clear why it ceased, although it has been suggested that its insular
family unit limited the possibilities for narrative development in the
longer term (Sydney-Smith, 2002: 98). Even so, the Producer seemed
baffled when he discovered that the Groves were to go: "How do we
explain this to the press? . . . Surely it is not our intention to throw away
a popular programme?"[73] The audience had been slightly depleted by the
competition from commercial television, although this did not appear to
usher in its demise. Nevertheless, before the decision was taken to end
TGF, the BBC engaged a strategy to try and hold on to their viewers
which is highly recognisable to us today. The Producer placed an article
in the *Radio Times* which read:

> *The Grove Family* have been on your screen for exactly three years.
> [But] . . . we should like to know what you think about *The Grove Family*
> still to come. Is Daphne being encouraged enough with her . . . art? . . .
> [S]hould [Pat] still live at home and help Mum . . . ? Do you think Jack
> should . . . get married? . . . *The Grove Family* has always been strictly
> your programme.[74]

It is clear that rather than anticipating the end of the Groves, the
Producer was aiming to map the family's future in ways which were
directly shaped by audience interests and desires. This was a further site
upon which the programme negotiated its generic identity, as the
responses revealed how "violence and murder . . . proved extremely
unpopular", while "a wedding and, ultimately, babies are wanted".[75]
Most of the 300 responses received were from female viewers. Does this

suggest that, in aiming to provide "something for everyone", the BBC had underestimated the significance of the female audience? Does this point us toward the programme's identity as a "soap", or away from it, with *Coronation Street* soon to pick up what *TGF* had patently "failed" to provide? Given that this chapter began with the intention to drop in and spend some time with the Groves, this appropriately leaves the front door ajar – for those "neighbours to the nation" to be revisited (again and again).

Notes

1 *The Lime Grove Story: The Grove Family* (BBC, 26 August 1991).
2 *John Bull*, 5 February 1952.
3 "Mrs Dale's Diary", undated editorial policy. R19/779/2.
4 *Daily Herald*, 3 December 1951.
5 In comparison, an opposition between the rural and suburban seemed to play down discussions of class where *The Archers* was concerned.
6 *The Times*, 29 October 1952.
7 *Birmingham Weekly Post*, 23 March 1951.
8 Audience Research Report, *The Archers*, 22 November 1954.
9 *Daily Mail*, 17 March 1954.
10 As above.
11 "The Groves of Lime Grove", *TV Mirror*, 10 April 1954, p. 22.
12 As above.
13 *Evening News*, 8 October 1954.
14 Viewer comment in "Some Observations on Listeners' Reactions to Mrs Dale's Diary", 19 September 1950. R19/779/2.
15 As above.
16 John Warrington to Head of Light Entertainment, 31 May 1954. T12/137/1.
17 "The Groves of Lime Grove", p. 22.
18 See general correspondence in the file on *Meet the Huggetts*. R19/720.
19 Untitled press review, 10 April 1954.
20 Viewer Research Report, 21 March 1956.
21 Viewer Research Report, 28 June 1957.
22 Undated memo, c. 1953. T12/137/20.
23 Ronald Waldman to Controller of Programmes, Television, 25 September 1953. T12/137/1. My emphasis.
24 As above.
25 "Some Observations on Listeners' Reactions to Mrs Dale's Diary", 17 September 1952. R19/779/2.
26 *TV Times*, 20 February 1956, TVTip database.
27 *TV Times*, 22 September–31 March 1955. TVTip database.
28 *Daily Sketch*, 5 January 1955.
29 John Warrington to Head of Light Entertainment, 6 June 1956. T12/137/20.

30 Senior Planning Asst to Controller of Programmes, Television, "Points on planning method", 11 July 1958. T16/149/2.

31 *Everybody's*, 10 April 1954.

32 John Warrington to Head of Light Entertainment, 31 May 1954. T12/137/1.

33 *The Lime Grove Story*.

34 John Warrington to Head of Light Entertainment, 10 December 1954. T12/137/1.

35 Assistant Head of Copyright to Head of Light Entertainment, undated. T12/137/2.

36 *Everybody's*, 10 April 1954.

37 Viewer Research Report, 21 March 1956.

38 *Evening News*, 8 October 1954.

39 John Warrington to Head of Light Entertainment, 9 September, 1954. T12/137/1.

40 John Warrington to Head of Light Entertainment, 4 April 1955. T12/137/20.

41 Synopses in envelope. T12/137/5.

42 As above.

43 See in particular "How True to Life is Television Comedy?", *The Times*, 21 October 1961. ITC press cuttings.

44 Viewer Research Report, 21 March 1956.

45 Viewer Research Report, 31 October 1956.

46 Evidence all taken from the programme scripts (on microfilm).

47 Andy Medhurst, *The Lime Grove Story*.

48 John Warrington to George Campey, 17 January 1957. T12/137/3.

49 "Fear", episode 129, first part transmitted 27 February 1957.

50 *Daily Telegraph*, 29 February 1957.

51 *Daily Telegraph*, 6 March 1957.

52 Kenneth Adam to Director of Television Broadcasting, 5 March 1957. T12/137/3.

53 Edition no. 46. Scripts.

54 Michael Pertwee to Ronald Waldman, 10 January 1957. T12/137/3.

55 At the same time, and as in television drama more widely, it was often the case that (single-camera) filmed inserts rarely matched the tempo or lighting of the live studio scenes, thus potentially fragmenting the illusion of reality (see also Jacobs, 2000: 127).

56 In this respect, and with regard to the series as a whole, it is interesting that Roland Pertwee's background as a scriptwriter for the Gainsborough film melodramas is kept in check.

57 Viewer Research Report, 28 June 1957.

58 *Evening News*, 8 October 1954.

59 *Thoroughly Modern Antiques* (BBC4, 14 March 2006).

60 *Daily Mail*, 23 January 1957.

61 *News Chronicle*, 10 July 1956.

62 John Warrington to Head of Television Design, 26 November 1956. T12/137/2.

63 John Warrington to Eileen Diss, 10 November 1956. T12/137/20.
64 Edition no. 23. Scripts.
65 Edition no. 38. Scripts.
66 *The Lime Grove Story.*
67 Alice Lowman to John Warrington, 21 May 1957. T12/137/20.
68 The Groves – Home and Away', *Radio Times Annual*, 1955, p. 52.
69 Undated editorial policy. R19/779/2.
70 Edition no. 16. Scripts.
71 Edition no. 22. Scripts.
72 John Warrington to Assistant Head of Copyright, 19 May 1954. T12/137/1.
73 John Warrington to Head of Light Entertainment, undated memo, but c. June 1957. T12/137/20.
74 Undated article prepared for *The Radio Times*, but c. early 1957. T12/137/20.
75 Alice Lowman to John Warrington, 21 May 1957. T12/137/20.

3

"The 'Give-Away' Shows – But Who is *Really* Paying?": rethinking quiz and game shows on 1950s British television

As for the give-away quizzes, we all like the possibility of getting something for nothing. To see someone else getting it at least keeps the possibility alive. (Viewer letter, *The Star*, 8 October 1955)

With all their variations, these give-away shows have a common core. They make a straight appeal to cupidity and often, to sadism. They encourage people to expose themselves to public humiliation, and others to gloat over it. They represent knowledge as something with an immediate – and grossly disproportionate – cash value. They are a symptom of the disease of a sensation-loving, money-mad society which reckons all values in terms of possessions. (Maurice Wiggin, *The Sunday Times*, 24 March 1957)

More so than any other genre explored in this book, the quiz or game show has been used to map sharp differences between the BBC and ITV in the 1950s. The quiz and game show, or to use the dominant term from the time, the "give-away" show, is used to represent ITV as giving the audience what it wants, apparently unencumbered by concerns about critical distaste and cultural value. The genre is also invoked as the epitome of ITV's claim to be "people's television", in part because it offered viewers representations of "themselves on screen" (Thumim, 2004: 35). Furthermore, discussion of these programmes has consolidated the perceived relationship between commercial television and Americanisation: not only is ITV seen as eagerly embracing American quiz and game show formats, but America is often identified as the home of the genre itself. At the level of British television historiography, the relationship between ITV and the "give-away" show has also been cemented by the famous Pilkington Report (1962) which singled out the genre for its apparently inherent display of "triviality".

This perception is part of a much longer heritage of critical disdain for the quiz/game show which, as Bourdon notes, is seen as the "bad genre"

– "a damning synecdoche for the whole . . . medium" (2004: 287). The Introduction noted how the game show represents one of Bourdon's six "ghosts" – the genres and issues which he argues have haunted public service television's relations with the popular (game shows, stars, seriality, ratings, "America" and voyeurism). It is only in the context of the game show that these "ghosts" can be combined into one spectacular event: "a game show of US origin with a popular and vulgar host occasionally humiliating the participants, stripped in prime time, instantly gaining huge ratings" (Bourdon, 2004: 299). According to existing histories, it was with the advent of ITV that this "nightmarish" spectacle had truly arrived.

"Quick – change the channel! It's time for one of those 'Give-aways' on the ITA . . ."

The prevailing historical picture implies that ITV introduced the genre to Britain, with the programmes bursting onto the scene to delight audiences and offend critics in equal measure. But this view fetishises a particular juncture in the British history of the genre. Mittell (2004a) points out a similar isolation of the 1950s American quiz show scandals, when *Twenty-One* and other Big Money quiz shows were exposed as rigged and placed under legal investigation. The scandals are regularly explored within a "generic vacuum" (Mittell, 2004a: 32), yet the reaction to the events ("how *could* this happen?") implied that certain generic expectations were already in place. Mittell's aim is less to reconstruct the succession of texts which lead to rigged shows, than to trace how the genre, as a "cluster of definitions, interpretations and evaluations" (ibid), created a discursive framework in which the television scandals would unfold.

This chapter differs from the others in this book in that, rather than focus attention on specific case studies, it takes the category *itself* as the object of analysis (Mittell, 2004a: 30). Given the focus of the book and its aim to explore the BBC's relations with popular programme culture, the intention is to contextualise ITV's contribution to the genre by bringing the BBC more firmly into the picture. It is commonly perceived that on radio and early television, the BBC merely dipped its toe into the genre, providing certain types of quizzes and panel games which avoided the spectacle of prize-giving, and which were more befitting of a public service broadcaster. There is some truth in this perspective, but it is also too totalising and generalised, and the BBC's historical relations with the genre have never really been examined. It was the BBC which played a crucial role in developing the broadcast conception of the quiz or game show well before ITV was part of the cultural landscape, and it was the BBC which introduced the genre to television.

Game on: the programmes in question

It has been suggested that the "quiz show" involves the display of factual knowledge through questions and answers (Hestroni, 2004: 134), while the game show incorporates a wider sense of competition, often involving physical performance, within the sphere of fun and games (Hoerschelmann, 2006: 7). As Olaf Hoerschelmann has demonstrated, the distinction between *quiz* and *game* show is quite important historically where the US context is concerned. Following the quiz show scandals in the 1950s, the broadcast industry sought to reposition quiz shows as "game shows", shifting them from prime-time to daytime, downplaying the use of serious factual knowledge, and associating them with play, leisure and consumerism (2006: 18). The distinction (and shift) which Hoerschelmann describes does not have the same currency in Britain. In British radio and television, and across the 1940s and 1950s, there were many generic terms in operation, ranging from the quiz show, the panel game, the parlour game, a "Brains Trust", the gift show, the give-away, the audience-participation programme to the "stunt" show. On BBC radio in the 1940s, the term "quiz" was dominant, foregrounding the focus on question and answer. In the 1950s, and in relation to television, the term "give-away" was pushed to the fore, effectively becoming the main generic label for a wide range of programmes. In comparison, the BBC preferred the public-service-orientated term "audience-participation" programme (although this term actually originated in the American context). While examining particular historical labels, this chapter also recognises that the discursive boundary between quiz and game shows is difficult to maintain: the terms are often used interchangeably, or in different ways in different national contexts. I use both terms here, but more often invoke the category of the *quiz show* as an overarching term for the genre as a whole (see also Hoerschelmann, 2006: 18).

Quiz shows are cheap to make, and this has historically made them attractive to both commercial and public service broadcasters. But quiz shows were particularly central to the building of the audience for commercial television. By early 1957 there were between eight and ten per week (depending on the region), a move which later prompted the ITA to demand a reduction to one per day (Whannel, 1992: 182). The first three to achieve popularity were *Double Your Money* (ITV, 1955–64) hosted by Hughie Greene, *Take Your Pick* (ITV, 1955–68) hosted by Michael Miles, and Tommy Trinder's *Beat the Clock* section in the popular *Sunday Night at the London Palladium* (ITV, 1955–67). Although varying considerably in format, many of the ITV shows were adapted from Radio Luxembourg and/or the US, and the significance of

Radio Luxembourg should be noted here on two counts. First, the BBC was not the sole provider of the genre prior to the advent of ITV, and second, ITV introduced some of the most popular formats to *television*, but not to British audiences in general. *Double Your Money* and *People Are Funny* (ITV, 1955–56) were already familiar to the British audience from broadcasts on Radio Luxembourg.

ITV adapted a number of formats from the US, including *The $64,000 Question* (ITV, 1956–58), *Twenty-One* (ITV, 1957–59), *Hit the Limit* (ITV, 1956), *Criss-Cross Quiz* (ITV, 1957–67), *Dotto* (ITV, 1958–60), *Do You Trust Your Wife?* (ITV, 1956–57), *Bury the Hatchet* (ITV, 1957), *Make up Your Mind* (ITV, 1955–58), *Two for the Money* (ITV, 1957), *Lucky Spot Quiz* (ITV, 1957), *Spot the Tune* (ITV, 1956–62) and *State your Case* (ITV, 1956–57). Almost immediately after ITV began, ATV adapted the American success *People Are Funny*. Referred to as one of the "stunt" shows in the US (Mittell, 2002), it involved contestants participating in set-ups and embarrassing situations in exchange for cash, or prizes such as washing machines, radios and refrigerators. ITV also screened panel games such as *I've Got a Secret* (ITV, 1956–58), in which panel members had to guess a challenger's secret by asking them questions, and *My Wildest Dream* (ITV, 1956–57), in which Tommy Trinder, Terry Thomas and others aimed to guess the "wildest dreams" of studio challengers. As the secrets and the dreams could sometimes edge toward the risqué (one woman's secret was that she worked in a factory which produced outsize bras), critics found both programmes rather "unsavoury".

The ITV shows, despite their considerable range, were primarily attacked by critics for fostering a morally unhealthy attitude toward money, for rewarding trivial displays of knowledge, and for engaging participants in exploitative and degrading performances. In the context of this chapter and its aim to situate the ITV shows within the genre's wider broadcast heritage, it is pertinent to examine exactly what was "new" here. But before examining three key themes, principally 1) the regulation of prizes, 2) the use of knowledge, and 3) the role of "ordinary" people as performers, it is necessary to give an overview of the range of programming in circulation.

Quiz/game shows on radio and television appropriated an existing cultural appetite for games, and find their roots in the diverse class contexts of fairground sideshows, Edwardian/Victorian parlour games, and the popular press (Whannel, 1992: 181). While broadcasting may not have invented the genre, it is recognised as one of few forms which did not emerge as an adaptation from existing entertainment in literature, cinema or theatre (Mittell, 2002: 320). The BBC later claimed that radio's 1937 Inter-regional Spelling Competition in *Children's Hour*, adapted from the spelling bee craze in the US, represented the birth of the "quiz programme" on British radio.[1] But the majority of radio's long-running quiz formats emerged in the 1940s, and after the restructuring of the BBC's radio service, they were primarily broadcast on the Home and Light Programmes.

First, there was a strand of programming which focused on general knowledge and competition. This could encompass competition between teams, whether in *Transatlantic Quiz*, which aired simultaneously over BBC and NBC during the war, or the regional *Round Britain Quiz* (Light, 1947–present). Other programmes focused on competitions between individuals, most famously in *What do You Know?* (Light, 1946–present), where the aim was to find the "Brain of Britain". *Puzzle Corner* (Light, 1946–48) was a combination of general knowledge and crossword puzzles, and the *ABC Spelling Bee* for adults was another example of British broadcasting adapting the American spelling bee craze (Home, 1947). The well-known *Top of the Form*, an inter-school quiz with teams of four pupils, began in 1947 (Home, 1947–75), and there were many quiz formats aimed specifically at children. Quizzes also made a regular appearance in film magazine programmes such as *Picture Parade* (Light, 1949) and *Film-Time* (Home, 1948–53) (see Holmes, 2005a), as well as in sports and music features.

The Brains Trust began on radio in 1941, and while it was originally conceived as a quiz format, it ultimately became a discussion programme, with questions sent in by the listening audience. The panel included the philosopher C.E.M. Joad, zoologist Julian Huxley and Commander A.B. Campbell, and the first question was "What effect would it have if women were able to exert more power in professional politics and diplomacy?" This was followed by such philosophical musings as "What is happiness?" and "Are thoughts things or about things?"[2] Deliberately positioning itself at the opposite end of the class spectrum was *Have a Go!* (Light, 1946–67). Including a quiz based on general knowledge which largely focused on popular culture, *Have a Go!* was presented by the popular Yorkshireman, Wilfred Pickles. With the tag-line "Presenting the People to the People", it was organised around the idea of allowing "ordinary folk" to perform, and the quiz element was secondary to the banter between contestant and host.

From sound to vision

When it came to adapting the genre for television, certain BBC personnel felt that with its verbal basis in question and answer, the quiz show had a "non-visual" quality.[3] But the 1950s saw many of the radio programmes make the move onto television, while new formats also emerged. The popular "Brain of Britain" competition (*What do You Know?*), made the shift in 1955, and in *Ask Me Another* (BBC, 1955–63), intellectual geniuses also competed in teams of three. Prior to this, *The Brains Trust* (BBC, 1955–61) and *Top of the Form* (BBC, 1953–75) had already made the transition to television.[4] At least as early as 1950, the radio title of *Puzzle Corner* was reused as the name of a quiz section in the magazine programme *Kaleidoscope* (BBC, 1946–53), presented by MacDonald Hobley, while *The Charlie Chester Show* (BBC, 1951–60) began in 1951. This included a "Pot Luck" section in which members of the public participated in games for forfeits and prizes, while in the early 1950s, *Michael Miles' House Party* (BBC, 1951) similarly engaged participants in games and forfeits. *Know Your Partner* (BBC, 1951) quizzed couples about their knowledge of each other, while, drawing on aspects of *Have a Go!*, the popular *Ask Pickles* began in 1954, and saw Wilfred and Mabel Pickles celebrating the talents of "ordinary" people. Although the programme also included fun and games, it was mainly comprised of surprises (e.g. reuniting people), or viewers writing in to ask if their family member, friend or neighbour could come on TV to perform their "talent" (a song, a dance or a comic turn).

The early 1950s also saw the flourishing of the television panel game. The most popular of these was undoubtedly *What's My Line?* (BBC, initially 1951–62). Hosted by Eamon Andrews, it revolved around panel members such as Gilbert Harding, Isobel Barnett, Barbara Kelly and David Nixon trying to guess the unusual occupation undertaken by a member of the public. Other panel games included the crossword-based *Down You Go* (BBC, 1953–56), *Why?* (BBC, 1953), *Guess My Story* (BBC, 1953) and *The Balloon Game* (BBC, 1953–54). There was also the more sober *Animal, Vegetable or Mineral* (BBC, 1952–59) in which host Glyn Daniel presided over the efforts of bespectacled archaeologists and professors as they aimed to guess the status of an artefact (such as the "bronze figure of a horse found near the Obrany settlement about 500 BC"). As with ITV, many of the BBC's programmes were originally American formats, ranging across *What do You Know/Ask Me Another*, *The Brains Trust* and *What's My Line?*

Whether showcasing the knowledge of experts or inviting "ordinary" people to perform, the programmes incorporate a wide variety of cultural referents. In doing so, they demonstrate John Fiske's point that the genre can be read in terms of its interaction with a range of cultural domains, including schooling and education, shopping and consumerism, as well as leisure and social relationships (1987: 274). These cultural referents are important in approaching the historical reconstruction of the genre, providing available access points through which to consider the quiz/game show as a form of cultural expression.

Prizes and the regulation of reward

In dealing with prizes and money, quiz and game shows offer insight into attitudes toward consumerism in the 1950s, particularly as these were shaped by discourses of class. The idea that the appeal of the quiz/game show pivots on greed, representing the "apotheosis of the urge to consume" (Holbrook, 1993: 51), has a long history. But such associations must begin somewhere, and it is notable that mass consumerism and the rise of mass television develop together. Any assessment of this relationship must consider the institutional and cultural history of prize-giving in the genre, including the BBC's approach to this issue, and television's aesthetic impact on this sphere.

One of the earliest references to competitions in broadcasting, and thus prizes or rewards, appears to be in 1926, when a BBC memo notes: "It [is] . . . felt that the conduct of competitions should be carefully considered by the Programme Board before they were entered into by any department, and that under any circumstances no more than one a month should be held".[5] The need for careful consideration was elucidated in 1930 when a producer enquired about including a puzzle competition in *Children's Hour*. He explained:

> While I entirely agree with the Board that competitions of any obvious type, which are more in the nature of lotteries than anything else, are to be deprecated, I feel that the right kind of competition which stimulates thought and creates intelligent interest has something to recommend it.[6]

This indicates how competitions, here associated with gambling, are seen to be in tension with the values of public service, unless they are carefully marshalled and controlled. The aim of fostering "intelligent interest" sat at the core of public service, and this was itself conceived as the reward that the BBC aimed to offer its listeners. As elaborated later in 1958, and in ways which link prizes to a commercial conception of the audience, competitions "inevitably introduce an element of bribery rather than adequate reward as a means of stimulating interest".[7] While the BBC often positioned this attitude as differentiating their ethos from that of American broadcasting, and the American quiz/game show in particular, the American Federal Communications Commission (FCC) also voiced concern about programmes representing "on-air lotteries" that were not "in the public interest" (Mittell, 2002: 320), and precisely the same terminology is used to express a distaste for "buying the audience" (Mittell, 2002: 322). The extent to which the meanings of the American quiz/game show are *re*cast in the British context is a running theme in this chapter.

Although particular BBC producers and other personnel occasionally raised the matter of prize-giving in different contexts, there seems to have been little discussion on the matter until the 1940s. It was acknowledged internally within the BBC that a certain culture of prize-giving had grown up on radio during the Second World War, although this was more in relation to general competitions (scriptwriting, short stories) rather than games as such.[8] In 1949, however, it was asserted that any cash prizes should "gradually be eliminated, and the pre-war policy of a ban . . . reinstated".[9] But whether referring to radio or television, it seems that the notion of a "ban" is too strong a term. A later memo by Cecil McGivern outlined how the desire to receive a prize is in fact a natural "human weakness", and that the BBC's best plan of attack was to "cater to" this desire, while "trying to control it and keep it decent".[10] What might be described as this *negotiated* approach characterises the BBC's involvement with the quiz and game show in the 1940s and 1950s.

This approach fosters essentially two strategies. First, there are programmes in which the competitors win prestige as opposed to a tangible reward (*What do You Know?*, *Ask Me Another*, *Top of the Form*). Contestants on radio and television's "Brain of Britain" received a diploma and book tokens to the value of £5. Second, there is the offer of limited cash or commodities only when the programmes are not really about the prizes (or indeed knowledge), but rather pivot on participation, camaraderie and the experience of meeting the host. Radio's *Have a Go!* offered monetary reward, and the programme's famous catchphrase was "Give 'em the money, Barney", which referred to the Producer, Barney Colehan, who handed out the cash. But despite this catchphrase, the conventional prize was a modest 38s 6d. Everyone appeared to be rewarded with the same sum of money and in the press, Pickles emphasised how the money was "just for fun", and that "often it is returned at the end of the programme to help some good cause" (see Figure 2).[11] Equally, there was a persistent fudging of *where* the money actually came from ("Father Christmas"),[12] and it was unceremoniously produced from a brown paper bag. Aside from a concern about encouraging gambling, as well as a distaste for promoting acquisitive desires, a key worry here was public perception: the BBC felt that giving out large prizes would lead to accusations that they were "using licence-holders' money wrongly".[13]

Figure 2 'Give 'em the money, Barney': Wilfred Pickles hosts *Have a Go* (1947)

In *Have a Go!*, the brown paper bag reflected the aural nature of the programme, and this was convenient given the desire to play down the presence of a prize. But the idea of aiming for an *image* of restraint necessarily took on new meanings where television was concerned. As the Director of Television, George Barnes, suggested in 1951: "The question of giving visible prizes of negligible value has not arisen in sound".[14] Television did not initially prompt explicit discussion concerning the BBC's prize-giving policy, but the consideration of its different aesthetic demands clearly impacted upon this sphere. Early examples in this respect were the "Puzzle Corner" section in *Kaleidoscope* and *The Charlie Chester Show*.

From the early 1950s, the magazine programme *Kaleidoscope* included a section called "Puzzle Corner" which offered a cash reward. If viewers wanted to play the game, which included four general knowledge questions, they were to place a copy of the *Radio Times* in their window. The outside broadcast team would then pick a house in a particular region, and as the outside broadcast footage of the van patrolling the streets was shown, Hobley would comment how "it might be here, it might be anywhere".[15] Exploiting the liveness of the medium, as well as the "unwritten" rhetoric of the game, this articulates the democratic myth of participation ("it could be you") which Fiske (1987) argues permeates the genre. But rather interestingly, at least in terms of the exploration of television's possibilities, the chosen competitor would be called by Hobley on the telephone when it was time to give their answers. The competitor was heard but not seen, and this reliance on sound, particularly when placed side by side with the roaming vision of the OB unit, was apparently shaped by the difficulty of recording inside someone's home on the spot. (It was not until the mid-1950s that the newly developed portable tape recorder could capture people talking in their own environment) (Laing, 1986: 161). The visually absent competitor was at least rewarded with an invitation to Alexandra Palace to see the making of the next *Kaleidoscope* programme, and they also won £2 or £4 the following week if the prize had accumulated. While this sounds like an incredibly small sum today, in 1954 the chief wage earner in a working-class family would bring home around £9–£10 per week (Hoggart, 1958: 9), and this suggests that the prize in "Puzzle Corner" was not entirely insignificant.

"First TV gift show": "Give 'em the money, Charlie"
It was *The Charlie Chester Show* in 1951, produced by the Light Entertainment Department, which was categorised by the press and the BBC as the first prize-giving programme on television. *The Charlie Chester Show* was greeted with some surprise by the press, with headlines such as "New TV Show Will Give Presents: BBC Breaks Rules for Quizzers", "First TV Gift Show", or simply (referring back to *Have a Go!*) "Give 'em the money, Charlie".[16] Comedian Charlie Chester had previously fronted the successful radio shows, *A Proper Charlie* and *That Man Chester*, and when Chester's programme was adapted for television in 1951, the "Pot Luck" saw members of the studio audience at the King's Theatre, Hammersmith, compete in a range of games. In its earliest years it included features such as the "Sit and Stand" game (in which people had to sit on the word "stand" and stand on the word sit), and sporting questions put to the "memory man". *The Charlie Chester Show* was essentially a variety format, screened at 8:30p.m. on a Saturday night. The "Pot Luck" sections were interspersed between skits and sketches, musical acts and dances, to some extent prefiguring ITV's insertion of "Beat the Clock" in *Sunday Night at the London Palladium*.

The dominant term used to describe the programme in the press was the "TV gift show", a label which implies a more benevolent and well-intentioned act than the descriptor of the "give-away" later in the decade. This was perhaps shaped by the nature of the prizes on offer – a string of cosmetic pearls, ties, handkerchiefs, nylon tights, an electric iron, a lamp, a razor blade, a packet of crisps, or football, boxing or theatre tickets. The Head of Light Entertainment, Ronald Waldman, told the press how the "prizes would be severely limited in cost . . . No big American stuff here . . . We don't want to buy viewers . . . The programme is the thing, not the prizes. We can't have people queuing for tickets to furnish their homes".[17] Waldman clearly exaggerates the image of viewers being hypnotised by the consumer allure of the television screen, but his comment is also a reminder of the still austere conditions of everyday life at this time. In 1951 much rationing was still in force (Addison, 1985).

If the BBC was again aiming for an image of restraint, this took on new, and more literal, meanings where television was concerned. *The Charlie Chester Show* appeared to pivot on a tension between wanting to provide sufficient visual interest and yet wishing to avoid an image of extravagance. When it began the Controller of Television, Cecil McGivern, emphasised that the prizes must be modest in cost ("i.e., up to and around £3 is modest, but £10 is not"), and he went on to insist: "The prizes must in the greater majority be visual and of the type given at fairs . . . (E.g. large teddy bears but *not* an expensively dressed doll from Liberty's)".[18] Compared to a cash reward, McGivern recognises here that commodities can be more easily categorised in terms of class, and thus "taste". From his point of view, it is evidently better that the BBC sacrifice good "taste" in favour of protecting its reputation as a guardian of public funds: a doll from Liberty's is too extravagant, but a fairground prize is better. The concern with the doll, here identified with a particular store, also related to the perennial fear over advertising. But despite McGivern's emphasis on the need for prizes to be visual, as well as the fact that the show *did* keep to a modest budget, the programme was still wary of showcasing its goods. Several press reviews reported how "complaints came from viewers" because the prizes were handed to the on-screen participants in boxes.[19] Although the BBC claimed that this aptly reflected the theme of "pot luck", while also foregrounding how participation (not prizes) was the point of the show, critics and viewers were not convinced. While *The Charlie Chester Show* is a clear example of the BBC negotiating their relations with the genre (catering to a prize-giving desire while "trying to control it and keep it decent"), the outcome of this for *television* was the sight of hidden prizes in boxes being shuttled across the screen.

"You can see the prizes, your mouth waters . . .": will the BBC agree to give prizes?

This discussion of how the BBC approached the prizes and the values associated with the quiz and game show reflects a longer history in which, according to the Marxist analysis of Mike Wayne:

> Under public service broadcasting, examples of the quiz/game show genre
> tend to foreground such values as camaraderie, for example, *It's a Knockout*
> and *The Generation Game*, or specialist knowledge, e.g. *Mastermind* or
> *University Challenge*, or physical/problem-solving skills such as *The Crystal
> Maze* . . . but the more exchange values permeate television, the more we
> can expect consumerism, consumer goods, individualism and hard cash to
> be at the centre of the game show. (2000: 200)

This chapter aims to demonstrate how the quiz/game show has never had
an easy relationship with an ethos of public service, but what seems
lacking in Wayne's analysis is an acknowledgement of how there is no
inherent relationship between the values of a quiz/game show, the prizes
on offer, and their association with a public service or commercial broadcaster. As Matt Hills points out in his discussion of the relationship
between ITV1 and *Who Wants to be a Millionaire* (ITV, 1998–), there is
no "natural affinity" between big prize quiz/game shows and commercial television: this is the product of a cultural and institutional construction (2005: 179). The same can be said of the values which Wayne
associates with public service quiz/game shows, and what is so valuable
in returning to the earlier broadcasting context is that we can see this cultural construction *in process*. From Pickles's references to the benefactor
Father Christmas, McGivern's insistence that an "expensively dressed
doll from Liberty's" is too posh, to the mysterious gifts sitting in concealed boxes on "Pot Luck", we see a *performance* of restraint, an
attempt to shape the public perception of how the BBC spends its funds.
Certainly, the BBC could not have matched the thousands of dollars
offered by American quiz/game shows on radio and television, but they
could have afforded more than they spent.

With the emphasis on visual display, television did seem to pose more
challenges in this respect. The BBC also felt more pressure to consider
these challenges once commercial television was on the horizon, and
perhaps also once standards of living began to rise. In 1954, and less than
one year before the advent of ITV, McGivern describes a very different
aesthetic approach to the quiz/game show to that seen in *The Charlie
Chester Show*:

> There is no doubt that the awarding of prizes gives considerable strength
> and extra tension and excitement to television programmes. You can see the
> prizes, your mouth waters, and the progress from the "ten dollar question"
> to the "hundred dollar question" creates tremendous atmosphere.[20]

Given the reference to dollars, McGivern is possibly drawing on experience of viewing American television here. He is certainly imagining a

more self-consciously commercial aesthetic, both in terms of how the programme beckons the viewer to watch, and with regard to the images on offer. But consolidating the argument above, we can see quite clearly how the BBC face a *choice* here, a choice which is both institutional and aesthetic. The memo goes on to detail McGivern's belief that:

> our competitors will use this ingredient to an important extent. . . . [E]ven with expensive prizes, the programmes are cheap, easy and exciting; and only a ban by the ITA Board could stop them. . . . [T]here is no doubt that such programmes . . . could very easily steal a majority audience. Will the BBC agree to give prizes? I think the point should be considered <u>before</u> competition starts. It would look very weak to agree to prizes in programmes <u>after</u> we have obviously been asked to re-consider the point because of the "success" of competitive television.[21]

This chapter has questioned the concept of a prize "ban" in the first place, but the BBC's programmes were not really reshaped by ITV's success with the genre. By 1955 *The Charlie Chester* show offered the possibility of winning £5, in addition to the small commodities it had offered before (and as the term enjoyed its most liberal use, the programme was actually reframed by the press as a "give-away", rather than "gift show"). But when it was still running in 1960, the prizes listed in the scripts, such as an electric razor, an electric toaster, a small tent or a travelling rug, stubbornly mirror what passed for consolation items on ITV's *Beat the Clock*.

A *"symbol of our buy now, buy quick (and pay later) society"*: consuming class

This history enables a more complex understanding of the "give-away" phenomenon, and the cultural responses it attracted in the 1950s. Certainly, in thinking about the advent of ITV, we need to acknowledge the considerable rise in prize funds in the genre, the like of which had not been seen on BBC radio or television. The top prize on *Double Your Money* was £1,025. In 1957 it was reported that British TV "Gives Away a House", a headline which referred to a £5,000 property won on *Take Your Pick*.[22] Aside from the increase in prize value, a key difference was how the prizes were promoted. Clearly eschewing the discursive impression of restraint, the *TV Times* would eagerly regale viewers with detailed information on prize funds, jackpots and winners.

But the visibility of the genre was also shaped by changing social and cultural contexts, particularly debates about consumerism, affluence and class. As part of a much wider study of how television circulated discourses of consumerism at this time, Turnock (forthcoming) has argued that the "give-away" show became a visible cultural occasion for the expression of elite and middle-class attitudes toward working-class consumption. In reading the press commentary at the time, we get glimpses of how the genre is discussed as part of a wider distaste for a shiny new consumerism. A critic in *The Times* observed how, "Collectively, these . . . [give-away] programmes leave a dominant impression of money and goods changing hands at a feverish tempo, a symbol of our buy now, buy quick (and pay later) society".[23] At the same time it is worth noting that many of the prizes reviled by critics on the quiz/game show (fridge, washing machine) were also seen at the time as commodities which represented the *closing* of a class gap (see Obelkevich, 1994: 149). Was the critical antipathy toward the prizes, and the consumer ethos of the "give-away" show in general, as much about the apparent waning of distinctions?

When it comes to prize-giving in British quiz shows, the juncture often foregrounded is the moment when the ITA, and then the Pilkington Report (1962), suggest that the value of prizes be reduced, and their distribution more "closely link to *skill and knowledge*" (Whannel, 1992: 184; original emphasis) (see also Sendall, 1982, Hills, 2005). The ITA announced in 1960 that there would be "no more big money", and stipulated that prizes should now be limited to £1,000.[24] This decision was apparently prompted by two key concerns. First, the American quiz show scandals appeared to cement a connection between large prizes and corrupt production practices. Second, the ITA felt that the channels were now simply competing to see "who could hand out most cash".[25] But when we situate this moment in relation to the wider history of the genre, it looks less like an isolated intervention than part of a network of continuing concerns, with changing emphases and contexts.

The reception of the ITV programmes was no longer bound up with concerns over the use of public money, but when it came to a distaste for "buying the audience", it is possible to trace a line right through from the BBC's first reference to competitions in 1926, to the intervention of the ITA in 1960. At the same time, the visibility of the "give-away" show in the 1950s, and the cultural debate it seemed to attract, was shaped as much by attitudes toward the changing consumer context as it was by ITV's impact on the genre *per se*. Furthermore, this section has also aimed to reconnect the popular roots of the genre *with* the BBC. From *Have a Go!* and *Kaleidoscope* to *The Charlie Chester Show*, we are hardly presented with programmes which, in the words of Andy Medhurst, "blended entertainment and education in a way that adhered securely to the prevailing Reithian ideology of broadcast entertainment" (1991: 61). As the next section explores, the genre's links with education were in any case contested on a regular basis.

"The question is – is it all *worth* knowing?":
Knowledge, education, class

Fiske (1987) argues that quiz/game shows occupy flexible and multiple relations with a range of cultural domains. Some of these domains might appear to contradict each other, such as education and consumerism (which in turn translate into an opposition between work and leisure). But from a historical perspective in particular, this is not necessarily the case. For example, the Tory emphasis on consumerism may have been foregrounded in debates about "embourgeoisement" and changing class boundaries, but the idea of collective social provision, including health, transport and education, and as initially set up by Labour's Welfare State, was also linked to this argument (Laing, 1986: 13). In approaching the genre's relations with education, schooling and knowledge, this section situates quiz shows in relation to discourses on education in post-war Britain.

In the cultural reception of the "give-away" show in the mid-to late 1950s, emphasis was placed on a decline in the difficulty of the questions – something consistent with ITV's populist image and dismissive views of its mass appeal. The generic label of the "give-away", in conjunction with references to a "workshy paradise",[26] suggested that the money was not being *earned*. One critic offers a typical response when he observes that:

> commercial shows offer bribes – sorry *prizes* – . . . To win a mere pound or two, all you need to know is your own name. You might even get away with not knowing *that*. One young woman wasn't quite sure if she was Miss *or* Mrs.[27]

Since this time, concerns about declining standards of knowledge have recurrently circled around the genre, and continue to do so today (see Holmes, 2005c). Yet the ITV shows were more varied in their use of knowledge than the quote implies. Shows such as *People are Funny* were not about knowledge at all, but focused on "ordinary" people taking part in set-ups and stunts. But *Double Your Money*, and especially *The $64,000 Question* and *Twenty-One*, positively embraced an emphasis on factual/academic knowledge. This suggests how although the "stunt" and forfeit shows dominated public and regulatory debate, there remained a range of programmes in circulation. Furthermore, once we examine the earlier context and the BBC's relations with the genre, we can see that the status of knowledge in the quiz show had been a subject of debate for some time.

"This is far from education properly . . . described"

On radio, the BBC's *Round Britain Quiz*, for which listeners sent in the questions, was conceived as "primarily an entertainment and not a competitive examination",[28] while radio's *Top of the Form* was keen to ensure that it was not "too academic" and that the questions were kept "as general as possible".[29] With regard to the more discursive format of *The Brains Trust*, the BBC received up to 3,000 questions per week from listeners, and they emphasised how it was not the aim of the series to allow "clever people to show listeners how really clever they are". Rather, it was for questions to be answered concisely, so that "as many [listeners] as possible may hear their questions asked".[30]

This may have expressed a cultural ambivalence toward the display of cleverness – particularly given class-demarcated assumptions about intellectuality and (related to this) the extent to which broadcasting aimed to build a "common culture". But the BBC's hesitation was perhaps also shaped by the fact that the educational value of the quiz show was subject to considerable cultural debate. Certainly, there were voices which praised the BBC's quiz programmes. Commenting on everything from *Round Britain Quiz* to *Top of the Form* to *Ask Me Another*, listeners/viewers often wrote to the press to emphasise the educational value of the programmes, particularly where the younger audience was concerned. Equally, BBC Audience Research reports consistently confirmed that the programmes could be "Intelligent without being too highbrow; stimulating because one can try to answer questions too; instructive when one can't".[31] But at the same time, there was a wider chorus of disapproval over the educational value and wider social influence of the genre, well before ITV emerged. Throughout the 1940s, the 1950s and beyond, critics in the "quality" press consistently questioned the quiz show's relationship with education, and its potential influence in shaping conceptions of learning and knowledge. Providing a variation on the argument that the genre promotes "wealth without work", one critic described its pervasive appeal as a "social malady" which promised an easy, "quick-fix" education rather than reflecting an "insatiable thirst for knowledge":

> [This] is far from education properly . . . described, but it may give a pleasant glowing feeling to the listener or viewer. This type of programme panders to the secret longing of many lazy people to become well-informed without taking any of the necessary steps toward that praiseworthy end.[32]

Some emphasised how the programmes valued a computer-like ability to store and recall answers, while others foregrounded the decontextualised nature of the knowledge used. In an article entitled "BBC Quiz Shows

Misguided", Professor Cannon from Manchester University gave a warning talk to 500 school boys:

> Do not follow the lead of the BBC in their accursed quiz programmes and think that mere knowledge of facts is education . . . The whole idea is utter nonsense and is definitely against the ideas of education which the teachers are trying to instil in you.[33]

These responses complement subsequent academic work on the genre. Critics such as John Tulloch (1976) and William Boddy (1990) have noted the quiz show's bid to define knowledge as an accumulation of facts in a way that abolishes explanation, and penalises thought and reflection. But as the quotation from Professor Cannon makes clear, the conception of quiz show knowledge as an "accumulation of facts" at one time emerged from a particular historical context. Critics such as Hoerschelmann (2000) and Whannel (1992) have explored the historical nature of knowledge in quiz shows: the degree to which it may appear to be ahistorical, but is shaped by social, cultural and national contexts. The criticism of the BBC shows, however, might be seen to point less to the specific content of the knowledge, as it indirectly circles around contemporary discourses on educational practice.

Britain had witnessed radical shifts in education in the period following the Second World War, and integral to the egalitarian promise of the Welfare State, the Education Act was passed in 1944. Put simply, it emerged from the sense that British society had failed to make education more widely accessible (Addison, 1985: 141). Shaped by the wartime spirit of "fair shares" and a desire to see a reduction in privilege, the Act made a period of secondary education compulsory for every boy and girl. School leaving age was raised, and there was a greater emphasis on the concept of adult education (Bernbaum, 1967, Smith, 1957). But these shifts also intersected with changing theories of educational practice which can be traced in educational literature from the time. In 1949 the book *The New Secondary Education* described how "in every secondary school, attention must be paid not only to the intellectual but also to the social, emotional, physical and spiritual growth of the child" (Dent, 1949: 116). There had been not only a growth of psychological and scientific interest in childhood development and education, but an emphasis on education as a "life-long process" (Smith, 1957: 20). As W.O. Lester Smith explained in *Education*:

> Teachers . . . previously accustomed to rigid requirements . . . concentrated on the practice of drilling young children in . . . what they regarded as essential knowledge; for them education was literally a process of knocking facts into empty heads . . . [But] the modern teacher thinks of the child,

not as a passive recipient of imparted knowledge, but as learning most readily when actively pursuing some problem or project – exploring skills which might later be pursued in outside contexts. (1957: 21)

It is not surprising that a programme such as *The Brains Trust*, in which questions were explored, debated and pondered, would be received more favourably within this context. Indeed, Smith's book specifically praises the programme for "making [its] subject matter accessible" to a wide audience (1957: 27). While also mindful of the need to address a mass audience (and perhaps aiming to minimise accusations of elitism), it is little wonder that the BBC were hesitant to emphasise the educational value of the quiz show when it was often subject to "expert" critique.

"Fair Shares?": Knowledge and class

The dominant theme in academic analyses of the genre has been the ideological relationship between knowledge, class and education (Tulloch, 1976, Fiske, 1987, Hoerschelmann, 2000). Fiske's work provided an influential taxonomy of knowledge in the quiz show, ranging from the academic (questions about history, science geography or art) to the "everyday" (knowledge with a different epistemological basis, such as guessing the prices of commodities, or predicting popular opinion). Academic knowledge is more highly valued by modern societies (Hestroni, 2004), and as access to educational opportunity and the cultural capital (Bourdieu, 1986) it cultivates is not equal "for all", the quiz show functions as an "enactment of capitalist ideology":

> Individuals are constructed as different but equal in opportunity. Differences of *natural* ability are discovered, and the reward is upward mobility into the realm of social power which "naturally" brings with it material and economic benefits . . . Such an ideology . . . grounds social or class differences in individual natural differences and thus naturalizes the class system. (Fiske, 1987: 266)

This also reproduces the structure of the education system in Western societies, and Fiske's point is that it is ideological to perceive the chance of success as related to "natural" ability given that all individuals are not, and cannot be, equal in opportunity here. While still relevant today (see Holmes (2005c) on the discussion which has surrounded the class status of jackpot winners on *Who Wants to be a Millionaire*), this raises particularly interesting questions when looking back to the early British quiz show. After all, discourses surrounding the equality of opportunity in education had been a dominant theme on the political agenda.

The Education Act had aimed to guarantee for every citizen an education that was "appropriate for his age, aptitude and ability" throughout the period of full-time compulsory schooling (Smith, 1957: 102). The outstanding feature of the Act was the pledge to introduce free secondary schooling for children over the age of 11–12, and this was in place of the elementary schooling which was previously experienced by approximately 90% of the population (Addison, 1985: 140). Fees for grammar schools were abolished in 1945, and arguments about "embougeoisement" were linked in two key ways to educational provision. On one hand, general improvement at all levels of the system was seen to offer an equality of opportunity, while educational achievement was now to be "the route to social position – the creation of a meritocracy, a system of social stratification and differential rewards based on ability not heredity" (Laing, 1986: 24). This idea of creating an elite of meritocrats notably dovetails with the mythic promise of the quiz show later described by Fiske.

Such changes did lead to an increase in the number of working-class children attending grammar schools, but the attack on the grammar school system did not really begin in earnest until the mid-1950s. Despite being the programme which could have been most directly affected by these changes, the BBC's *Top of the Form* seems relatively isolated from them. The school teams are drawn from grammar schools – often establishments boasting suitably elite names – and they showcased the talents of students who were clearly privileged in their academic and social backgrounds. Jeffrey Richards recalls the programme as the utter "embodiment of grammar school culture",[34] an identity which continued well into the 1960s. But perhaps *Top of the Form* also speaks indirectly to the limited nature of the change which occurred. Much debate had circled around how best to provide secondary education for all, and the structure which emerged was the tri-partite framework of grammar, technical and modern. But the technical and modern schools never attained the same prestige as the grammar, and the latter enjoyed better facilities, teaching resources and attainment. By the 1950s, investigations indicated the clear part that class continued to play in educational opportunity (Bernbaum, 1967: 113). It was not until the late 1960s, some time after the period under discussion, that *Television Top of the Form* began to appear somewhat outmoded. This was notably under the push toward comprehensivisation – Labour's bid in the 1960s to revise the failures of the previous decade where educational provision was concerned (Laing, 1986: 25).

In this respect it is important to consider the kind of knowledge utilised and valued by the BBC programmes in general. *Have a Go!* was the only programme to persistently feature questions on popular culture. Across radio and television, other programmes such as *Trans-Britain/Round*

Britain Quiz, *What do You Know?/Ask Me Another*, predominantly concentrated on the spheres of history, science, geography, literature and contemporary affairs. Questions on radio's *Round Britain Quiz* enquired: "Do you know why Brasenose College at Oxford is so named?", "Who said 'Dr Livingstone, I presume?'", while radio's *Trans-Britain Quiz* asked: "What poets have given their names to London telephone exchanges?", "What is George Bernard Shaw reputed to have said on these three occasions . . . ?". The "Brain of Britain" on television asked for answers to such questions as: "What is the chemical symbol of gold?", "Who is the prime minister of Italy?", "Where would knights have worn the piece of armour known as the habergeon?" There were more popular touches on each of these programmes ("For which county does cricketer Freddie Trueman play?", "What sports or games do you associate with the Wolves, Penguins and Lions?"), but the received academic subjects appeared to predominate.[35] It is perhaps no surprise that contestants competing for the title "Brain of Britain" tended to emerge from more privileged class and educational backgrounds. When Mr Henry Button, a civil servant from Ealing, won the title in 1958, the BBC circulated information on his education at grammar school and the Universities of Cambridge and Bonn, his writing for newspapers and magazines, and his interest in studying old businesses, about which he "hoped to publish a book one day".[36]

When we get to the mid-1950s and the emphasis on "idiot contestants and give-away shows" on ITV, we are being asked to recognise a shift in the knowledge utilised by the genre. Yet this is far from clear-cut. *Double Your Money* featured a wide range of contestants where educational background and occupation was concerned, and when host Hughie Greene asked the contestant, "What do you want to talk about today?", many of the categories on the board occupied traditionally academic spheres (Geography, History and Vocabulary) in ways which mirrored the programmes on the BBC. It is also true, however, that *Double Your Money* included a range of subjects which emerged from what Fiske describes as "common social experience . . . rather than the education system" (1987: 267). Contestants could also answer questions on Music Hall, Railways, Good Housekeeping, Fashion and Gramophone Records (categories which were also more inclusive in terms of gender, as well as class).[37] Furthermore, in the opening sequence of the first edition, the programme specifically invokes the referent of education so that it can be rejected or undermined. The sequence begins with three school children in uniform sitting at their desks, while the female assistant asks, "What's 2 plus 2?" As the children give the correct answer, she comments: "It's so easy – even children at home can play it". Host Hughie Greene then emerges from behind a fourth desk, dressed to comic effect in a school uniform. Peering round the desk lid he rolls his eyes and protests, "But I'm the host!" when he is prompted to answer the next question. In this sequence, *Double Your Money* illustrates Fiske's point that quiz shows may draw on the referent of education in order to re-cast its meanings (1987: 274). *Double Your Money* uses the imagery of schooling so it can play down the traditionally less inclusive referent of education, and then position itself as disrupting the formality and regimentation of the "classroom". This was certainly in stark contrast to something like the BBC's *Ask Me Another*. Here, two elite teams (comprised of Drs, Professors and other experts who displayed quite startling levels of knowledge) compete in a space which is more akin to the austere atmosphere of the exam room – something accentuated by its very slow pace and static camerawork.[38]

"The miner who knows literature"

In this sense, the early history of the British quiz show has a complex relationship with the discourses of egalitarianism which Fiske (1987) suggests are integral to its ideological form. In terms of the programmes focusing on question-and-answer, the formats on both channels tended to value academic knowledge, although commercial television does seem keener to stress the "open" nature of its competitions, and to play down their association with education and school. But this is where a cross-cultural comparison with the American context, especially in relation to format adaptation, is particularly revealing. Olaf Hoerschelmann (2000) and Kent Anderson (1978) have examined how some of the Big Money quiz shows on American television aimed to "erase . . . the social differences" implicit in their class-based knowledge (Hoerschelmann, 2000: 190). While the frequent appearance of highly educated contestants mirrored the significance placed on high culture and academic knowledge, this was more apparent in *Twenty-One*. The first and most successful format, *The $64,000 Question*, which began on US television in 1955, was different. Not dissimilar to a programme like *Mastermind* (BBC, 1979–), *The $64,000 Question* invited contestants to select their own specialist category (which might range from the history of boxing, to Italian cuisine, to opera). They climbed a ladder of plateaus, returning show after show, and after answering the $32,000 question, the contestant was given several reference books in their category and was allowed to draw on expert assistance if they chose to tackle to top question (Anderson, 1978: 7). In the American version there was the elevation of "folk heroes", such as "the cop who knew Shakespeare" or the "cobbler who knew opera", fostering the egalitarian claim that "We're all pretty much alike and we're all smart" (Anderson, 1978: 39).

It is true that traces of this egalitarian myth can be discerned in relation to the British adaptation of *The $64,000 Question*. Take, for example, Producer John Irwin's initial emphasis on how he was looking for:

> Unusual people to take part – a miner who can answer questions on any aspect of literature, or a lift attendant who is master of the history of cooking . . . Competitors will really earn their money. It is a show for experts.[39]

While suggesting how the programme sought to distinguish itself from the "give-away" label, we might note how it paradoxically needs to be made moderately elite (a show for "experts"), so that discourses of egalitarianism can come to the fore. As Hoerschelmann observes in relation to the American shows, the interest of such contestants stems from an acknowledgement of the "contradiction between the class and the cultural capital they deal with" (2000: 190). In America, such images of social mobility were the product of a carefully crafted construction: the "cop who knew Shakespeare", for example, was also a postgraduate student of English literature, and the true educational levels of the contestants were regularly submerged by the programmes (Anderson, 1978: 39).

It is impossible to say whether this sublimation also occurred in the British context, but the question is in many ways redundant. Despite the Producer's initial emphasis on the desire for "unusual" contestants – the miner who is also a literary expert – he seems to be laying down this framework as part of the format "package" inherited from the US. These discourses are not apparent in the UK once the programme gets going. The press remain fascinated by following the contestants through the game, with some returning to compete five or six times. But other factors come into play to construct the ordinary/extraordinary status of the players. For example, there is an emphasis on age ("He's only 21!", "Little Old lady wins £3,520 on TV!"),[40] and discourses of "ordinariness" lose their articulation with discourses of class. The Big Money quiz shows were "the newest translation of the Great *American* Dream" (Anderson, 1978: 20; my emphasis), and it goes without saying that the emphasis on a "classless" discourse had a special relationship with American society. But such myths also have a historical currency in shaping constructions of success and opportunity in modern capitalist societies in general (Dyer, 1998). It was after all in the post-war period, with the promise of affluence and increasing prosperity, that there was a clear bid to hail the dawn of a "classless" society in Britain. Sites such as consumerism, as well as the education system, seemed to hold out the "egalitarian" promise of equal opportunity for all. Of course, beneath these promises, as the discussion of the "problem show" in Chapter 4 of this book makes clear, lay the continued persistence of economic inequalities. It is perhaps because Britain was more used to perceiving itself as an inherently *stratified* society that the egalitarian myth had less currency where the quiz show was concerned.

This section has considered the complex relationship between quiz shows, knowledge and class in relation to the early history of the genre. It has argued that there was no clear shift in the construction of knowledge with the advent of ITV. The emphasis on "idiot contestants and give-away shows" foregrounded programmes which did not pivot on question and answer, while expressing a wider distaste for ITV's working-class appeal. Furthermore, the BBC's programmes had always attracted criticism where the construction of knowledge was concerned. This may have been primarily related to the *form* of the knowledge rather than its content, but *Have a Go!* at least had long since been described as rewarding displays of "simple ignorance".[41] There is no straightforward or direct relationship between the education system and conceptions of education and knowledge in the quiz show. But it is at least interesting here that, despite the public debate surrounding (class) equality in education, there is an automatic acceptance of order, stratification and hierarchy. At the same time, it is possible to suggest that the main focus of popular debate was invested elsewhere: enter the "ordinary" person as television performer.

"Ordinary" people and the "intoxicating indignity" of television fame

The fact that the ordinary person has become an increasingly valued commodity on television, largely due to the explosion of popular factual programming, has led to a growth of discussion on the subject (Couldry, 2000, Teurlings, 2001, Bonner, 2003, Holmes, 2004a, 2004b, Biressi and Nunn, 2005). According to Jan Teurlings, "Television . . . has entered the age of the ordinary" (2001: 249). While to conceptualise this as a shift is not necessarily problematic, we have little sense of the historical contours of this field. The quiz or game show is one of the few broadcast spaces where ordinary people historically appeared as a matter of course. In this respect, ITV's use of "ordinary" people in the 1950s, particularly in the context of the quiz/game show, has underpinned a range of discourses associated with the advent of commercial television in general. There is an emphasis here on popularisation and democratisation – the bid to let the people "decide for themselves", as well as *appear themselves*. But as recent debate has suggested, television's increasing appetite to display the performances of ordinary people is not in itself evidence of a democratising impetus in the medium (Couldry, 2000, Turner, 2004). Instead, and given that the concept of the ordinary is produced within discourse, attention has been focused on television's construction of "ordinariness", and the contingent and complex nature of the performative context involved.

It is difficult to offer a clear definition of what "performance" means here. Everyday life has long since been understood as demanding a particular "presentation of the self" (Goffman, 1972), but as Myra Macdonald argues, when the notion of everyday performance "is transferred to the public arena of television . . . more explicitly performative abilities come into play" (2003: 82). Karen Lury has provided a useful template for analysing this arena, particularly when it comes to what she calls our "uneasy ambivalence in the appreciation of the ordinary performer" (1995: 126). As is now played out in the debate surrounding Reality TV, the concept of authenticity represents a key frame of reception. Lury explains how this is because "the otherwise accepted duality of character and actor is made problematic when we witness real people perform. For if real people convincingly 'put on an act' where can sincerity, authenticity and real emotion be located with any conviction?" (1995: 126). At the same time, we may "empathise uncomfortably" if we perceive the performer to lack control, or we may occupy a sadistic position, hoping that the person may be "punished or humiliated for his or her 'unseemly' desire to perform" (ibid). Lury's discussion captures some of the key responses which circulated around the "ordinary" person as performer on 1950s British television. But that is not to imply that it can be interpreted as something of a transhistorical paradigm. For example, while Lury refers to people convincingly putting on an "act", Macdonald describes how perceptions of authenticity change over time, because we have all seen "enough televisual performances to have learned the rules" (2003: 82). But what of a context in which this familiarity is not yet secure? How are these appearances situated when, in the case of television, the apparatus itself is not yet entirely "ordinary"?

"Good evening Mr. Privilege, it's a proper pickle to meet you": ordinary people Have a Go!

In order to frame the reception of what was "new" here, it is necessary to consider some of the existing perceptions of the relations between ordinary people-as-performers and radio. The most significant example here was undoubtedly the BBC's phenomenally popular radio show, *Have a Go!*

Have a Go! initially began on the North Regional Programme in 1946, but it went on to attain a national popularity. The persona host Wilfred

Pickles was central to the programme's appeal. Here, and unlike some of the quiz shows discussed earlier in this chapter, the "success myth" (Dyer, 1998) *did* have a clear currency. Press and magazine coverage emphasised how Pickles's broadcasting career had represented "his deliverance from the horrors of poverty",[42] and it foregrounded his humble beginnings in Halifax, Yorkshire. Pickles had featured in a number of plays on BBC radio, including those on the highbrow Third Programme, and he was also famous for reading the BBC news in his broad Yorkshire dialect. But it was *Have a Go!*, in which he boomed "Ow do – ow are yer?", or "Ad a ard live, ave ye?", which made him a national institution, and he was later joined in the programme by his wife Mabel, who also enjoyed considerable fame.

The press intermittently reported that social investigators were aiming to explore the show's popularity, and the explanation regularly given by Pickles, the press and the BBC was that it "presented the people to the people". Playing out broadcasting's aim of mobilising a sense of national belonging and "we-feeling" out of an abstract collectivity (Chaney, 1993), Pickles opens one edition by explaining:

> When I say "presenting the people to the people", I don't mean just a mass of abstract humanity, but people with names, with hopes, fears, ambitions, and most of all, a sense of humour. People, just people. Folks whose names maybe will never reach the headlines in the newspapers. People like the folks who live next door.[43]

Pickles identifies "ordinary" here in terms of participants *unversed* in the world of media performance, as well as in relation to the shared, "the everyday" and the familiar. But evident in Pickles's colloquial construction of community is a sense of working-class life. The association of the "real" and the "ordinary" people with the Northern working class has a long history in British popular culture, with some of the most famous examples being the British Documentary Film Movement, "kitchen sink" drama (literature, theatre, film or television) and television soap opera (Geraghty, 1991). *Have a Go!* is part of this history and as with these other media examples, it made its claim to the real by defining itself against the wider class context of its address. In press and magazine interviews Pickles would emphasise how the secret of bringing "ordinary" people to the microphone was to get rid of any "BBC atmosphere": "It's a pity, but . . . people are a bit overawed by the BBC".[44]

The BBC actually exploited this perception, and promoted *Have a Go!*'s relationship with the working-class community on an almost ethnographic level. We learn, for example, "of old crafts and ancient customs, of folk-lore and local superstitions which still survive",[45] a description which also carries the sense of venturing into an unknown world. Indicating the level of authenticity and respect conferred on a light entertainment series, one critic remarked how the programme assembled a "gallery of Dickensian individuals from what seemed at first no more than a cheerful crowd and raise[d] light entertainment to an almost documentary status".[46] The programme was broadcast live in front of a studio audience, and *Have a Go!* regularly insisted on the unscripted nature of the participants' dialogue. While Pickles tended to use stock questions such as "What is your secret ambition?", or "Is there anything you'd like to do before you die?", he routinely emphasised how: "We don't have scriptwriters. No scriptwriter could ever match the true story of the little boy who had swallowed a dice by mistake and whose first question after the doctors had been called was 'Dad, was it a six?' "[47] When asked about "the best types for interviewing" he replied, "Nervous types. And never rehearse them or see them before the programme . . . I'll never forget the woman who was so flustered she said: 'Good evening Mr Privilege, it's been a proper pickle to meet you!' "[48]

Pickles's recurrent emphasis on the *unscripted* nature of the show can be understood as an implicit reaction to the debates which had circled around the appearances of "ordinary" people on radio. As Scannell and Cardiff explain, while also making an appearance in entertainment-based programmes (such as *Harry Hopeful* beginning in 1935), working-class people had been brought to the microphone in the 1930s, in features and documentaries such as *Other People's Houses* or *Time to Spare*, which dealt with poverty and unemployment. These were attempts to cut through the "established discursive forms" of broadcasting, and their attendant implications of class distance (Scannell and Cardiff, 1991: 143). However, there was also an ambiguity as to the extent to which speakers were "helped" in the production of their dialogue (the "occasional literary turn of phrase aroused suspicion" (ibid)), and Pickles's eagerness to insist upon the unscripted nature of *Have a Go!* may have been intended to counteract such perceptions. Either way, concerns surrounding authenticity appear to be kept at bay at this point, but they were to surface in new and explicit ways with the advent of television. In fact, from the vantage point of the following decade, *Have a Go!* was often invoked as representing a more innocent "golden age" where the relationship between ordinary people and broadcasting was concerned. What had changed?

"We make them eat a bowl of jelly with chopsticks": television torture
British critics in the mid-1950s helped to construct the controversial status of what were known as "stunt" or forfeit shows in the US. The

most famous example here was *People are Funny*, but forfeits were also part of the BBC's *The Charlie Chester Show* and ITV's *Take Your Pick* and *Beat the Clock*. Hosted for most of its run in the US by Ark Linkletter, *People are Funny* began as a successful American radio show in 1942, transferring to American television in 1954. In Britain, the pro- gramme had already been broadcast from 1953 on Radio Luxembourg, but it was ITV, and thus television, which quite literally increased its vis- ibility in the British context. Hosted in Britain by the comedian Derek Roy, *People are Funny*, along with *Candid Camera*, is now seen as a pre- cursor to a whole group of practical joke/hidden camera shows. Although the lavish merchandise and large cash prizes awarded in America were replaced in Britain with washing machines, radios, refrig- erators and beauty sets, contestants would be invited to play a practical joke on others who were unaware of the set-up, and going through the task would earn them a prize. Some of the "stunts" reported by the British press included a competitor throwing a brick through the window of his own shop and calling the police, children impersonating orphans, a woman loaded up with suitcases knocking on a stranger's door and saying she had come to stay, and a woman clasping a toy doll approach- ing a stranger in a bus queue and telling him he was the father of her child.[49]

From the very start the programme attracted claims of "bad taste", and a series of articles appeared in the press in January 1956 which detailed the efforts of an MP from Deptford to get the show banned. He felt that local residents had been humiliated when the programme visited the area. But on a wider level, concern circled around the humiliation of *both* the contestants and the unwitting performers in the pranks, despite the fact that the former had clearly consented to appear. Although the programme was forced to remove its more "questionable incidents" (such as "the invasion of homes and the impersonation of orphans"), this was not enough, and Sir Kenneth Clark, Chairman of the ITA, stepped in to give the first warning to commercial television about a programme exhibiting "questionable taste".[50] After being forced to censor its stunts more and more, the show was ultimately withdrawn in March 1956.

At issue here was first that ordinary people were often seen as having less agency in the stunt and forfeit shows. The formats were seen as more explicitly engineered and contrived, and the sense that they constrained the agency of the participants was frequently yoked to an emphasis on humiliation and, related to this, concerns about the investment of the television viewer. Mittell observes a not dissimilar response to the rise of the "stunt" show on American radio in the 1940s (2002: 327), and he notes how such formats altered the ways in which "competition and vicarious participation factored into the genre" (2004a: 43). Yet it seems impossible to consider this shift in "vicarious participation" without confronting the impact of television itself.

A representative example of the press discussion here is offered by Victor Anant's article, "The 'Give-Away' Shows – Who is Really Paying?", published in *Picture Post* in 1955:

> The pattern of civilised sport hardly changes. We still derive the greatest pleasure from watching one man in a large arena being baited. The Roman gladiator faced a lion. The Spanish Matador fights a bull. And, in the age of television, chosen members of a live audience confront the Quiz Master . . . Television has evolved a subtler technique of man-baiting . . . If he triumphs, the Average Man will expect prize . . . If he fails he will pay a forfeit. This, again, is in keeping with our times. We do not destroy those who have lost. We make them eat a bowl of jelly with chopsticks. (Anant, 1955: 27)

Not confining his critique to programmes on commercial television, Anant primarily refers to the BBC's *The Charlie Chester Show* and ITV's *Take Your Pick*. He goes on to suggest that the programmes are not the "harmless" fun they appear to be ("they win fine prizes – but how much do they lose?"), and that such public exhibitions of indignity are "socially dangerous". Furthermore, it is intriguing that the examples recalled by critics in these discussions worried less over miners, farmers and shop assistants suffering the "intoxicating indignities" of televisual fame, than bank managers, educators and businessmen. In *Take Your Pick* a bank manager "who did not know the difference between 'tonsorial' and 'sartorial' had to curtsey like a debutante . . . with an imaginary bouquet of flowers" (Anant, 1955: 28), while in *The Charlie Chester Show* a teacher and newspaper critic had to "sing I Belong To Glasgow standing on his head while wearing a corset".[51] As these examples suggest, the concerns also appeared to have a *gendered* inflection: professional men in what are conceived as "feminised" (and feminising) displays of public performance are the main target for distaste. As with the responses to commodities discussed earlier in this chapter, concern here circles less around the perceived working-class appeal of these shows than the *mixing* of class cultures in one space.

The referent of gladiatorial combat and torture is not confined to the 1950s where the quiz and game show is concerned. The more recent shift toward the meaner psychological quiz show has explicitly drawn upon the referent of torture (e.g. *The Chair*, *The Chamber*), and the less punitive arena of *Millionaire* conjures up the visual connotations of what one critic described as a "Perspex and chrome amphitheatre" (Sutcliffe,

2000). But in the 1950s, this rhetoric structures the common parlance used to discuss the relationship between contestant and host. Descriptions of the quiz host as the "official torturer" appear without quotation marks, suggesting a shared understanding of this language between critic and reader. As Maurice Wiggin of the *Sunday Times* had to admit, the apparent capacity to endure punishment and humiliation contradicted the idea that these programmes were a "work-shy paradise" in which money was distributed for free.[52] It is not so much the acts themselves which are conceived as "harmful" (notwithstanding that dangerous mixture of jelly and sharp objects), as the fact that such games are subject to the *public* gaze. In their persistent return to issues of exhibition and display, these debates speak to television's mediation of public/private spheres, and the position then offered to the television viewer.

As television historians have noted (Spigel, 1992, Jacobs, 2000), from the very start television was promoted as a technology which *blurred* the boundaries of public and private. The apparatus of television was envisaged through metaphors of travel, taking the viewer *out* to distant events and locations, or bringing another world *into* the home (Jacobs, 2000). Particularly in relation to British television in the 1950s, scholars have tended to foreground television's ability to connect the viewer *to* public space, referencing the key event of the Coronation (1953), or the centrality of the outside broadcast in promoting the possibilities of the new medium (Holmes, 2005a: 179–193). In relation to the American context, Spigel has also discussed the series of "confusions about the spaces that television brought *into* the home" (1992: 115; my italics), involving debates about the "ultimate merits of bringing spectacles indoors" (117). But these discussions don't seem to cover how television provided access to images which, for all their "mediated publicness" (Dahlgren, 1995: 44), felt *private*, and which people would otherwise not have seen.

Conceived as inhabiting a self-referential televisual space which exists only under the bright lights of the studio set (announcing itself as an openly performative space constructed for *public* view) (Butler, 2002: 83), the quiz/game show is not a genre which has readily been discussed in relation to discourses of public/private. But while the quiz and game show did not emerge as an adaptation of existing entertainment in literature, cinema or theatre, it did adapt an existing cultural appetite for games – from "parlour" and party games to the popular press (Whannel, 1992: 181). For example, while one critic noted how quizzes, game shows and parlour games were "cropping up like mushrooms . . . over the graves of the jolly domestic variety of parlour games which have died in our homes . . . since it became possible just to turn on television for one's guests",[53] the Pilkington Report insisted that:

> The criticism that the "party" game items . . . often humiliate the members
> of the public. . . . is, in our view, justified. That people need not take part,
> or that they positively want to . . . is not . . . an answer to the criticism. Nor
> it is it relevant to say that these games are much the same as those people
> play in private. One may, of course, make a fool of oneself among relatives
> or friends because one is then participating in an intimate and lively human
> relationship: to do so for the amusement of millions of others, who are both
> unseen and unknown, is to risk being merely a foolish spectacle. (Pilkington
> Report, 1962: 55)

Critics in the 1950s could still recall the relative autonomy of the cultural
antecedents of the genre. Indeed, as the critic above hints, we might spec-
ulate that the increasing mediatisation of the home rendered such cultural practices more obsolete. Within this process, the Pilkington Report
is clearly concerned about the nature of the "para-social relationships"
(Horton and Wohl, 1956) engendered by television – as suggested by its
ambiguous reference to those "unseen and unknown" others watching
at home. While the Report classes the face to face relationships of families and gatherings as "intimate and lively", it seems to be precisely the
uncomfortable and acute intimacy of *viewing* these spectacles on television which sits at the core of the distaste. This is particularly so given the
emphasis on the close relationship between contestant and viewer. But
there is also a concern about this relationship breaking down, or rather
the impossibility of seeing how the performance is actually received. This
in turn circles around the "vicarious investment" (Mittell, 2004a: 43)
which is imagined to be offered to the viewer (see also Chapter 4 on the
"problem show"). While in practice, the contestants may have been
having the time of their lives, as they frequently protested when questioned by the press, this is not how it was perceived by the critic-viewers
producing these discourses. These responses represent a particularly self-
conscious dramatisation of the "uneasy ambivalence" which characterises our appreciation of the ordinary performer on television – the
oscillation between an uncomfortable empathy and a sadistic pleasure
(Lury, 1995: 126). But in the 1950s, this was shaped by the experience
of witnessing the translation (or transformation) of the genre across cultural practices and media forms.

"Keep your face up a bit – we get a better camera shot": performing for television

Reports of the thousands of people queuing to appear on quiz and game
shows suggest an immediate recognition of television as a "special
space", a "higher" order of reality which sits at the centre of social life
(Couldry, 2000). At the same time, as Nick Couldry has explored, it is

through the construction of the "ordinary", the claim to offer a common reference point for all, that television can claim this centrality in the first place (ibid). While the label of the "give-away" show focused attention on the prizes, there was equally a recognition in the 1950s that the *real* prize was "your 15 minutes of fame" (Whannel, 1992: 182), and critics were often amazed by, and concerned about, just what people would do in the pursuit of television visibility. But in the 1950s, emphasis on a distaste for opportunistic fame-seekers remained subordinate to stress on the exploitation of "ordinary" people. While clearly not an attitude confined to this period, this expressed a newly emergent anxiety about the commercialisation of the medium (will the broadcasters *know when to stop?*) as much as a concern for the participants themselves. While ITV was at the centre of these debates, they also included the BBC.

This image of a ruthless television industry, deviously manipulating ordinary people in the pursuit of TV ratings, was most clearly brought into view by the quiz show scandals which rocked American television in the late 1950s. But little is known about how these events impacted on other national contexts, or that they were in fact only the most visible examples of how "corruption and treachery" permeated the genre on an international level (Bourdon, 2004: 287). Rather than an isolated event, the scandals existed as part of a *continuum* of debates about the status of authenticity in the genre, particularly once it had transferred to television. This circled around television's difference from radio, and the perception that it involved ordinary people in a different type of performative context.

Even now, the quiz show competitor should ideally display some nervousness, exitement or awe about being on television, signifying their status as a competitor-viewer. In shows where contestants are chosen for their "personalities", they are also required to express these personalities in ways which "internalise and reproduce the conventions of public display" (Whannel, 1992: 193). Whannel observes how women are expected to "respond cheerfully to the flirtatious approach of the compere", while "bibliographic details are material for 'spontaneous' comedy" (1992: 193). Furthermore, "ordinary" people must also occupy the role of the "good sport", and generally perform "social roles . . . they may not wish to inhabit" (ibid).

In the programmes from the 1950s, contestants were very much required to act as the straight foil for the comedic talents of the (always male) host. In this respect, while appearances by ordinary people have been cited as a key mechanism through which broadcasting negotiates its sociality (Scannell, 1991), Turnock rightly points out that this needs to be understood as a form of *structured sociability* which pivots on unequal power relations (Turnock, forthcoming). It is certainly the case that in the existing footage, the imbalance of power between host and contestant is *acutely* apparent, and the press picked up on this in ways which did not emerge in the discussions of radio. This was perhaps in part because the contestants exuded a hesitancy about the new medium themselves. People are not yet *sure* if they have internalised the "conventions of public display" required for television (Whannel, 1992: 193), precisely because these conventions are still being explored. This is quite literally played out in existing footage of *Take Your Pick* when the host Michael Miles tells contestant Elizabeth Flynn "to keep your face up a bit, we get a better camera shot", physically tilting her face as he does so. The sense of being unsure about performing television's rituals of exchange went beyond understanding the specifics of shot or camera position – as is particularly apparent in the first television edition of *Double Your Money*, screened in 1955. Led on by the smiling blonde assistant, Hughie Greene welcomes "our oldest married couple", Mr and Mrs Wally ("married for 55 years – isn't that wonderful?"), who are 78 and 73 respectively. Dress, speech and demeanour position the couple as working class, but age is also important here: blinking warily under the studio lights, the couple come across as bewildered and vulnerable, although clearly pleased to be appearing on the show.

When Greene asks them to pick a knowledge category from the board, Mr Wally answers uncertainly ("I'm not sure there is much we can talk about at our age"), and Greene has to signal that the game has begun by suggesting possible subjects. Before the couple are questioned on the subject of Old Time Music Hall, Greene engages them in an exchange about their past, and asks, "Where did you meet?" After a pause, Mr Wally answers:

Mr Wally: In the Mile End Road.
Greene: I see . . . [pause]
Mr Wally: I asked her if she'd like to have a drink.
Greene: [turning to address the viewer while rolling his eyes] It's been a *long* drink, hasn't it?

Greene is evidently slightly thrown by the man's answer – he was expecting a type of place and not a road – but he regains control of the exchange with his joke. When he asks, "And where do you live now?", only to receive the hesitant reply "In, . . . in the Boursbon Road", Greene just repeats the answer ("Boursbon Road, I see"), before moving on to begin the game. It is the *localness* of Mr Wally's responses that disrupt the smooth patter of the proceedings here. His responses seem to be addressed to the "public" audience in the studio (perhaps his road is just round the corner), rather than the unseen, mass audience viewing him at home. At the same time, the awkward, stilted and self-conscious nature of the appearance can be seen to work in the service of authenticity, and thus the genre's wider claim to showcase "real" people. As Corner argues in a different context, in relation to the documentary *Housing Problems* (Anstey and Elton, 1935), the "very awkwardness of non-professional performance . . . can be seen as a guarantee of communicative honesty" (1996: 68). While age is just as important in assessing the connotations of this performance, it seems fascinating for enacting the still new experience of appearing *on* television. When Mr Wally says his wife will "have a go", Greene rolls his eyes and jokes, "Not Have a Go! That's another *programme*!", and the studio audience roars with laughter. Yet this intertextual link is quite apposite: it seems possible to imagine that the couple *could* have wandered into *Have a Go!*, only to find themselves illuminated by the bright studio lights of television and ushered along by the sparkling wit of Hughie Greene.

Have a Go! was partly repositioned at this time as representing an innocent "golden age" where broadcasting's use of "ordinary" people was concerned (and as Harry Hopkins notes, although it continued into the 1960s, the ethos of the programme was really rooted in a wartime spirit of community and camaraderie (1963: 229)). Even the socialist *Daily Worker*, in an article titled "I can appreciate Pickles now after a basinful of *People are Funny*", saw fit to comment:

> All this American-style entertainment has made me think more kindly of Wilfred Pickles. It's easy to see through his showman's tricks – the easy sentiment, the cheers for anyone over 80. . . . But he doesn't hurt or humiliate people he interviews, and he does, for a minute or two, let them speak for themselves.[54]

These comments arguably tap into the wider perspective (also discussed in Chapter 2), that traditional working-class culture was under threat from the new mass entertainments of the 1950s. In fact, while Richard Hoggart's *The Uses of Literacy* has relatively little to say about radio or television, it specifically refers to *Have a Go!* as an example of how "older attitudes [of working class culture] manage to survive" (Hoggart, 1958: 137). When Hoggart notes how *Have a Go!* values "good neighbourliness", "openess" and "loyalty" as opposed to the "commercial values" of "outdoing your acquaintances, show for its own sake [and] conspicuous consumption" (ibid), he could literally be comparing it to the newer television quiz show. Hoggart's position on working-class culture seemed to be doubly invoked where the quiz/game show was concerned: ITV was already positioned as "smuggling American values into British broadcasting and displac[ing] an organic working-class culture" (Bignell, 2005a: 19), while the "give-away" show was seen as the textual embodiment of this influence. Hoggart was later a prominent member of the Pilkington Committee which consolidated the view that ITV's quiz/game shows were something of a malign force.

It not necessary to endorse Hoggart's position in order to probe how perceptions of television's impact on the genre were relevant here. In this respect it is crucial to bear in mind that *Have a Go!* was *the* key reference point where broadcast appearances of "ordinary" people were concerned. It was also one of the most popular programmes on BBC radio – if not *the* most popular (Crisell, 2001). When it came to the claim to access the texture of regional voices and spaces, the importance of location had been central to *Have a Go!* Recordings were made in places such as factories, holiday camps, railway centres, collieries, an OAP club and a NAAFI canteen, and Pickles was very vocal about the extent to which studio-based productions, *especially* on television, compromised this authenticity. In comparison, the television quiz show has been conceived as inhabiting a self-referential television space which exists only under the bright lights of the studio set (Butler, 2002: 83). The Big Money quiz shows in the US had also introduced an increasingly elaborate set design and visual style. Producers paid careful attention to the dramatic construction of the shows – making use of using a theatricalised mise en scène, split screens juxtaposing battling contestants, and close-ups of anxious faces (among both the contestants and the studio audience) (Boddy, 1990: 105). While the BBC rejected much of this elaborate aesthetic framework, the ITV shows were quick to exploit it in their adaptation of these formats.

It seems that the visual iconography of the television quiz show shaped the perception that the performances of ordinary people on television were more forced and contrived. The sense that the ordinary person on television has been "manipulated by technicians, producers and bullying presenters" (Lury, 1995: 126) was discussed in quite literal terms in the 1950s. As one critic noted in relation to *Double Your Money*:

> With the face squeezed into close-up against the tick tick of the clock, and the [contestant] . . . squashed into that box, I'm surprised he could remember who he was amidst that ridiculous paraphernalia – never mind where the mouth of the Orinoco river might be.[55]

Far from reflecting back a mirror of recognisable humanity to the viewing audience, the self is seen to be *lost* in this televisual scenario.

"Are TV quizzes fixed?" (Maybe in America, but not over here . . .)
As this suggests, questions of authenticity focused on the *context* of the
appearance – the vivid sense that contestants were not given communicative, physical and visual space to "be themselves", and were effectively manhandled by the genre's aesthetic frame. Concerns about
authenticity in the genre took on a range of meanings in the 1950s,
moving from the contrived nature of the stunts to the aesthetic framework of the genre itself. In the late 1950s the rigging of the competitive
space, the casting of contestants, and the possibility that they might
"fake" a performance, also entered the discursive field, apparently courtesy of the Big Money shows in America. The 1956–57 season saw the
first public surfacing of the idea that the American programmes were not
the straightforward contests of knowledge they appeared to be. Articles
in national magazines such as *Time* and *Look* bluntly asked "Are TV
quizzes fixed?" (Anderson, 1978: 88). The suggestion here was that producers were manipulating the outcome of shows, both to ensure the
return of favourable contestants, and to maximise the dramatic excitement of the game. According to Boddy, while the quiz show was represented as an "uncontrolled and unpredictable contest . . . between
non-actors, producers were sensitive to their affinities with traditional
dramatic forms" (1990: 104). Boddy's point implies that the scandals
only gave a more visible expression to the contradictory pressures
which structured the genre. Peter Conrad has observed, for example,
how we can now actually describe the "corrupt" American producers as
pioneers:

> Though the medium reviled them, they were actually doing its work,
> turning the quiz show from an aural examination into a visual spectacle,
> training contestants to be actors . . . Was this malpractice, or was it merely
> the medium's early, astute recognition that whatever happens on it must be
> a performance, and therefore a simulation? (Conrad, 1982: 91)

The contours of Conrad's argument are brought out vividly by the British
discussion of the American version of *Dotto*. This was the first show to
be placed under investigation in America. A US contestant explained in
The Times:

> You'd think I was Marlon Brando. I was told how to bite my lips, clench
> my fists and look agonised as I supposedly struggled to find the answers.
> They even told me how, at the last moment, to make my face light up as
> if the answer had suddenly come to me. It made the whole thing very
> dramatic.[56]

Sequences in the film *Quiz Show* (Robert Redford, 1994) corroborate the
story told by the *Dotto* contestant. *Quiz Show* dramatises the most

famous scandal which surrounded *Twenty-One*, when Charles Van Doren, the "tall, handsome, young Ivy Leaguer with the engaging smile", was cast against Herbert Stempel, "the stout Jewish student from CCNY" (Anderson, 1978: 56). After being forced to lose to Van Doren, Stempel aimed to expose the cheating scam to the media, but his story was not accepted until August 1958 (Anderson, 1978: 117). What is crucial about the scandals in terms of the analysis here is how they enable a certain reframing of the quiz show in the British context (and a wider site upon which to negotiate the difference between "British" and "American" television), while they also had a direct impact on the institutional regulation of the genre in Britain.

Much of the British commentary was smug and moralistic, telling British viewers the "awful truth" about the "carefully-scripted and well-rehearsed spectacles" which had deceived the American public.[57] This is despite the fact that *very* similar debates had been going on closer to home in relation to certain British shows. But in the context of this book it is important to note that it is at this point that the BBC bows out of the quiz show narrative: existing evidence does not imply that they were implicated in the rigging debates, and it is only *here* that we can draw a clear marker of difference between the channels.

The most visible case in Britain similarly centred on *Twenty-One*, and while the American trials were ongoing in October 1958 (they finished after nine months of deliberations in June 1959), the programme, produced by Granada, faced similar accusations of foul play. With headlines such as "We were given details of quiz subjects",[58] and "Irregularity in game, says man who took part",[59] the *Daily Express* printed accusations from two contestants which stated that they had been given the headings of subjects beforehand (including "motoring, UNO, and drink").[60] It was Granada, and not the ITA, which asked for an independent inquiry to be launched, and the popular show was pulled from the air. Sir Lionel Heald QC acquitted Producer Bob Kesten of any serious malpractice, but he did find that he had used "highly imprudent" methods to make the show more exciting (Sendall, 1982: 349). Although it remains unclear exactly what these "imprudent" methods entailed, and despite the fact that Kesten protested his innocence, he did express the apparently incriminating view that there was no visual entertainment value "in having people stand up before the cameras, look blank, and answer 'I don't know' ".[61]

Despite the suggestion that the claims of fakery, foul play and rigging were simply aping the American context (with the contestants painted as copycats and publicity seekers), closer scrutiny indicates more of a parallel development. In 1956–57, before the main scandals had broken in the US, the Producer of the British *$64,000 Question* keeps reiterating the fairness and honesty of the format, assuring us of its stringent security measures and the sound-proof contestant box which "prevents any tampering".[62] Very soon, the Producer of *$64,000 Question*, John Irwin, was reiterating the authenticity of the show in response to complaints, questions and critiques. The British press ran a series of articles which variously asked "How Fair is the [British] *$64,000 Question*?": "How are the challengers chosen? Is it a 'professional' audience? How are the subjects selected?"[63] The emphasis on a "professional audience" is particularly intriguing here: during the show "close-ups are given of agonised members of the audience and it has been suggested that [they] . . . are actors".[64]

While this audience was part of the on-screen spectacle, inserted into the same framework as the contestants themselves, the example reflects on the ambiguous positioning of the audience within the scandals. In America, the main people prosecuted came from the group of contestants (they were not convicted for television fraud but for lying to a grand jury) (Anderson, 1978: 182). This was because the scandals were not deemed to constitute a fraud in the traditional sense, as they were seen as lacking a clear victim (Anderson, 1978: 134). This image of a system "protecting the powerful while prosecuting the weak" (Anderson, 1978: 182), however, reinforced the characterisation of the contestants as powerless and manipulated, and the television industry as ruthless exploiters. In both national contexts, these roles in the debates remain relatively fixed, and an analysis of the British situation foregrounds how this was part of the wider discursive construction of ordinary people as television performers in the genre. But the role which is more ambiguous, fluctuating between "victim" and perpetrator, is the role occupied by the public. Some of the American producers claimed that "to give the viewer what he wants . . . the producer has to set up some kind of controls" (cited in Boddy, 1990: 104). This ambiguity surrounding the role of the viewer is quite literally dramatised in the discussion of the British *$64,000 Question* above: apparently innocent onlookers are imagined to be part of the deception, and we are encouraged to scrutinise their faces for signs of performance, deviousness and fraud. While certainly an attempt by the producers to shift ethical responsibility onto the viewer, this also suggests how the genre, and specifically the concerns over rigging, gave expression to broader debates about the institutional regulation of television, and particularly the spectre of commercialisation. The extent to which television should "give the audience what it wants" had clearly enjoyed a particular currency in relation to the advent of ITV, and the history of the "give-away" show on 1950s British television suggests the importance of examining how these debates were articulated through, and shaped by, the specificity of different generic contexts.

The British scandal was also productive for British television, in that it was paradoxically used as a marker of differentiation between the two contexts. As the *Evening Post* argued, for example, while the shows may be "faked" in the US, they "aren't over here. It is good to see this kind of strong reaction [in Britain] to suggestions of malpractice. We must keep the phoney and corrupt out of British television".[65] The *Birmingham Mail* explained how "television really is an entertainment *business* in the US – we may have gone 'commercial', but we are a long way from all that".[66] The ITA's decision to draw up more stringent rules for the regulation of quiz shows (each programme had to be accompanied by a book which set out the rules of the game and the procedure for selecting contestants (Sendall, 1982: 349)), as well as the decision to cap the prize limit at £1,000, was in part a product of the accusations over rigging in *both* national contexts. Yet this apparently rigorous and quick intervention bolstered the emphasis on the institutional, moral and cultural difference of British television (despite the fact that the scandals had a more lasting institutional impact on American television) (see Anderson, 1978, Boddy, 1990). In tracing this process, what is so interesting is that a genre initially seen as an odious American import, an intrusive commercial alien on the British television screen, is reframed as reassuringly playing out the overriding dominance of a public service framework.

Not the final answer . . .

This suggests how the ITA's intervention to "steer the quiz form away from the spectacular direction it took in the USA" (Whannel, 1992: 184), and even the characterisation of the genre in the Pilkington Report, was not simply the product of innate distaste – a middle-class derision for gambling, or a suspicion of a form which promoted "wealth without work". These attitudes *are* important, and they continue to have a currency in the cultural and critical reception of the genre. But the ITA's intervention did not come out of nowhere, and it needs to be placed in relation to the complex and fascinating set of discourses which surrounded the genre on British television in the 1950s. The American context is crucial here. There is a clear material relationship between Britain and America (the adaptation of American formats), as well as a clear discursive interaction (the American quiz show scandals shape the cultural reception of the genre in Britain). Given the paucity of historical work on the genre, comparisons with other European contexts would be revealing and productive (see Bourdon, 2004). This is particularly so when, as with Chapter 2 on the "soap opera", any bid to write this history feels the weight of the American context, not simply in relation to the origin of the formats, but also at the level of television historiography. Other histories, including the British, can seem less spectacular, "excessive" and scandalous – pale imitations of the "real" history of the genre which was unfolding in the US. This conception has undoubtedly shaped the experience of researching the early British history, but this need not be cast in terms of conceptual straitjacket. Part of examining the institutional and cultural specificity of the British context *is* to explore how the relations between "America" and the quiz show were used, discussed and rejected to shape the British conception of the genre.

In this regard, this chapter has argued that *the impact of television on the genre has often been mistaken for the impact of ITV*. These spheres cannot be separated, and it is precisely for this reason that we need to examine the picture from a wider perspective. This perspective includes the genre's history on radio, and this can elucidate the aesthetic, institutional and cultural impact of television on the quiz and game show, while it also cautions against an approach in which television examples are explored in a "generic vacuum" (Mittell, 2002: 319). This chapter has not aimed to cast the relations between radio and television in one way: we get a different picture of these relations as we move across the regulation of prizes, the use of knowledge, and the construction of ordinary people as performers (even while in practice, these spheres must be viewed as inextricably intertwined). This wider perspective is not simply about expanding the media focus of the genre. It also demands that we write *the BBC* back into this history, with regard to both radio and television.

As such, this chapter has taken a slightly different approach to its material than the other chapters in *Entertaining Television*. The "known" framework here, albeit one painted in very broad strokes, related to ITV. This chapter has aimed to reconstruct and analyse this history by drawing on new archival research, while also reconnecting it with the broadcast roots of the genre and the contribution of the BBC. We *can* trace differences in how the channels approached and conceptualised the genre, but to argue that this is a clear-cut opposition, or that ITV ushered in a radical break where the generic components of the quiz/game show were concerned, is problematic. After all, as Maurice Wiggin of the *Sunday Times* rightly observed in 1957, we should not forget that:

> The odium of having introduced the American import to Britain belongs [not to ITV but] to the BBC. Long before [now] . . . *The Charlie Chester Show* offered modest prizes . . . to anyone willing to submit themselves to

such hilarious indignities as having a bucket emptied over his head . . . No student of the give-away quiz phenomenon can ignore this [fact].[67]

Notes

1 "And that's how quiz kids were born!", *Evening Express*, 7 November 1958.
2 See Frank Gillard, "The Story of 'Any Questions?'", *Radio Times*, 18 September 1953, p. 3.
3 Ronald Waldman to Kenneth Adam, 29 June 1955. T12/455.
4 Although it has been suggested that *Top of the Form* did not make the transition to television until 1962 (when it was called *Television Top of the Form*), this was not the case, although its television appearances were intermittent in the 1950s.
5 "Minutes of Control Committee Meeting", 13 January, 1926. R19/989.
6 "Competitions", Director of Talks to Director General, 3 July 1930. R19/989.
7 "B.T.H.A and Listener Competitions", J.B. Clarke, 13 January 1956. R34/595/2.
8 Director Secretariat to Norman Collins, 6 April 1946. R34/595/1.
9 Controller, Entertainment, 5 September 1949. R34/595/1.
10 Cecil McGivern to George Barnes, 29 November 1954. T16/160.
11 *Yorkshire Evening News*, 30 January 1950.
12 *Evening Telegraph and Post: Dundee*, 29 December 1949.
13 "News Chronicle Competition", Deputy Director of Television to Director General, 7 August 1958. R34/595/2.
14 George Barnes to Cecil McGivern, 8 August 1951. T16/160.
15 *Kaleidoscope* script, 12 May 1950.
16 See BBC Press Cuttings, 1951–52.
17 "New TV Show Will Give Presents: BBC Breaks Rules for Quizzers", *News Chronicle*, 6 December 1951.
18 "Prizes in Programmes", Controller of Television Programmes to Head of Television Light Entertainment, 16 August 1951. T12/302.
19 *Daily Herald*, 27 December 1951.
20 Cecil McGivern to George Barnes, 29 November 1954. T16/160.
21 As above; original emphasis.
22 *Daily Mirror*, 8 March 1957. (ITC.)
23 *The Times*, 22 October 1958.
24 *Daily Express*, 13 July 1960. (ITC.)
25 As above.
26 *Sunday Times*, 24 March 1957. (ITC.)
27 As above.
28 "Round Britain Quiz", Acting Controller, Light Programme, 23 March 1948. R51/519/2.
29 "Headmaster with a Class of 12 million", *Daily Mirror*, 10 October 1950.
30 "The Brain's Trust Talks Too Much", undated memo. R41/22/2.

31 BBC Viewer Research Report, *What Do You Know?*, 15 January 1959. R19/1970/1.

32 "Parlour Games and Quizzes on Radio and Television", *Glasgow Herald*, 4 November 1953.

33 "BBC Quiz Shows Misguided", *The Times*, 14 October 1959, p. 8.

34 *The Top of the Form Story* (BBC4, 9 April 2006).

35 Questions taken from scripts for *Round Britain Quiz, Trans-Britain Quiz, Ask me Another*.

36 "Background Information on Mr. Button", BBC press release, 28 July 1958. R19/1970/2.

37 There were a number of reports in the 1950s which observe how women were less likely to apply to be quiz and game show contestants. Explanations often made recourse to "natural", "biological" differences between the sexes – women's "natural" reluctance to be competitive, for example (see *TV Times*, 22 February 1957, p. 7). These discussions now have a long heritage where the quiz show is concerned, and the issue of women's relative invisibility in the genre was debated explicitly around the British and American versions of *Who Wants to be a Millionaire?* (Holmes, 2005d). In terms of the British context in the 1950s, the issue of gender inequality in education, as well as the gendering of knowledge itself, could be explored in more detail than is possible here.

38 Existing audiovisual episode of *Ask Me Another* (15 May 1960).

39 *Birmingham Mail*, 17 November 1956. (ITC.)

40 *News of the World*, 14 October 1956. (ITC.)

41 "So Personal – But No Offence", *John Bull*, 14 May 1949.

42 "So Personal – But No Offence", *John Bull*, 14 May 1949.

43 *Have a Go!* script, 11 May 1949.

44 "Presenting the People to the People", *TV Mirror*, 23 January 1953, pp. 18–19.

45 "*Have a Go!*: 1963/1964 – Programme Notes". R44/911/1.

46 "Television Competitions and Parlour Games", *The Times*, 22 October 1958, p. 9.

47 "Now 'Have a Go' Comes up for Round 13", *Evening Gazette*, 6 September 1958.

48 "Tales from the BBC", *Daily Mail*, 16 June 1950.

49 *Daily Mirror*, 23 November 1955. (ITC.)

50 *Daily Express*, 18 January 1956. (ITC.)

51 "First TV Gift Show", *Daily Herald*, 27 December 1951.

52 *Sunday Times*, 24 March 1957.

53 "Parlour Games and Quizzes on Radio and Television", *Glasgow Herald*, 14 November 1953.

54 *Daily Worker*, 27 January 1956. (ITC.)

55 "Last Night's TV", *Daily Mail*, 15 March 1957.

56 "US Inquiry into Quiz Shows", *The Times*, 28 August 1958, p. 7.

57 *Evening Post*, 26 November 1959.

58 *Daily Mail*, 5 November 1958. (ITC.)
59 *Daily Mail*, 31 October 1958. (ITC.)
60 *Daily Mail*, 5 November 1958. (ITC.)
61 *Mail on Sunday*, 26 May 1995, p. 45.
62 *Daily Telegraph*, 17 November 1956. (ITC.)
63 *Daily Mail*, 2 February 1957. (ITC.)
64 *Daily Mail*, 2 February 1957. (ITC.)
65 *Evening Post*, 26 November 1959.
66 *Birmingham Mail*, 16 March 1959.
67 *Sunday Times*, 24 March 1957. (ITC.)

4

The problem show
"An . . . unmarried mother sat in a wing-backed chair on TV last night": BBC Television asks *Is This Your Problem?* (1955–57)

The previous chapter focused on the quiz/game show and its claim to offer a utopian television space – the promise of "wealth without work", and what critics saw as a never-never land of consumer dreams. As Richard Dyer explains, light entertainment must provide an "alternative to the world of work . . . drudgery and depression" (1973: 23), a sphere in which the real world of work, poverty and social problems does not intrude. But if the "give-away" show appeared to represent an accelerated image of the affluent society, with the riches of consumerism on daily display, it also sat alongside a less sparkling image of life in post-war Britain. In this image, the real world of everyday struggle, inequality, personal hardship and social exclusion did intrude. In fact, it was actively ushered into public view by television itself. Enter the 1950s problem show.

It was while researching the quiz and game show in this period, sifting through fragments of stale newsprint in the BBC's Written Archives, that the existence of the problem show came to light. Amidst the complaints about "idiot contestants and giveaway shows", and the distaste for the ecstatic celebration of washing machines and fridges, a different headline came into view: "An Unmarried Mother Hid her Face on TV last night". Tantalised by the promise of "Real-life cases", I read on:

> A middle-aged unmarried mother sat in a wing-backed chair on TV last night, her face hidden from the cameras, while three men gave her advice. . . . Viewers saw only the mother's hands – twisting and turning a pair of gloves. There was a bag on her lap and a ring on her finger. Her voice was halting, subdued and reluctant.[1]

There was immediately something fascinating about this image, precisely because of its transgressive air. Much like the woman's hands, the image wouldn't sit still when positioned in the context of historical assumptions about 1950s British television, and BBC television in particular. While the BBC is characterised as "stuffy", "paternalist" and "priggish" (Thumim, 2004: 27), the popular image of post-war reconstruction pivots on its bid to (re)consolidate family life, with television imagined as a catalyst which might renew such values. At the same time, the press report also spoke to these prevailing perceptions: it says that the woman "hid her face", but it is possible that the BBC also hid it *for* her, and the visual capacities of television appear to be cautiously reined in. The scenario is also saturated with patriarchal and middle-class moral values, and the spectacle of the "unmarried mother" – "subdued and reluctant" – is framed within its power.

The review was referring to the BBC's *Is This Your Problem?* (1955–57) (hereafter *ITYP?*), a programme in which members of the public appeared on television to present a problem to an expert panel consisting of a doctor, a University Vice Chancellor and a representative of the clergy. The problems covered by the programme varied considerably, although the press reported that the biggest batch of letters "dealt with housing difficulties, matrimonial conflicts, as well as erring husbands, delinquent children, adoption . . . emigration and people made unhappy by. . . . physical disability".[2] The reviewer above goes on to denounce the programme as a "cheap, shoddy, shameful business", while BBC Audience Research recorded how certain viewers could "not . . . overcome the feeling that [it was] . . . not suitable for television entertainment – despite the undoubted attraction of the human stories".[3] There is much here which seems to prefigure more recent debates about "tabloidisation". More specifically, the discussion of *ITYP?* speaks to the cultural debate which greeted the talk show in the 1990s. In recognising Corner's caution about the danger of fostering an "undue proximity" between past and present (2003: 277), I am not suggesting that the talk show and the 1950s problem show are "really" the same. But the chapter does work on the premise that there are conceptual and textual links here which reward close consideration. These links are doubly interesting given that, whether in the UK or the US, studies of the talk show have paid more attention to print precursors than they have to those emerging from television itself (e.g. Shattuc, 1997, Glynn, 2000).

The description of the "unmarried mother" above incites the desire to look, but the possibility of looking at *ITYP?* is now circumscribed by more than the BBC's camera arrangements. The programme was broadcast live, and it is the only series used as a main case study in this book which has not survived in audiovisual form. Aside from photographs of the host, the analysis of the programme is based on archival research into press reviews, scripts and the internal documentation of the BBC. In using this evidence, Chapter 4 situates *ITYP?* within the historical circumstances of its circulation, exploring what it can contribute to knowledge of British television's aesthetic development at this time, the medium's negotiation of public/private, and its production of social and cultural identity.

The chapter begins by exploring some of the social and cultural contexts from which the programme emerged, particularly the emphasis on post-war social problems and the role of the Welfare State. It then considers the institutional development of *ITYP?*, before moving on to an analysis of the programme as a form of television talk. In looking at case studies on *ITYP?*, and making comparisons with the talk show, the analysis foregrounds the contradictory power relations at the core of the programme. The chapter then examines the extent to which gender (or more specifically, the feminine) informs the key tensions here, before moving on to explore the programme in relation to the subsequent explosion of confessional and therapeutic cultures on television.

"It might be anyone's window . . .": television looks in on post-war troubles

Like many programmes on BBC television at this time, *ITYP?* was screened on a fortnightly basis. It initially appeared on a Wednesday at 9:15 p.m., but later moved to 10:15 p.m. As young people were understood to be viewing between 6 and 9 p.m., it was policy that programmes "portraying the break up or degradation of family life [should be] . . . kept for later in the evening",[4] and *ITYP?* was evidently perceived to fit into this category. The programme was initially produced by the distinguished Huw Wheldon. Later known to viewers as the presenter of the BBC's arts programme *Monitor* (1958–64), Wheldon was to become a leading figure among BBC programme makers in the 1960s, and a top BBC administrator in the 1970s, ultimately becoming the Deputy Director General. But contributing to the programme's near effacement from British television history, it is difficult to find reference to *ITYP?* in descriptions of Wheldon's early years at the BBC, and when afforded a quick reference, it is described as "one of the most embarrassing disasters of his career".[5]

ITYP? was previewed by a trailer before it went on air, and this trailer soon became the permanent opening title sequence. It begins with an aerial shot of a city, imagined by Wheldon as being London at dusk or by night. The camera then moves in, dissolving into nearer shots of roads and streets, then dissolving into further shots of single houses, and ending

Figure 3 Edna Romney, the hostess of *Is This Your Problem?* 'It might be anybody's window, mightn't it?'

on an approach to a single curtained window with lights inside.[6] Filmed in close-up, the host, Edana Romney (see Figure 3) then adopts a direct address to the viewer:

> It might be anybody's window, mightn't it? Might be yours – might be mine. Every night there are millions of windows all over the country looking just like that – curtains cosily drawn, the light glowing behind them, all that suggests a happy home inside. But it isn't *always* so, is it? Any night you like – tonight – behind so many of those curtains there is somebody fretting over a personal problem that makes happiness impossible.
>
> And there are so many different problems. One of you may long to have a child, who's now with foster parents . . . Maybe you're being blackmailed for some small indiscretion, and you don't know what to do. Maybe you're a widow, and you are thinking of marrying again, but your children resent the man who would take their father's place. And you are trying to make up your mind what is best for them, for him, for you. Heartbreaks – divided loyalties – duties. It was this that made [us] . . . wonder whether in some way, Television could not be used to help.[7]

Romney asks any interested viewers to write to her, and if the programme thinks it can help, the viewer will be invited to meet the group of advisors:

"This meeting will be televised; but you needn't have any anxiety. Your name need not be given and in [some] . . . cases you needn't even be seen."[8]

One of the most fascinating aspects of this sequence is how it seems to capture an image of a shift toward a more privatised society at this time. But rather than the private suburban home appearing as a "potent utopian fantasy" (Spigel, 1992: 34), it is imagined to be a state of existence which is fraught with problems. The trailer for *ITYP?* invokes the "underside", or rather the unseen "inside", of the post-war ideal, in which a sense of community has declined. *ITYP?* is then positioned as recreating its own community through a complex relay of television identifications. The trailer beckons the lonely viewer to step into the television space, and thus to share the problem with an on-screen community. But it also inserts the subject into a community of viewers who, in the process, must then be imagined as sharing similar troubles themselves. The title is addressed to the individual viewer as an empty signifier ("Is this *your* problem?"), while in reality it aimed to reach out to the millions of viewers who made up television's growing mass audience. In this regard, it is impossible to say whether there is a direct relationship between *ITYP?* and the emergence of commercial television, but they did both begin in September 1955. While it is more appropriate to suggest that the advent of ITV coincided with, or at best accelerated, the class expansion of the television audience (Hand, 2003), *ITYP?* offers a particularly interesting example of the bid to address a more heterogeneous public. It is precisely *through* this shift, what might be seen as a rather Gramscian (1998) bid to engage in "negotiations with opposing groups, classes and values" (Turner, 1996: 178), that *ITYP?* is born.

The BBC's family serial, *The Grove Family*, discussed in Chapter 2, generally presented a reassuring image of post-war family life. It did play out the experience of a suburban existence, with the family relatively isolated from their neighbours. But it did not make any overt attempt to tackle contemporary or social issues on a regular basis. In society at large, however, there was a recognition that not all families were as happy and cohesive as the Groves (Sydney-Smith, 2002: 48). Claims about the disintegration of family life took on many meanings in the 1950s, covering juvenile delinquency, working mothers, divorce and racial tension. On a broader scale, the war had opened up cracks in family life, and the question in the following period was about how to repair such wounds (Wilson, 1980).

This picture suggests how the prevailing social mechanisms were inadequate to manage the reconstruction of family life, while it was evidently also through these mechanisms that such "problems" were spoken. The

landmark development here was the Beveridge Report of 1942, and
the Welfare State constructed a vision of Britain in which the citizen
would be cared for from the "cradle to the grave" (Walker, 1991: 188).
Although Labour assumed that the New Conservatism represented by
the government that was elected in 1951 would renege on the commit-
ment to the Welfare State, the policies were generally upheld (Hill,
1986: 5). The late 1940s had seen the infrastructure of the Welfare State
emerge, with the introduction of policies for social security, health, education, employment, housing and personal social services. This effectively legalised state intervention into family life at large (Walker, 1991:
191), setting forth an extended network of "specialists" who were
backed by statutory authority. As these structures were also ideologies,
defining and regulating the "normal" (Walker, 1991: 207), it is little
wonder that there were concerns about the usurpation of private choice
and freedom, or that arguments about the condition of family life in post-
war Britain also "involved a fear of state intervention" (Wilson, 1980:
78). Yet defenders of the Welfare State argued that absolute privacy could
only exist if the state were to take no responsibility for its citizens at all
(Walker, 1991: 210). The relationship of public to private was being rene-
gotiated here, not simply at the level of everyday life, work and leisure,
but also in terms of the relations between self and state.

Television, itself an agent for reworking the boundaries between public
and private, then enters this context, bringing *ITYP?* in its tow. But
despite its gesture to anxieties concealed behind closed doors, the problems explored by the programme were not otherwise invisible. *ITYP?*
occasionally referred to newspaper headlines to indicate the topical relevance of a problem, and British cinema turned toward the social problem
film at this time (see Hill, 1986). Perhaps most crucially, television itself
participated in exploring this sphere from an early stage. Building on the
socially democratic impetus of documentaries in the 1930s, as well as
BBC radio documentaries from the same period (see Scannell and
Cardiff, 1991), television documentaries and current affairs contributed
to the media definition of social problems at this time. Between 1946 and
1956, the story-documentary – based on studio reconstructions with
actors and scripts – produced features on juvenile delinquency, marriage,
divorce, borstal, women at work, children in care and "maladjusted children" (Scannell, 1979: 101). In moving from the early 1950s to mid-
decade, Stuart Laing describes a shift from presenting the *operation* of
social service institutions (the courts, the medical profession, the police,
the prison), to focusing "on the problems of those caught up in, or
needing welfare institutions" (1986: 160). In 1955 the BBC produced
The Unloved, which focused on delinquent children, and in 1956 it

produced *Women Alone*, which focused on unmarried mothers. In the sphere of current affairs, *Special Enquiry* (BBC, 1952–57), which mixed unscripted statements from ordinary people with authoritative commentary, as well as *Panorama* and ITV's *This Week*, all concerned themselves with "*the state* of Britain today", with social problems very much a part of this agenda (Thumim, 2004: 46; original emphasis).

ITYP?, then, was far from an isolated example of television engaging with the problems which were affecting people's everyday lives, and the prevalence of this perspective begins to question how all-encompassing the emphasis on the affluent "good life" actually was. Yet while some of the topics or problems are similar, *ITYP?* differed from these other programme contexts on a number of levels. Unlike documentaries or current affairs which could claim to "get close" in order to take a "public look" (Jacobs, 2000: 159), *ITYP?* could boast no such legitimacy. This was not television casting its emerging "social eye" (Scannell, 1979) across the British social landscape, but a carefully crafted television occasion in its own right. Like the quiz/game show, *ITYP?* constructed a television reality. It invited people into the studio space to meet the host, panel and home viewer, and the problems were refracted through a more individualised and personalised framework. It is this which made the programme both innovative and controversial.

Developing a private life programme: contexts and concerns

When it came to the press, *ITYP?* was most often described as a problem show, but it was also dismissively called a "heartbreak corner" – a term which invoked gendered, feminine, associations. The BBC used the term problem show, but equally adopted the more public-service-spirited label of the "counselling programme", or they called it a "private life programme"[9] if it was being scrutinised as an object of institutional concern. These descriptors also indicate how *ITYP?* drew its roots from various media contexts, including problem pages in the press and magazines, and existing formats from British and American broadcasting. In the initial discussions about *ITYP?*, BBC radio's *Can I Help You?* is mentioned as a precursor programme which dealt with problems. *Can I Help You?* began in 1939, and the *Radio Times* explained how "Questions which are puzzling listeners in these difficult times are discussed each fortnight in this series of talks".[10] The nod to these "difficult times" clearly referred to the Second World War, and while the programme continued in peacetime, it initially addressed issues raised by the wartime context, including evacuated children, wartime benefits, or widows claiming on personal insurance policies after their husbands had been killed in service. In the early 1950s, the programme dealt with such topics as how to apply for an old age pension, legal definitions of disability, or problems relating to the Rent Act or buying a house. The programme was actually run in its initial years by the National Council of Social Services, and speakers from the Council were paid by the BBC to take part. The BBC felt that it would be most attractive to working-class listeners who "would make use of these bureaux",[11] apparently because they were seen as less likely to "understand" such matters, and less likely to ask for official help. Listeners were encouraged to send any correspondence with questions or problems to the Council, rather than the Corporation. (By the later period of 1961, *Can I Help You?* was run by the Citizen's Advice Bureau[12]). The problems or questions did reflect concerns raised by listeners, but they were presented as general or hypothetical problems, rather than individual, real narratives. Furthermore, and as the topics suggest, *Can I Help You?* could not be conceived as addressing social problems as such, nor as touching on "private" or intimate issues which affected listeners. The point of the programme is well captured by one listener's view that it contributes to listeners' "education as citizens".[13]

The idea of a problem show covering more intimate, "private" issues really seems to emerge *with* television. The closest companion to *ITYP?* could be found in the BBC's daytime television programming for women. *Family Affairs* (1955) began the same year as *ITYP?*, and it was a magazine programme which generally dealt with child and family healthcare (Thumim, 2004: 61). In conjunction with *Mainly for Women*, Thumim notes how it also included a panel of experts – a doctor, an educational psychologist, the Director of the NSPCC and a children's magistrate – who answered questions and problems sent in by viewers (ibid). But while the problem forum was sandwiched in between items such as "Feeding problems in young children", "Caring for the sick child" or "the child who stammers",[14] it also addressed a wider set of concerns than the emphasis on childcare might imply. These concerns ranged across alcoholism, falling out of love with one's husband, and the loneliness of a young widow. The problems were clearly real and individualised, and the letters (notably edited by the programme makers) were read out on air by the doctor: "Problem No. 5. 'I have a son aged 32 who is far too fond of alcohol' ".[15]

The fact that the closest companion to *ITYP?* is found in *Family Affairs* indicates how the maintenance of relationships, and the social and psychological health of the family, are seen as part of the traditionally feminine work of personal intimacy. But the idea of a problem forum was evidently also perceived by the BBC as a flexible format which could be adapted for, and addressed to, a wider evening audience. Only weeks after *ITYP?* went on air, ITV also began its own problem show called *As Others See Us*. The *TV Times* details how Godfrey Winn "suggests a solution for family, sociological and domestic problems which trouble viewers".[16] While *Family Affairs* dealt with anonymous problems sent in by absent viewers, ITV's *As Others See Us* was apparently more akin to a reconstructed story-documentary. Godfrey Winn acted as the narrator while actors played out the problem in a two-minute scene, and the suggested solution was then also performed.

In contrast, *ITYP?* included the person *with* the problem as part of the programme itself. It was produced live, with the participant and panel occupying the same space. The idea of doing such a programme was in fact initially mooted by Religious Broadcasting. This was a time of debate about the impact television could have on religious culture,[17] as well as a time of experimentation with its television possibilities (see Briggs, 1979: 783). Although *ITYP?* was ultimately a general production by the Talks Department and not a religious programme *per se*, the presence of a religious framework remained apparent, not least of all because it had a representative of the clergy on its panel. According to the BBC memos, the decision to include an on-screen role for the "questioner", as they were called, was prompted by formats on American radio and television, and these formats were first noted by the Religious Broadcasting Organiser, Colin Beale. After seeing an idea on US television which had a "presenter and a secretary" (the title of the show is not given), Beale initially suggested that "People could be invited to ring up [via a number in the] . . . *Radio Times* . . . [This programme] might be able to stimulate the general pastoral work which the clergy can do with the outside."[18] (In ecclesiastical terms, the 1950s seemed to offer an optimistic future, but by the end of the decade, churchgoing was in precipitous decline (see Davie, 1994).) The Head of Religious Broadcasting entered into a number of exchanges with BBC contacts in New York to ask for further information on "American television programmes of the religious counselling kind – personal problems of a moral or religious nature".[19] But it is clear that he also had some pressing concerns:

> If a telephone is used will this provide sufficient visual interest for [a] 15 minute [television] programme? Are there any programmes of this kind in which questioners are actually in the studio, although anonymity is preserved by keeping them out of vision? More serious, do American programmes of this kind seem to entail a violation of personal privacy which would be distasteful to English viewers? What safeguards against exhibitionism on the one hand, or the presentation of problems which can only be answered in strict privacy on the other, are used?[20]

In addition to discussions of the soap opera or the quiz/game show (see Chapters 2 and 3), this is further evidence of how the BBC negotiated its own identity by invoking the perennial "other" of American broadcasting. Here, and as with the treatment of celebrities (Chapter 5), the emphasis is on American broadcasting as having less regard for personal privacy than the BBC, something the Corporation saw as a product of different cultural mores, as well as the rampant dangers of commercial television. But more crucial at this stage is the recognition that a television problem show involves competing pressures which are specific to its textual form. There is a rather bourgeois obsession with the relationship between privacy and "good taste", yet in the same breath, there is the clear acknowledgement that "visual interest", and thus appeal, cannot be ignored. This ultimately spoke to a wider tension in the development of *ITYP?*: the difficulty of balancing public service ideals with the need to produce a programme which appealed to – and even entertained – a mass audience.

From private life programme to public sphere

Notions of what is private are always premised on what is seen as public (and vice versa) (Dahlgren, 1995), and in this respect, work on the television talk show has engaged with Jürgen Habermas's (1984) conception of the rational, critical public sphere (Shattuc, 1997, Lunt and Stenner, 2005, Livingstone and Lunt, 1994). Habermas understood the public sphere as a realm of social life in which issues of common concern can be debated, views can be exchanged and "something approaching public opinion can be formed" (Habermas, 1984: 198). The "public sphere" "takes place" when "citizens . . . gather as public bodies to discuss issues of the day, specifically those of political concern" (Dahlgren, 1995: 44). Habermas's conception of the bourgeois public sphere was rooted in the contexts of Britain, France and Germany in the eighteenth century, and as is well known, he traces the decline of this sphere in the context of industrial capitalism and the social welfare state of mass democracy (ibid). The State, and large institutions such as the media, are seen as agents of commercialisation and institutionalisation. Given his emphasis on the need for a forum outside the control of particular interests, Habermas was critical of the extent to which media institutions could create the conditions for public deliberation. Instead, such institutions are seen as creating only an "illusion of participation" (Lunt and Stenner, 2005: 60).

Habermas's position has been critiqued from a number of perspectives. Feminist work has drawn attention to the gender and class bias of the public sphere, while others have suggested that it was an ideal to be striven for, rather than a reflection of real historical circumstances. We can also ask whether it feasibly reflects how society now operates (although it should be noted that this does not in itself invalidate the trajectory of Habermas's argument). As Peter Lunt and Paul Stenner ask, how can deliberation now "take place without mediation given the logistical problems of co-ordinating the participation of large, geographically spread, diverse populations?" (2005: 60). Work on the talk show has found no easy relationship with Habermas's conception of the public sphere, particularly in light of the generic shift from "personal issues connected to social injustice" toward the individualised, interpersonal conflicts of the 1990s talk show (Shattuc, 1998: 212). But Habermas's work has nevertheless been used as a starting point, as Lunt and Stenner describe in their survey of the field, to consider "whether talk shows are sufficiently free of institutional control; provide freedom of access and voice; and constitute a viable framework for the formation of public opinion" (2005: 60). At the same time, critics such as Joshua Gamson (1999) suggested moving beyond the bid to assess the talk show as a public sphere, and as Lunt and Stenner expand:

> Instead, commentators should accept that the talk show provides an institutionally constrained space that nevertheless offers the opportunity for the expression of marginal voices that would otherwise not be heard in public . . . [T]he focus of cultural analyses should be on questions of voice and expression as moments in a wider process of public deliberation rather than as microcosms of the whole process of deliberation as implied by the public sphere concept. Talk shows are unusual and interesting public spaces . . . creating novel combinations of people who normally live separate lives. (2005: 61–62)

The contemporary talk show is very much the product of a number of social, cultural and political shifts, including the rise of identity politics, the increased visibility of once marginalised identities, and the triumph of confessional and therapeutic cultures (Shattuc, 1997, White, 2002, Wilson, 2005). In this respect, there is clearly a considerable historical distance to be taken into account when it comes to making connections with the 1950s. Nevertheless, in describing a television space which performs social interaction as a form of public participation, the conceptual framework described by Lunt and Stenner resonates with *ITYP?* This is absolutely an "institutionally constrained space" on a number of different levels, but if the programme is shaped by the sense that public service broadcasting can act as a powerful means of promoting social unity, this also demanded that it open its doors to a sharp juxtaposition of social identities. It is through this act that *ITYP?* emerges as a rather contingent, unstable meeting of *power* between institution and public.

Problem perspectives

The set of *ITYP?* approximated the pseudo-domestic appearance of the magazine programme, housing a mahogany veneered cabinet, a leather topped desk, leather-bound books, one bowl of flowers and a red leather wing-back chair.[21] As the host of the programme, the film and television actress Edana Romney introduced each edition, before the camera panned right, in medium close-up, taking in the faces of the panel. Three problems were dealt with in each edition, and it is important to emphasise that the out-of-vision strategy was not used for all the problems, as this would depend on the nature of the subject being explored. The BBC would judge the nature of the "delicate" and the "intimate", and presumably took into account the wishes of the questioner themselves. If the subject's face was not to be seen, the chair was placed in the middle of the set, turned toward the panel but away from the cameras. The cameras would then alternate between shots of the panel and images of the person's arm, hands or feet, or offer an over-the-shoulder shot from behind their chair.[22]

When it came to the panel, the doctor was always introduced as a "consultant physician who specialises in psychological medicine in one of our national hospitals", and in the early editions he was joined by "Canon Bryan Green, Rector of Birmingham", and "Mr J.F Wolfenden, former headmaster of Uppingham [school] and now Vice-Chancellor of Reading University". (The panel varied between editions, but some of the core roles remained constant.) The composition of the panel further foregrounds the programme's precarious balancing on the boundaries of public/private space. Members of the clergy or the medical profession often have access to the private lives and stories of others, but these stories were now to be heard within the public space of television, and before the eyes and ears of thousands of viewers. At the same time, and downplaying its status as a public spectacle, there was to be no studio audience (something which would also have undermined the anonymity of many of the participants).

In terms of their use by television, confessional and therapeutic strategies are seen as something of a recent shift. But the set-up of *ITYP?* does beg a comparison with a confessional space, at least at the level of its imagery and roles. Michel Foucault's (1990) famous discussion of confession in Western society explores how it produces identity within relations of power. Confession is a strategy for disciplining the self, and one confesses within the presence of an interlocutor who "prescribes", "judges" and "intervenes" (Foucault, 1990: 61). Given the composition of the panel in *ITYP?*, the currency of confession seems resonant, even if the dominant religious discourse was always Christianity, and not Catholicism.[23] Furthermore, the out-of-vision strategy could be interpreted as consolidating this link. The descriptions of images showing restless hands but no faces, twitching arms but no legs, conjure up a visual perspective which might be glimpsed from a confessional box. While the intention was clearly to offer the questioner a sympathetic space, this visual framework surely carried connotations of guilt and shame, and the idea of interlocutors "prescribing" and "intervening" is set up by the premise of the programme itself. At the same time, scholars have since emphasised how television "initiates a significant shift in terms of the confessional transaction", as the positions of confessor and interlocutor "proliferate and create multiple possibilities for engaging viewers" (White, 2002: 314). This seems apt given that, across scripts, BBC memos, press discussions and audience responses, the viewer of *ITYP?* is variously imagined as a troubled citizen, judging interlocutor, prurient snooper or guilty Peeping Tom. This idea of competing discursive frames also emerges when the relations between questioner, host and panel are examined.

As an example of television talk, *ITYP?* engages participants in a prearranged discursive event that is to be seen and heard by an absent audience (Haarman, 2001: 32). To this effect, it stages a variety of communicative roles (Goffman, 1981) which regulate the interaction of those on screen, and which shape the positions offered to the home viewer. As the direct-to-camera host, Romney had the privilege of addressing the viewer, and according to the Producer, Romney's role was to "explain the problem as it affects or as it is felt by the single person concerned"; and it was explicitly "not objective".[24] She would then hand over to co-host Edgar Lustgarten. His role was to tease out the problem further, to clarify it and to ask the person questions which will "immediately suggest themselves to viewers". Romney was to shed a "rosy light" on the problem, while Lustgarten was to bring out the "facts", positioning the situation under a "clinical light".[25] Once Lustgarten had finished procuring the facts, the panel would then take turns to give their view on the problem.

There are clearly gender divisions at work here, with the female role associated with the subjective and the personal, and the masculine roles equated with the objective and the rational. This was partly responsible for what one reviewer saw as the programme's "schizophrenia of tone",[26] or what might be recast as its contradictory orchestration of communicative roles. For example, Romney's introductions certainly sought to animate the problem from the perspective of questioner, and this is interesting given that the out-of-vision strategy may have inadvertently implied guilt or shame. Despite the sensational headlines used in the press, the unseen and "unmarried mother" in the first edition is actually introduced by Romney as a vulnerable, timid and rather mousy character. In mapping the woman's dilemma, Romney explains how it all began:

> Margaret Burns, as we shall call her, is a greying gentle little Scots woman of 41. She is a clerk, and I would say there isn't a mean thought or ounce of malice in her. Four years ago she took a clerical post abroad, the consequences of which she is now paying for. I suppose it really was a need for affection – whatever it was she fell in love with a married man who was also by himself. Two years ago Miss Burns returned to England to have this man's son . . . As . . . she says, whatever feelings of misery and resentment you may have . . . you become a mother when [the child] . . . is put into your arms for the first time. "My son", she says, "is the best thing that has ever happened to me, but I have so little to give him". . . . [S]he does two jobs a week in order to bring her net income up to £7 . . . £3 of which goes to an exceptionally kind woman, who takes care of the child . . . Miss Burns sees him three times a week, and he knows her as "Mummy".[27]

Romney goes on to explain that although the father pays maintenance, he now wants to bring the boy up within his own family context, and give him the material benefits that this will offer. As Romney concludes her introduction she explains: "Make no mistake – she certainly wants to keep her son, but her fear is he might one day accuse her of depriving him of his rightful heritage".

The problem is then handed over to Lustgarten, who is seen in medium close-up over the shoulder of the chair. The broadcast transcription runs as follows:[28]

> Lustgarten: I gather that . . . if you just put your own inclinations first and foremost, you'd keep David at any cost?
> Miss Burns: Yes
> Lustgarten: That's what you'd want to do – however much effort or trouble it might give you?
> Miss Burns: Yes.
> Lustgarten: But if you were absolutely convinced in your own mind that it was in David's best interest, you would give him to his father?
> Miss Burns: I can't honestly even say that, because I want to keep my boy so much.
> Lustgarten: I understand that that so well. I do understand too though, that you do want us to deal with this problem on the basis of what is best for David?
> Miss Burns: Yes
> Lustgarten: You do?
> Miss Burns: I do, yes.

Lustgarten: . . . It's an unselfish point of view, and I can assure all viewers that you live absolutely up to Miss Romney's description of you.

The construction of this scene follows the editing pattern for most of out-of-vision cases (and there was usually at least one in each edition). Filmed with four cameras, the scene begins with a high-angle shot of Lustgarten and the chair. As Miss Burns speaks we cut between images of her hands and medium close-ups of Lustgarten. This economy of shots is repeated, and at the end of the exchange the camera tracks Lustgarten as he rises and walks over to the table to pass the problem on to the panel.

The panel's responses are too extensive to quote in detail here, but the doctor proves the most sympathetic to Miss Burns by suggesting that the father "has sacrificed his claim on this boy, emotionally, completely" and that for the boy to go to a new family context would be too much of a wrench. In contrast, both the Vice Chancellor and the preacher advise Miss Burns to relinquish her son, with the VC suggesting that if he stays, "he will never have a father of any kind", so the "supreme unselfishness and self-sacrifice of letting him go might be right". The preacher suggests a trial period with the father, explaining that to give him up might be "the highest sacrifice, the noblest thing to do". Although the hosts did not always return to express a point of view, in this case Lustgarten indicates his agreement with the doctor, and Romney expresses a similar allegiance: "If [the boy] . . . goes to the father, he might one day accuse him of depriving him of his rightful heritage – his mother's love".

Needless to say, Miss Burns's identity carried a great deal of stigma in 1955. While the number of illegitimate births rose during wartime, they dropped during the 1950s, and after the Second World War, birth control, transformed into "family planning", sought to locate sexuality firmly within marriage (Wilson, 1980: 95). Nevertheless, it is clear from Romney's opening that while there is an emphasis on the consequences of the relationship, there is also a retreat from outright judgement, and a bid to foster identification with Miss Burns – to entertain her situation and dilemma. As Romney invokes aspects of Miss Burns's physical appearance and personality, we also see the bid to make the woman "ordinary". This was a recurrent strategy in Romney's introductions: a Mrs Moore is a "motherly sort of woman in her early sixties", while Mrs Harris's case is introduced by Romney explaining how: "I'd like to give you a mental image of her. I can't think of anyone she reminds me more of than our Gracie, Gracie Fields – and so of course she comes from Lancashire".[29] This was clearly an attempt to avoid stigmatising the person on screen, instead eliciting sympathy for their plight.

But the roles offered to the speakers within this framework are far from equal. Irving Goffman (1981) uses the term "footing" to refer to the alignment of speakers within a framework of spoken communication. Speakers can function as *authors* of their own words, *animators* of the words of others, or they can adopt the *principal* footing, speaking on behalf of an organisation or authority (see also Brunvatne and Tolson, 2001). Miss Burns is clearly not the author of her own story. In fact, Romney takes on the role of *animating* Miss Burns's narrative by literally voicing her words. This emphasises the constrained space of the questioner's role, and we also see how the "questioner" is really the questioned. The script headings for the sequences reflect this lack of agency: "Problem Stated", "Questioner Examined" and "Questioner Discussed". Questioning is a technique for exercising control over meaning (Bell and van Leuwen, 1994: 225), and we notably see Lustgarten steer Miss Burns's responses so that they more securely express the most "selfless" position. (It seems that although the answers were not literally scripted, the person knew what Lustgarten would ask.) Lustgarten's interaction with the questioner is indeed more "clinical". He not only moves out to a more external "objective" stance, but compared to Romney, he uses short clipped sentences to elicit those "facts". The responses from the panel are then given the most space and the principal footing in the exchange, speaking not only on behalf of authorities but *as* authorities, and by far the most time is given over to their deliberation. This may be a narrativisation of "ordinary" experience, yet the narrative is only marginally produced by the subject themselves.

But Miss Burns's case does begin to suggest what might have been meant by what one critic called the programme's "schizophrenia of tone".[30] The person's narrative is produced through different discursive frames and perspectives, and these appear to shift with each section and role. This is most clearly demonstrated by what now emerges as one of the most fascinating cases explored on *ITYP?*, particularly given historical perceptions of women's roles in the 1950s. With the participant this time in vision, Romney begins with characteristic gusto:

> If you were a single girl looking for a job, and you read this advertisement, would you go after it? "Housekeeper required – no off duty – full charge 4 children – no pay, except keep – hours 7:30am – 7:30pm, when there is ample leisure for darning, etc – no holidays. Required for sitting in at night".
>
> That was how Mrs McCleary first put her problem to me. She said, "isn't it amazing that thousands of women should apply for jobs like these . . . as housewives of course. Why is it that girls don't look beyond the white veil and orange blossom? . . . It can't be right to expect all women to enjoy housekeeping, any more than we should expect all men to be fitted for engineering or medicine."[31]

Romney goes on to detail how Mrs McCleary (33) was a hospital dispenser before her marriage, and although she is "devoted" to her husband and "adores" her children, she resents giving up her career and finds her daily life isolating and unfulfilling. The family's financial circumstances do not permit a mother's help, and Romney sets out Mrs McCleary's daily timetable hour by hour, and then asks the viewer: "So how can an intelligent, young woman be a mother and housewife and enjoy a full life . . . [without becoming] . . . a cabbage?"

Lustgarten asks Mrs McCleary whether she ever enjoys housekeeping, and if her husband knows how she feels, and although her role remains constrained, Mrs McCleary is a more vocal subject than Miss Burns, expressing her position beyond the information solicited by Lustgarten. She insists, for example: "But I feel that I am perhaps speaking for a lot of women who feel just the same way I do", or "I would like to get out and meet people . . . I enjoy talking to people and [at present] the great moment in my day is when the bread man comes and says 'will you have brown or white?'".[32] Women in working-class families had often worked outside the home, and it may be the case that the image of the 1950s housewife is based on middle-class ideals. Yet historians have also emphasised how home-making as a career was imparted to women of all social classes in the 1950s, even if this role was experienced by women from different classes in different ways. Either way, the idea of the housewife as a "domestic prisoner" clearly ran counter to popular constructions of femininity at this time (Williams, 2003: 145). Although dealing largely with college-educated women living in the American suburbs, Betty Friedan's *The Feminine Mystique* was one of the most visible attempts to foreground women's domestic confinement, but this was not published until 1963. In the UK, and three years later in 1966, Hannah Gavron's *The Captive Wife: Conflicts of Housebound Mothers* received a considerable circulation, and the original reviews of the book ran such headlines as "Alone with the Gadgets" and "Prisoners in their Own Home" or asked, "Is Your Wife Just a Bird in a Plastic Cage?" (Oakley, 1983: x). But these were both later texts, and even in 1963 Friedan had spoken of "the problem that has no name", suggesting that it lacked public articulation due to fear of shame and ostracism (Williams, 2003: 146). It thus seems striking that Mrs McCleary's problem is openly named on BBC television in 1955. Romney also ends by reaffirming Mrs McCleary's point that the perspective has been given *public* articulation, recognising its social currency for other women beyond the screen: "Well, many husbands may be recognising their wife's problem for the first time, and I hope they will be a little more sympathetic to it."

Romney's discourse makes possible a relay of identifications between subject and viewer – addressing both husbands and wives in different ways. In fact, it starts by asking the viewer to imagine themselves as a "single girl", while it ends with a nod toward the now "enlightened" husband, although the overall perspective seems to address, and even side with, the perspective of the housewife. The problem, however, was of course then circulated through the judgements of the panel, and given Romney's gesture toward previously "ignorant" husbands, this offers the rather incongruous image of Mrs McCleary being advised by a panel of men. The reverend emphasises the importance of retaining a sense of "dignity in any form of work" and encourages her to become more involved in her local church and community; the Vice Chancellor simply says her domestic load will get lighter as the children grow up; while the doctor suggests that she talk to her husband (who needs to "make clear how invaluable she is"), although he also notes that she will be able to "take more of an active part in *his* life [my emphasis]" in the later stages of family life. Notably, the advice of the panel prefigured the response to problem in the 1960s when, as Ann Oakley explains, the media "capitalised on the social isolation theme", precisely because it was remediable. In contrast, women's real ambivalence about their dual roles of worker and mother was not (Oakley, 1983: xiii).

Public interest? Public service?: Institutional constraints

Given that the panel literally embodied dominant social institutions, it is hardly surprising that the advice often offered a hegemonic point of view. There was an emphasis on protecting the sanctity of the traditional family unit, whether problems entailed housing, adoption or separation. But as Miss Burns's case implies, it would be unfair to suggest that the panel always agreed on how best to tackle the problems. This would in fact have been difficult for the programme given that, in the pursuit of impartiality and balance, the BBC did not want to cultivate the impression that they were giving individuals a platform to air their views, or that they were using speakers to propagate particular perspectives. This points to the programme's ambiguous positioning between the public and the State, highlighting the institutional constraints within which it operated.

On one level, the panel collectively represented a microcosm *of* the "state", speaking from the perspective of the dominant power bloc. It would also routinely promote the Welfare State (recommending, for example, the Marriage Guidance Bureau). But unlike radio's *Can I Help You?*, which was essentially a forum for the National Council of Social Services or Citizen's Advice Bureau to perform their work on air, *ITYP?*

was run by Romney and Lustgarten, and problem letters were simply sent to the BBC. *ITYP?* had a more ambiguous relationship with state services – precisely because it necessarily highlighted cracks in the social system: *why* was television's helping hand needed at all? From this perspective, the programme asks questions about the political agency and autonomy of BBC television.

As Scannell observes, the BBC effectively institutionalised a separation between the "political" and the "social". In discussing the early television documentaries which covered similar topics to *ITYP?*, Scannell describes the bid to position the programmes as examining "social issues of general concern" rather than "political" matters, and the overtly political was seen as pertaining to the "affairs of the government, major parties, individual politicians" (1979: 97). We now certainly operate within an expanded sense of what is seen as "political" (as the rise of the talk show itself suggests), and the term is used in this chapter to refer to the structuring of identity within relations of power. But the fact that a distinction between the "social" and the "political" was *impossible* to maintain had already been dramatised by the BBC's own programming. In the 1930s, for example, BBC radio broadcast documentaries which highlighted the acute problems of poverty and unemployment, such as *Other People's Houses*, *Time to Spare* and *SOS*. They drew what Scannell and Cardiff describe as "sharp reactions" from listeners, critics and politicians, and *Time to Spare* triggered an "explosive row between the BBC and the Government, for seeming to expose (quite unintentionally) the inadequacies of the . . . Government's handling of the problem" (Scannell and Cardiff, 1991: 58).

Although mainly in relation to news, the BBC's difficulty in maintaining political independence from the Government, which has jurisdiction over the survival of the BBC's licence fee at any one time, has been widely recognised and debated. This is because it foregrounds key tensions within the nature of public service: is broadcasting there to serve the state or the people? What if these needs contradict each other? (Scannell and Cardiff, 1991: 10). It is in relation to these questions that we gain the clearest insight into the difference between "public service" and "public interest", which returns to Habermas's (1984) argument about the institutionalisation of the public sphere. But it is enough to state here that *ITYP?* occupied a unique position in relation to these debates. On the one hand, its focus was more individualised and small-scale than the problems covered in documentaries and current affairs. But on the other hand, *ITYP?* was in a more precarious situation. Television was not simply going out and "finding out": it was setting itself up as a space for problem solving in the post-war world. Little wonder, then, that it was possible to discern in the programme itself an uncertainty about its own agency.

This can be seen in the editions dealing with housing problems. These appeared frequently, and as Laing describes, the shortage of new post-war housing remained an "awkward" issue for the affluence myth (Laing, 1986: 20). In this respect, the opening of *ITYP?*, with the camera swooping down across rows of uniform homes, was rather ironic given the prevalence of housing problems on the programme itself. Romney explains in the fifth edition:

> We all know that there are thousands of families on the waiting lists for better homes, but the object of our tackling this problem *is not to show how to jump the waiting list*, but to make the waiting bearable. Well Mr Mason is a decent, hardworking man of thirty-three . . .[33]

There is clearly an uncertainty about whether television should intervene here, and an anxiety that it might be accused of using its public visibility to enable people to jump the queue. Part of the difficulty involved acknowledging the currency of the issue at large. From the BBC's perspective, this was central to the public service functions of the show for viewers, while it also usefully bolstered the emphasis on a sympathetic community of viewers which flattened out class differences ("we're all in the same boat"). But in terms of the BBC's own conception of the "political", it was evidently more sensitive to indicate the wider prevalence of problems which reflected on Government provision and the Welfare State (such as inadequate housing, or care for the handicapped or the elderly). It remains clear, however, that other problems, from the story of the unmarried mother, to women's domestic role, to the difficulty of maintaining an interracial relationship, were no less "politically" sensitive within the wider social context of the mid-1950s.

Peeking at "freaks" and the titillations of the tabloid

The narratives centre on individual stories, and they are thus subject to individual solutions (we only need to look at the advice given to the isolated housewife Mrs McCleary). Yet as the examples above suggest, they are not always presented as individual problems, and this is an important distinction when it comes to approaching the programme's conceptual relationship with the public sphere. Nevertheless, at least in terms of the role offered to members of the public, *ITYP?* could not really be characterised as a debating space, or even a dialogue. Indeed, one of the key tensions involved in comparing it to the talk show is that the subjects were given little space to actually *talk*.

But even in work on the talk show, it has been suggested that the most interesting site of focus might be less the opportunity for discussion, than the juxtaposition of people who "normally lead separate lives" (Lunt and Stenner, 2005: 61). With the "unmarried mother" and the rector, or the housewife and the Vice Chancellor, *ITYP?* certainly offered such a juxtaposition. For the socially marginalised and people with less social power, this *in itself* represents a "crucial site for entry into public view and, at least to some degree, public conversation" (Gamson, 1999: 195). The recognition that the questioners emerged from the margins of society is evident in the conception and circulation of the programme.

Gesturing toward what she sees as lost souls turned social deviants, Romney explains how she developed the idea for *ITYP?* while on jury service: "I saw people in the dock who would never have been there if they had had the *right* advice at the right time".[34] In terms of surveying the social composition of the questioners as a whole, the BBC's files recorded how the "higher IQ groups and better-educated are rarely heard from"[35] – an apparently not-so-coded reference to the absence of more affluent viewers. But despite the air of class elitism here, this was still an attempt to create a television space which addressed the experience and presence of the less fortunate members of society. In this regard, we might also ask where else some of these people could have gone to be heard. For those with housing difficulties, the claim was that the official channels had been exhausted. For others, there was not always a clear authority or "expert" to which their problem could have been presented in the first place. Where would Mrs McCleary really take her dissatisfaction with daily domesticity? Who would take the time to consider whether Miss Burns should give up her son? Who would listen to Mr Ramani's experience (edition 4) of entering into an interracial, cross-cultural relationship in 1950s Britain? This may lend weight to the argument that it is too simplistic to suggest that spaces under media control cannot be understood as public spheres (Lunt and Stenner, 2005: 78). Yet it is nevertheless only within such spaces – with their attendant constraints – that such voices and perspectives might be heard. This chapter advances the argument that it is *through* its competing pressures and constraints that *ITYP?* emerges as a dynamic cultural object, dramatising its contradictory and unstable intentions across its surface.

While women and men appeared on the programme as questioners in roughly equal numbers, the fact that some of the most interesting and controversial cases were presented by women may consolidate the feminist critique of Habermas's public sphere: that it naturalises the public as encompassing the masculine, the political and the rational, and the private as encompassing the feminine, the personal and the emotional

(Livingstone and Lunt, 1994, Shattuc, 1997). Given the historical emphasis on a *bourgeois* public sphere, class inequalities are equally important. As van Zoonen reminds us, "television has contributed in a great many ways to disclosing the private realm hidden by Bourgeois mores" (2001: 671). At the very least, *ITYP?* seems to be peeping behind the door.

But this idea of "peeping in", perhaps naughtily, guiltily or furtively, fractures the programme's own attempt to construct a unified address – an inclusive television/ social community to which hosts, panel, questioners and viewers all belong. It also brings into perspective how viewers, as well as critics, were making judgements about the programme which related to its social implications as well as its aesthetic form. To be sure, there were some viewers who praised the public service functions of *ITYP?* They claimed that it "stimulated debate and discussion about problems" with friends and relatives,[36] or they explained how the advice was helpful in the context of their own lives. But such positive affirmations sat alongside more critical responses – responses which indicated an anxiety about the legitimacy of watching the programme. According to BBC Audience Research:

> Viewers expressed a concern that the problems served as an excuse for exhibitionism and an appearance on television. . . . Such criticisms spring from a feeling that on the one hand it is indecent of people to display their intimate troubles to the world at large and on the other hand it is degrading to those who watch and who find entertainment in the display. A Railway Clerk, for instance, who admitted to finding the programme very interesting, wrote: "I admit my interest is one of morbid curiosity. I often feel like one listening at a keyhole – a little shabby about it all".[37]

While some viewers openly revelled in the fact that there was "nothing as exciting or as tragic as real life", or exclaimed this is "real life with a capital 'L' ",[38] others claimed that the programme made them "squirm", and they "condemned it as nauseating, embarrassing and degrading":

> "A public show of self pity" is not suitable material for television entertainment, they said, and a taste for it should not be indulged by the BBC. A Civil Servant's wife went on to insist that: "Any programme which violates personal privacy, as this does, is utterly wrong and greatly lowers the standards of the BBC in showing it . . . It is a disgrace and should be taken off the air immediately . . . I am aware that the type of person who enjoys the more lurid Sunday newspapers may like this type of programme . . . [and it] encourages a liking for cheap sensationalism".[39]

The sensation of guilt ("I admit my interest is one of morbid curiosity") circles around the feeling that the material is compelling, but the worry that perhaps it *shouldn't* be. In relation to this, the reference to "keyhole" viewing and listening, perhaps also encouraged by the newly privatised experience of domestic spectatorship, spoke to the feeling that this was a *private* space being cracked open by television for public view.

Similar responses are described by Marsha F. Cassidy in her fascinating study of "sob" or "misery" shows on 1950s American television – programmes such as *Queen for a Day* or *Strike it Rich* in which women told hardship stories in exchange for the chance to win money or prizes. According to Cassidy, the vehement distaste for the programmes' "nauseating spectacles" and "morbid exhibitionism" (Cassidy, 2005: 116) was in part prompted by the fact that their collective imagery belied the emphasis on post-war optimism. The premise of the misery shows "mandated the . . . involvement of those who were socially marginalised – the sick, the poor, the unfortunate", causing an "irritation in the visual field" (Cassidy, 2005: 105). *ITYP?* was not so *clearly* marked as a space for the financially needy (people were not there to trade the public exposure of their problems for the chance to win prizes), yet issues of inequality were hardly submerged. But when Cassidy describes how the misery shows made the "repressed visible" (2005: 105), this is complicated by the visual dynamic of *ITYP?* The out-of-vision strategy seems rather symbolic when we consider Cassidy's emphasis on the disruptive implications of bringing the marginalised social body *into view*. In fact, the image of people literally "crawling out" into the visual field from somewhat undesirable spaces is visible in the early discussion of the programme. Romney told the press that "while there had been no star struck teenagers . . . there had been one or two fetishists and . . . people obsessed with some grotesque physical attribute or other".[40] The concern here seems to be that "ordinary" people might not be so "ordinary" after all.

In reading these responses today, it is difficult not to consider the resonance of debates about the tabloidisation of television, something which connects with the discussion of "popular aesthetics" discussed in Chapter 1. Particularly when wrested away from its origins in print media, tabloidisation is a rather elastic concept. It is used to encompass everything from an emphasis on human interest, a fascination with the bizarre and the "deviant", a dual impetus toward exposure and moral condemnation (Shattuc, 1997), an emphasis on the sensational and the melodramatic, and the blurring of the boundary between fact and fiction (Dovey, 2000, Glynn, 2000). As argued in the introduction to this book, the debate about the tabloidisation of television became particularly visible within the political economy of television in the 1980s/1990s, and its genealogy has largely been traced in relation to the political and cultural contexts of American television (see Glynn, 2000). But as the connection with print media clearly implies, such textual qualities are not in themselves new to the terrain of popular media forms. There is obviously the history of the tabloid press to consider (Fiske, 1992), and in this respect, it is no surprise that the history of tabloid television has been most carefully charted in relation to news and current affairs (Langer, 1998, Sparks and Tulloch, 2000). But an appetite for the sensational, and a fascination with the "bizarre and the deviant", has also been positioned as integral to the Victorian imagination (Singer, 2001) and more specifically, Shattuc (1997) posits the nineteenth century "yellow" press as a convincing precursor to the television talk show. (The viewer above links *ITYP?* to the diet of "lurid Sunday newspapers".)

Examinations of the tabloid turn in television might convincingly demonstrate institutional and economic reasons for its emergence. But it is questionable whether the same could be said of its textual contours. Indeed, Kevin Glynn describes how what actually unites many criticisms of the tabloid turn is a concern about the "unholy alliance between commercially interested broadcasters and the prurient interests of audiences" (2000: 105), and this dialectic is not new. Discussions about what constituted commercially driven television programming, *particularly* at the level of aesthetics, subject matter and audience address, were prominent in 1950s Britain, not least of all because this period witnessed the end of the public service monopoly and the birth of ITV. This was also a time when television was exploring forms of address which would appeal to a truly mass audience, and the collision of these spheres created the context for much of the concern directed at the programming in this book. But not all of the programming resonates with the tabloid debate, and if *ITYP?* does, it is worth recognising that the tabloid rhetoric is positioned as a conduit for "popular ways of knowing", and is more specifically seen as a bid to address (if not necessarily express) the interests of those with limited access to social power (Fiske, 1992, Glynn, 2000: 7). This chapter has argued that *ITYP?* can be understood as an explicit bid to address a more heterogeneous public, particularly at the level of class, and its material certainly operates at what Fiske describes as the intersection of "public and private life", continually juggling a curious mix of the "sensational . . . [the] moralistically earnest . . . and the populist" (Fiske, 1992: 48). Furthermore, as the chapter goes on to explore, the programme exploited what Fiske describes as a "fluid modality" between the fictional and the factual (often expressed through a melodramatic rhetoric), and it certainly turned out to be "offensive to masculine tastes" (Glynn, 2000: 7).

From the point of view of the BBC, it was precisely the incitement of "prurient desires" that they had aimed to contain. Reports of how "the camera took *occasional peaks* at a nervously wagging foot or a pair of anxiously fretting hands"[41] suggest a medium that is being forcibly restrained, while also one which, if unleashed, might have a *naughty mind of its own*. But it is not difficult to see from the responses that the out-of-vision strategy could have the opposite effect: it made for a highly titillating and sensational framework, inciting the viewer's curiosity when its intention was to block their gaze. When the BBC spoke of the dangers of soliciting "exhibitionists", this really referred to their concerns about the investment of the audience. The roles of voyeur/exhibitionist, while clearly implying a less than wholesome air, also pivoted on a separation between viewer and screen. In turn, this undermined the sympathetic community of viewers which the programme worked so hard to construct.

"A chemistry of corruption": Edana, ethics and entertainment values

The limited role offered to the questioner, the use of the out-of-vision strategy, as well as the concern about catering to the sensational, spoke to the BBC's wider unease about the entire idea of staging people's problems as television material. But that is not to imply that the potentially titillating nature of the out-of-vision strategy was lost on the BBC. (One viewer describes how he "especially liked the high camera angle from behind the chair"[42]). Rather than simply placing emphasis on the attempts to contain, rein in and *discipline* the wayward pleasures and possibilities of television, it is crucial to examine the format's negotiation of (what was seen as) a conflict between public service ideals and the entertainment values of popular appeal.

What would now be termed the ethics of care (Hill, 2005) involved in *ITYP?* were a subject of concern from the start. One critic asked how assistance with a personal problem could be met within the framework of "mass entertainment", and enquired: "Was it even decent to try? A chemistry of corruption takes place in the process of turning a personal problem into public property".[43] The Corporation were concerned about this "chemistry of corruption", and from the start there was a belief that television should *not* become a mass apparatus through which people were shuttled for programme purposes. But it effectively took on this status from the moment the programme began. Despite Romney's apparently personalised address to the viewer in the opening trailer (offering, to use the words of Heath and Skirrow, the sense that television is "direct for me" (1977: 54)), the Producer had already dictated a standard letter which read: "I deeply sympathise with the personal problem you are facing. Unhappily, I cannot deal with your specific case on the programme".[44] At the end of the memo he requested "5,000 copies 5,000 plain envelopes", and the addressee's name was to be inserted into a blank space. For those that made it onto the screen, the BBC remained concerned about squeezing serious personal problems into "3–5 minute conversations off the cuff",[45] and one of the key guidelines, which sat alongside the need to avoid "exhibitionists" and regularly to change the representatives on the panel, was that "dramatisation must be eliminated".[46]

Concern about television's eliciting of personal narratives, and how these narratives are subject to, and shaped by, commercial considerations, has structured both public and academic debate surrounding talk shows and Reality TV (Hill, 2005, Wilson, 2005). In the 1950s, however, and expressing a wary suspicion of television *form* itself, this process is seen as involving irreconcilable tensions. While, as Scannell outlines, all broadcast talk is "intentionally communicative", explicitly designed to be "heard by absent audiences" (1991: 1), it is the *prioritisation* of audience address and appeal, and thus the significance of television as the key force shaping production, which is approached with trepidation and concern. As the Head of Religious Broadcasting argued, "I would like to see personal problems dealt with in a serious . . . programme which makes no concessions to entertainment value".[47] This almost gives the impression that it would be preferable if the interaction were simply facilitated by the BBC, but not then filmed for television at all. Confirming perceptions of what Dahlgren (1995) terms television's "entertainment bias", we see the idea here that the values of public service are factual and transparent, whereas the pull toward the popular meddles with the material – trying to engage the audience with narrativisation and dramatisation. In invoking the objective versus the subjective, the serious versus the popular, this brought *gendered* discourses, and the gender divisions in the programme, into sharper view.

Perhaps recognising the fact that giving advice on problem pages in print media was more of a women's domain, the Producer initially requested a woman to answer some of the viewer's letters behind the scenes.[48] But when it came to imaging this expertise on screen, the female presence was to be carefully contained. In contrast, the resident expert on the BBC's daytime *Family Affairs* was Dr Winfred De Kok, a choice which reflected the perception that "women like to see women on screen".[49] From this point of view, *ITYP?* might be seen as a bid to "masculinise" the potentially female connotations of a "private life" programme, and it is clear that Edana Romney remained something of a troubling presence in the show. Scholars have explored how the advent of television as a cultural technology was bound up with discourses of feminisation (Spigel, 1992, Boddy, 2004, Thumim, 2004), and there is a much longer historical association between the concepts of the "feminine" and "mass culture" (Huyssen, 1986, Petro, 1986). But at a historical level, this has more often been explored in relation to the placement of television technology in the home. Spigel, for example, describes the fear that television might "emasculate" viewers and turn men into "passive home bodies" (1992: 61). Less has been said about how these discourses circulated around television's imagery and its emerging forms of address, and how these were negotiated by different genres. Given the gendered connotations of public and private, the concept of a "private life" programme provides a fertile case study in this respect.

The suggestion that it was preferable to somehow present the stories objectively contradicted the Producer's description of Romney's role as *subjective*. From this point of view, her role suggests an acknowledgement that, despite the BBC's concerns, some "concessions" must be made to popular appeal. As some of the previous excerpts from the programme have implied, Romney's introductions were not only subjective but deeply dramatic, and it would be an understatement to suggest that "dramatisation" was not eliminated. While in the contemporary talk show the host elicits and interrogates the personal stories and feelings of the guests, Romney's role was solely to animate – to vividly dramatise the problem on screen.

For example, in edition 4, a Mrs Taylor is introduced out of vision, and on this occasion the problem relates to her sister, "who we shall call Grace". Romney tells of how the sisters had not seen each other for years, and that during this period Grace had gone through a difficult divorce abroad. Then eight years ago Grace wrote to say that she was coming to England to have an operation, and asked if she could stay with her sister for a couple of months:

> [T]hat . . . turned into over two years. . . . This operation was the amputation of a limb, and the cause of this tragedy was a road accident – and the accident was caused by the very thing that brought Mrs Taylor here, because, you see, Grace was, and is, an alcoholic – a *secret* one – as she imagines! Mrs Taylor tells me that she has never succeeded in getting her sister to . . . admit it [and on one occasion Grace] . . . became quite hysterical and screamed, "don't talk about it! Don't talk about it! I swear I will never do it again!" With that [Grace] . . . slammed the door leaving Mrs Taylor alone in an empty room – the air thick with tension. But now [time has passed] how can she find the right words to approach her?[50]

Unlike Miss Burns or Mrs McCleary, "Grace" is not in the studio, and this perhaps accounts for Romney's less than sympathetic move to unmask her "hidden" identity. Based on the existing evidence, it is impossible to say whether her speech was accompanied by visual gestures, but here she literally enacts a scene before the viewer's eyes – using dialogue, and gesturing toward aspects of "set" and atmosphere. Exclamation marks were also prominent in Romney's introductions, signalling dramatic moments, climaxes or revelations.

In the first edition, which features the problem of Mr Hooper, who has been left alone to raise his daughters, Romney explains:

> [P]ut yourself in the place of a man suddenly landed with three young children . . . Mr Hooper doesn't want his children to go into a home – thank you very much . . . So now we come to the heart of the matter. His children's future! He has thought of all sorts of schemes. He even thought he could raise an insurance for them by trying to sell the cornea of his eye. Oh yes! But his real problem is how to ensure that the children . . . can grow up with a sense of security, and become good responsible people . . . Over to you, Mr Lustgarten.[51]

Given the polarisation of entertainment values ("dramatisation") against the factual/objective responsibilities of public service, Romney occupied the key role in discussions of the programme's ethics. In fact, the departure of Huw Wheldon as Producer in 1956 was specifically linked to this matter. In May 1956, Wheldon writes:

> [*ITYP?*] must play fair with people who submit themselves to it in good faith. This responsibility is the BBC's; and is not simply Edana Romney's. (In the final analysis, it is the BBC's responsibility absolutely). A problem elicited, disclosed and examined is inevitably open to every kind of varying emphasis and distortion, dependent on the fundamental attitudes of the elicitor and the examiner. These people should not have their problems distorted. This is possibly the main area where differences of approach have developed and hardened.[52]

While she was in practice neither the "elicitor" nor the "examiner", it is clearly Romney who is causing Wheldon the most concern. Wheldon leaves the show at this point, and is succeeded by a new Producer, Hugh Burnett. Burnett later became the Producer of the current affairs forum *Press Club*, as well as the interview-in-depth programme *Face to Face* (1959–62). As Chapter 5 outlines, *Face to Face* also ignited debates over television's invasion of privacy.

The idea that Romney is somehow out of place in the context of what should be a serious, moral and sensible programme is explicitly played out in the vitriolic reception of the *ITYP?* One reviewer found that the panel made a "wholesome impression", and along with the "meaty and dependable" Lustgarten, they came across as "matter-of-fact, practical realists, living in the world as it is and content to do so . . . Not so Miss Romney . . . She is. . . . tricksy, with one eyebrow working to distraction and a too insistent hand stabbing at the screen".[53] This paints an image of Romney as a twitchy, distracting and even hysterical hostess, and the wider circulation of her public persona shaped these judgements. Romney (36) was first and foremost an actress. She had starred in the British film *Corridor of Mirrors* in 1948, and was also credited as one of its writers, and her other film appearances included the British crime/mystery pictures *East of Piccadilly* (1941) and *Alibi* (1942). Although *Corridor of Mirrors* was a great success, press reports explained how the following years were difficult as "Dame fortune has not always smiled on . . . Edana, work dried up and she retired from showbusiness, defeated and bitter . . . And there were private problems, too. Four years later she divorced her husband".[54] She then made her "comeback" with the role of Princess Eboli in BBC television's production of *That Lady* in 1954.

This emphasis on "private problems" was clearly a bid to furnish Romney with personal credentials which might mediate the authenticity of her role, particularly given her privileged class background. But critics and viewers were unconvinced, and they often emphasised how her sincerity was compromised. Some of the BBC's viewers were apt to describe her as "over-dramatic", "lush" and "sentimental", and Romney attracted such comments as "she gives the impression of being completely bogus – why can't she forget she's an actress?", or "Romney's tragedy queen manner makes a revolting programme even more sickly".[55] Furthermore, one reviewer took great pleasure in explaining how:

> You see, she drives me nuts. Moreover, she used to be an actress and her problem is to try and convince us that she isn't acting now . . . . If she is acting, she's overacting to such a degree that she makes one want to smash one's set in with a hatchet.[56]

In expressing what Spigel elsewhere describes as "a mixture of misogyny and telephobia" (1992: 62), this was an extreme but not isolated response where Romney was concerned. But despite the emphasis on insincerity, as well as the extent to which the concerns surrounding ethics are laid at Romney's door, she also offered a space to identify *with* the subject – something which may be significant when we consider the perpetual irritation she seemed to cause.

The dismissal of Romney as a "tragedy queen" takes on a new resonance if we consider the thematic links with melodrama . In 1954 Gilbert Seldes observed that the American "misery shows" imitated soap opera's melodramatic storylines – "the same widows and orphans; the same deaths and trials and tribulations" (Seldes, cited in Cassidy, 2005: 187), and soap operas were evidently drawing on a longer heritage of melo-drama here. These plotlines were precisely the kind of stories that the BBC's serials, including *The Grove Family*, appeared to avoid. But they nevertheless seemed to receive an outlet in the apparently more sober, "factual" context of *ITYP?* We only need look at Romney's breathtaking introductions to see that there was a penchant for triumph-over-tragedy stories, missing parents, deserted children and lost limbs. Although apparently referring to performance style rather than narrative content, this sheds new light on one viewer's suggestion that Romney is "obvi-ously convinced this is the greatest tragedy part she has ever had and she conducts the programme in a theatrical manner worthy of Victorian melodrama".[57]

In the critical reception of the show this melodramatic rhetoric is notably set in opposition to the "practical realist" perspective offered by its patriarchal discourse (and a perceived opposition between melo-drama and realism circles around the different context of *The Grove Family*; see Chapter 2). But the melodramatic text has of course also been defined in terms of aesthetics, and Gledhill describes its "siphon-ing of unrepresentable material into the excessive *mise en scène*" (1987: 9). *ITYP?* carefully policed the possibility of an aesthetic in which close-ups, gestures and tears might produce an emotional on-screen spectacle. Nevertheless, when it came to the out-of-vision participants, there is undoubtedly something about those "twisting hands" that gestures toward a "hysterical text . . . bringing pressures close to the surface" (ibid). Furthermore, if melodrama "sides with the powerless" (Vicinus, cited in Gledhill, 1987: 21), the potentially melodramatic rhetoric of Romney's *verbal* narratives can indeed be interpreted as a "demand for significance unavailable within the constraints of socially legitimate dis-course" (Gledhill, 1987: 37). If the "socially legitimate" can be equated with the discourse of the panel, this offers a different perspective on why Romney, and her narrative role, seemed to be such a constant source of irritation.

From *Can I Help You?* to *Is This Your Problem?*: Nurturing therapy culture

Gendered discourses also implicitly shaped the space constructed for the questioner. Even when they were in vision, close-ups of the questioner were not used, and the programme deliberately avoided producing what Cassidy describes as "the kinetics of distress" (2005: 192) with regard to the 1950s American misery shows. The clipped tones of the panel, and halting sentences of the questioner, perhaps had as much in common with a dialogue at the Citizen's Advice Bureau as they did with a therapeutic, confessional "talking cure".

The contemporary triumph of confessional and therapeutic cultures is seen as key to understanding the emergence of the television talk show. As Minna Aslama and Mervi Pantti summarise:

> Interest in the emotions of other people seems to be very much a part of contemporary culture, as is the pressure to reveal emotions and talk in both public and private forums. We are . . . living in a "confessional" or "therapeutic" culture that celebrates individual feelings, intimate revelations and languages of therapy . . . [Television has emerged as] . . . a central public site for confessing one's innermost feelings. (2006: 167)

In tracing a shift from institutional definitions of citizenship to a narrower conception of the self based on psychological identity (Shattuc, 1998: 213), the talk show has represented a privileged television arena for debates about a confessional culture. Such shifting conceptions of selfhood account for many of the key differences between the period in which *ITYP?* was produced, and the contemporary cultural and media environment. Yet this trajectory is not best cast as a radical break with the past. It is possible to ask to what extent such cultures have a *currency* in the 1950s in such a way that is not simply reading back in time. Indeed, the 1950s is a key period for examining how therapeutics became a significant feature of Anglo-American culture (Furedi, 2004: 84).

In *Therapy Culture: Cultivating Uncertainty in an Uncertain Age* (2004), the sociologist Frank Furedi suggests that it was in the 1980s that therapy culture came to exercise a dominant cultural influence over society. By this he means that it became a truly cultural phenomenon rather than a clinical technique, emerging as a "dominant system of meaning" in everyday life (2004: 17). No longer confined to a functionally specific role, therapy culture colonised many professions and institutions in society, including education, justice, the welfare services, medicine, political life and the media. But as Furedi emphasises, cultural values change gradually, and the therapeutic sensibility has a long history. The interest in therapeutics coincides with the rise of modernity, and the explosion of therapy culture in the 1980s was preceded by a century-long expansion of the influence of psychology (Furedi, 2004: 84).

Nikolas Rose's *Governing the Soul: The Shaping of the Private Self* (1990) contributes to this history from a British perspective, examining how the Second World War, which enabled psychiatry to lose its "alien" overtones (Hopkins, 1963: 199), and then the rise of the Welfare State, provided key opportunities for the institutionalisation of therapeutic practices. As Rose explores, the post-war Welfare apparatus opened up the family up to a "range of gazes and therapeutic practices" (1990: 170). With an emphasis on psychiatry and clinical psychology, social workers were to be trained in "psychotherapeutic techniques", and armed with new scientific knowledge, they were set forth to deal with marital therapy or child/parent relations. The term "relationship therapy" also enjoyed an increasing currency (Rose, 1990: 171). In his social history of the period, Harry Hopkins also examines the popularisation of psychiatry in the spheres of film, radio and television, noting how "and *later on* TV, a 'psychologist' or psychiatrist [my emphasis]" provided a potent site of expertise, "the answer to the Worried Wife's prayer, the relaxer of the Over-Tense husband, the key to the Problem Child" (1963: 199).

In the context of this chapter, however, we might well ask what is meant by "later" where this reference to television is concerned. Hopkins implies that television enters this framework in the 1960s, yet *ITYP?* (along with ITV's *As Others See US*) emerges with the establishment of television as mass medium. In other words, this discourse is there from the start. Furthermore, while both Rose and Hopkins are referring to a context in which a therapeutic discourse is still functionally specific (associated with, and practised by, specific professionals), Hopkins nods toward it leaking into wider cultural domains – such as television. In *ITYP?*, we might recall that the doctor is not an ordinary GP, but a "consultant physician who specialises in psychological medicine in one of our national hospitals", and while everyday language was generally used, there was a good deal of emphasis, particularly in problems concerning children, on the significance of psychological growth. This discourse in the programme was at least strong enough for one critic to complain about the BBC dabbling in "public psychiatry" (which "might end sooner or later in a murder or suicide").[58]

What seems crucial here is that the rise of therapy culture, first at an institutional level and then as a pervasive part of everyday life, exploited key social and cultural shifts associated with the post-war period. These include the decline of organised religion, a more fragmented society which witnesses the weakening of social solidarity, and a context in which the "isolation of the nuclear family subjected it to particular stresses and strains" (Rose, 1990: 170). This is the same context exploited by *ITYP?*, and which appears in the programme's opening title sequence. After all, as Furedi reminds us, the shift toward a therapy culture pivots on a worldview that sees "closed doors" (or in the case of the opening title sequence of *ITYP?*, closed windows) as dangerous and repressive (2004: 77). Furedi emphasises here that therapy culture *cultivates* uncertainty and vulnerability, and without wanting to over-stretch the historical comparison, it is difficult not to observe a shift from radio's more tentative question *Can I Help You?* to television's invasive demand to know: *Is This Your Problem?* The title seems to ask not *if* "you" have a problem, but if the programme has included your particular troubles and concerns. Little wonder that some viewers accused the programme of discouraging self-reliance and cultivating a dependency on television as a site for self-formation in the post-war world.[59]

In conclusion, *ITYP?* is certainly a long way off television functioning as a "therapy machine" (White, 2002). But it nevertheless seems to offer the seeds of this framework, even if the main subject, the confessor, seems almost *absent* from a contemporary point of view. While the steady erosion of the boundary between public and private has been shaped by the wider triumph of therapeutic cultures, and television's role within this sphere (Furedi, 2004: 43), *ITYP?* approaches this boundary with some trepidation, pivoting on a mixture of hesitancy, distaste and concern. The aim here has not been to imply that the BBC were *really* producing a talk show (only they didn't know it), and the application of other generic or political frameworks could yield different results. But if we acknowledge that genres are primarily constituted at a discursive level (Mittell, 2004a), it is legitimate to foreground the similarity in cultural debate. It is also true that 1950s television, in both the UK and the US, has been largely ignored in explorations of televisual precursors to the talk show. While it may be that "inciting individuals to 'share' their personal problems with millions of viewers is the entertainment formula of a culture where . . . individual troubles masquerade as a public service" (Furedi, 2004: 74), *ITYP?* makes it hard to see this as something intrinsically new. In her analysis of the UK talk show *Trisha* (ITV1, 1998–2004, C5, 2004–), Sherryl Wilson argues that the programme represents a form of "public service . . . that encompasses commercial, popular television" and that, at a time in Britain when the "welfare systems are at the point of collapse, and within the increasingly powerful discourse of individualism and personal responsibility, *Trisha* offers a means through which to negotiate personal difficulties" (2005: 166). But *ITYP?* is evidence of how these contexts developed together, problematising a trajectory in which television steps in to care for the subject in an anxious, post-modern age. Given that the BBC were carefully constructing what they saw as guidelines for television's treatment of problem show material, it would be of value to trace the development of this programming in British television from the 1960s onwards.

ITYP? was the product of moves to address television's increasingly mass audience, and it is through this negotiation that its textual tensions emerge. In the context of this book, *ITYP?* stands as a unique site upon which public service broadcasting, and BBC television, negotiated discourses of the popular. This negotiation was often expressed as anxiety about the television frame itself, and the idea that television talk – particularly when it concerns "personal" matters – is a performed discourse which exists *solely for television* is being worked through. In fact, the extent to which *ITYP?* makes this process strange, usefully reminds us that going on television to confess one's inner troubles is actually not that "natural" or "ordinary" at all.

ITYP? also represents a unique research experience – one which, much like the programme itself, is situated on an uncertain border between public and private. I should "confess" myself to finding much of the material highly amusing, whether imagining the visual choreography of those anxiously tapping feet, or reading Miss Romney's quite extraordinary introductions. But especially in the form of the viewers' letters, the files also contain traces of the fact that these were people's *real* personal problems – they were reaching out to the BBC, to television, clearly quite desperate for help. The sensitive nature of the material is suggested by the fact that discourses of ethics and privacy *still* structure its status: I was asked to sign a special copyright agreement to say that I would not identify or follow up the names and addresses on the viewers' letters. The feeling of intruding into the private lives of others, but finding the material so compelling and fascinating that you can't turn away, perhaps shadowed at a distance of many years the contradictory experience of viewing *ITYP?* when it first aired.

When I was first beckoned by the description of "Real-life cases", and how "An Unmarried Mother Hid her Face on TV last night", it was hard to anticipate the world that *ITYP?* would uncover. Like any good tabloid headline, this titillating description rather spiced up the reality: she was, after all, a "greying gentle little Scots woman of 41". But as a historical case study, *ITYP?* does not disappoint. It is a fascinating reminder that our historical assumptions should be contradicted and challenged, while it invites reflection on the real pleasures this process involves.

Notes

1 *Daily Mirror*, 16 September 1955.
2 *Daily Mirror*, 26 April 1956.
3 BBC Audience Research report, *Is This Your Problem?*, 6 December 1956.
4 Gerald Beadle to Controller of Programmes, Television, 9 December 1958. T16/149/2.
5 Taken from Wheldon's biography at www.screenonline.org.uk/people/id/ 473425/index.html (accessed 6 August 2006).
6 Huw Wheldon to Alan Lawson, 22 July 1955. T32/1,777/1.
7 Trailer of *Is This Your Problem?*, 22 August 1955. T32/1851/1.
8 As above.

9   Secretary Director of Broadcasting to Controller of Programmes, Television, 26 January 1956. T32/1,777.
10 *Radio Times*, 29 December 1939, p. 23.
11 Source not identified, "Can I Help You?", 18 September 1939. R51/63/1.
12 *Radio Times*, 5 January 1961, p. 21.
13 Assistant Head of Audience Research, 31 July 1953. R51/63/7.
14 By 1959 the programme included a clinical psychologist dealing with "teenagers and sex before marriage" – much to the disgust of some female viewers who wrote to the BBC to complain about such "morally filthy" material. See T32/901/1, viewers' letters.
15 Excerpt from *Family Affairs* script, undated. T32/652/1.
16 *TV Times*, 29 October–4 November 1955.
17 See for example, "Television: A New Religious Medium", *Methodist Recorder*, 21 April 1955.
18 Colin Beale to Head of Religious Broadcasting, 4 May 1955. T32/1,777/1.
19 Head of Religious Broadcasting to Alec Sutherland, 16 May 1955. T32/1,777/1.
20 Head of Religious Broadcasting to Alec Sutherland, 16 May 1955. T32/1,777/1.
21 *ITYP?*, script 1.
22 *ITYP?*, scripts.
23 Although in terms of BBC radio and television more widely, "other faiths" could be given space "from time to time", the fact that the BBC's task was to make Britain a more "Christian country" was never up for debate (Briggs, 1979: 765).
24 Huw Wheldon to Director of Television Broadcasting, 28 September 1955. T32/1851/1.
25 *Truth*, 12 September 1955.
26 As above.
27 *ITYP?*, script 2.
28 The original scripts do not indicate the exact programme as broadcast, nor include the words of Lustgarten, the questioner or the panel. Fortunately, however, the majority of the programmes were transcribed by the BBC as broadcast, and this evidence has been used where possible.
29 *ITYP?*, transcript from programmes 7 and 10.
30 *Truth*, 12 September 1955.
31 *ITYP?*, transcript of programme 5.
32 *ITYP?*, transcript of programme 5.
33 *ITYP?*, transcript of programme 5; my emphasis.
34 *Daily Mirror*, 17 September 1955.
35 Secretary Director of Broadcasting to Controller of Programmes, Television, 26 January 1956. T32/1,777/1.
36 BBC Audience Research report, *Is This Your Problem?*, 10 November 1955.
37 BBC Audience Research report, *Is This Your Problem?*, 6 December 1956.
38 BBC Audience Research report, *Is This Your Problem?*, 8 December 1955.

39 BBC Audience Research report, *Is This Your Problem?*, 10 November 1955.
40 *Truth*, 12 September 1955.
41 As above; my emphasis.
42 Audience Research Report, *ITYP?*, 13 October 1955.
43 *Truth*, 12 September 1955.
44 Huw Wheldon to Alan Lawson, 22 July 1955. T32/1,777/1.
45 Colin Beale to Head of Religious Broadcasting, 4 May 1955. T32/1,777/1.
46 Secretary Director of Broadcasting to Controller of Programmes, Television, 26 January 1956. T32/1,7771.
47 Reverend R. McKay to Director of Television Broadcasting, 23 January 1957. T32/1,777/1.
48 Huw Wheldon to Controller of Programmes, Television, 18 August 1955. T32/851/1.
49 *News Chronicle*, 11 January 1955.
50 *ITYP?*, transcript of programme 4; original emphasis.
51 *ITYP?*, transcript of programme 1.
52 Wheldon to Asst Head of Television, 25 May 1956. T32/1,777/1.
53 *Truth*, 12 September 1955.
54 Untitled, press review, "Why Edana Wants to Help", 17 September 1955.
55 Audience Research Report, *ITYP?*, 10 November 1955.
56 *Spectator*, 4 May 1956.
57 BBC Audience Research report, *Is This Your Problem?*, 13 October 1955.
58 *Evening Standard*, 21 December 1955.
59 BBC Audience Research report, *Is This Your Problem?*, 13 October 1955.

5

From "Serialitis" to "Torture, Treacle, Tears and Trickery": framing television fame

The previous chapter explored the BBC's "problem show", *Is This Your Problem?* While the title of the show, as well as the address of its female hostess, appeared to be both direct and personalised ("Is this *your* problem?"), the majority of viewers who wrote to the programme would receive a standard response ("5,000 copies . . . in 5,000 plain envelopes").[1] This image resonates with one of the storylines in Ealing's satire on television, the film *Meet Mr Lucifer* (Anthony Pelissier, 1953), in which Hector McPhee (Gordon Jackson) falls in love with television's "Miss Lonely Hearts" (Kay Kendall) after responding to her singing and heartfelt words of comfort, which seem to constitute a personal form of address. This illusion is strengthened by the framing of Miss Lonely Hearts in tight close-up, as though engaging in face-to-face interaction. Mr McPhee builds a shrine to the singer and has her poster on his wall, and she when announces that she will be leaving the air he writes her a letter which begs: "Please come back to TV, my life is wretched without you". The scene then cuts to a factory set-up in which, against a back-drop of noise from chugging machines, women are printing and sending millions of standard "Miss Lonely Hearts" replies. But when Mr McPhee receives *his* reply he again imagines it to constitute a personal form of addresses, and he "hears" the words on the page spoken in Miss Lonely Hearts' sugary voice: "Dear Lonely Hearts, I was very touched to receive your letter – how could I *ignore* such a tender appeal?" The star comes back to television due to popular demand but soon announces that "America beckons". Miss Lonely Hearts will be going overseas to feature in a programme sponsored by "a delicious new breakfast cereal" (which she can't of course name on the BBC). Mr McPhee is left feeling foolish, angry and betrayed, especially as he has discarded his real friends in the pursuit of an intimate relationship with television.

Meet Mr Lucifer explores the various ways in which television might have a negative impact on sociability, and there is no reason to assume that real viewers were as naive as Mr McPhee. Chapter 4 of this book detailed how the host of *Is This Your Problem?*, Edana Romney, was frequently dismissed by viewers for being "completely bogus" and insincere. Rather than conveying true sentiments, she was seen as "merely acting [a] . . . part".[2] These comments would not look out of place next to Richard Hoggart's expression of antipathy for the new slew of "TV cabaret stars . . . specialising in fake intimacy" (1958: 162). Writing at the same time, although from a slightly less negative standpoint, Donald Horton and Richard Wohl (1956) were also exploring the "para-social" relationships fostered by television, with a particular emphasis on the medium's careful fostering of "intimacy-at-distance".

Canonical conceptions of television fame have emphasised the qualities of intimacy, familiarity, proximity and ordinariness (Langer, 1981, Ellis, 1992). But these accounts don't readily take questions of history on board. (Indeed, as a singular comment on the emergence of television fame in 1953, the example above offers a cross between the idolisation associated with film stardom proper, and a fascination with the increased intimacy and proximity which television may provide.) The quantity of historical work on film stardom far outweighs that devoted to television, but this lack of interest in television's historical, and still early, relations with fame is especially apparent in the British context. American scholars have built up a small but significant body of work on early television and radio stardom (Murray, 2005), as well as the shift of film stars to the home (Mann, 1992, Marshall, 1997, Desjardins, 2002, Becker, 2005). Interest in British television and stardom has been more limited and sporadic (Medhurst, 1991, Holmes, 2005a), and there is no equivalent to Susan Murray's extensive American study, *Hitch Your Antenna to the Stars: Early Television and Broadcast Stardom* (2005).

Although reflecting the slightly elitist air of British television historiography, this points to the different institutional contexts of British and American television. Bourdon argues that television fame is one of several areas to foreground tensions in public service television's relations with the popular: its difficulty in finding a compromise between its status as an "instrument of education and culture" and a mass medium which delivers entertainment. Bourdon describes this tension as a "contradiction between personal popularity and public service" (2004: 290), and the idea that there might be an uneasy fit between the BBC and "celebrity" culture is hinted at in existing histories (e.g. Briggs, 1979, Camporesi, 1993). This perception is no doubt strengthened by the fact that ITV, with its institutional and economic links with variety theatre (see Sendall, 1982), is more readily seen as the natural home of "showbiz". But celebrity culture was one of the most visible and often controversial sites upon which BBC television also negotiated its appeal to a growing mass audience.

In apparently counterpoising the historical and the conceptual, the intention is not to imply that the paradigms offered by Langer and Ellis are misleading or problematic. Their arguments resonate with the discourses in circulation in the 1950s, perhaps even *more* so because of the self-conscious bid to debate the "newness" of television fame in relation to the perceived qualities of the medium. But there is something slightly generalising and ahistorical about these paradigms. They don't seem to readily account for change or fully recognise significant distinctions within television fame (see also Lury, 1995, Jermyn, 2006). A key aim of this chapter is to bring out the different meanings which circulated around television's relations with fame in the 1950s. As part of this, it recognises that television constructs its own "personalities", while it simultaneously circulates personae from other domains. Returning to this earlier context also raises important questions. Where do these later conceptual claims about television fame locate their historical roots, and to what extent are discourses of "ordinariness", familiarity and intimacy historical? How might we approach the specificities of television fame, and to what extent were the debates surrounding it inherited from radio?

The chapter first sets out some of the discourses which circulated around television fame, particularly with respect to perceptions of cultural value. Expanding on Chapter 2, which focused on *The Grove Family*, it then moves on to consider television-produced fame in relation to the Groves, before examining, in relation to *This is Your Life*, television's controversial role in recirculating and reshaping the wider sphere of celebrity culture.

From "Star Wars" to "TV oomph": constructing the value of television fame

As Valeria Camporesi observes, there is some truth to the suggestion that from the earliest days of radio, the BBC "discourag[ed] the development of 'stars'" which they associated with the commercial values of American radio (1993: 142). This association is still apparent in 1949 when Sir William Haley, the BBC's first post-war Director General, contrasts the development of television in Britain and America. He felt it likely that American television would be built around "personalities", while British television favoured "ideas":

> In America, the attractiveness of the performer is everything, his material is secondary. In the BBC the position is first to look at the quality of the

material. There is little interest in America whether television does plays or ballet or opera. There is every interest in who is becoming popular. (Haley, cited in Briggs, 1979: 284)

Haley's construction here conflates the BBC's perennial distaste for the commerciality of American broadcasting with an insistence on the star as the centre of false value (a symbol which prioritises packaging over content, or surface over substance). This perspective can also be related to the BBC's wider historical ambivalence about the extent to which, as a public corporation, they should engage in publicity generation. The BBC had a Publicity Department, and this included a Television division by the mid-1950s. But even this expressed a distaste for "the bally-hoo ... the press party, the interviews, the glamour photographs, the screen-trailing, the Sunday paper story", especially when "nothing succeeds like a good programme".[3] At the same time, it should be recognised that this cultural attitude is not specific to the BBC. In negotiating its difference from Hollywood, British cinema has equally been associated with an "anti-star inflection of stardom" (Babington, 2001: 20), which cannot simply be explained by its more limited economic base.

But just as there were keen advocates of star-building within British cinema (such as the Rank Organisation or Associated British Picture Corporation) (Macnab, 2000), so a range of attitudes can be discerned within the BBC. In contrast to Haley, other personnel embraced television's ability to showcase existing stars, as well as its capacity to bring new faces into public view. The BBC's Programme Organiser, Cecil Madden, was well known as a figure who was keen to keep BBC television in touch with showbusiness, and he sought continually to discover new talent (claming to have done so with Petula Clark, the Beverley Sisters and Jimmy Edwards) (Briggs, 1979: 224). In the sphere of the popular cinema programme, it was also Madden who pursued the strongly star-driven culture of the BBC's *Picture Parade* (1956–62) (see Holmes, 2005a). Equally, in terms of mooting the possibility of stepping *into* a career in television, Brian Tesler, Producer of the BBC's popular television programme *Ask Pickles*, recurrently featured in the popular press and fan publications to talk about the Television Auditions Unit, the "most constant source of new television talent".[4] *Top Town* staged regional talent contests, with application forms placed in the *Radio Times*, while, in terms still familiar today, *It's Up to You* (1956–57) invited viewers to "choose the most promising new television artists" with advice from "a panel of experts".[5] These programmes also competed with ITV's talent show contests, such as *Opportunity Knocks*, beginning in 1956, and *Chance of a Lifetime* (1955–56).

By the mid-1950s, it is impossible to separate the more interested atti-tudes of Madden and Tesler from the fact that the BBC were now com-peting with ITV. At the level of public discourse, the BBC certainly becomes more vocal about foregrounding its talent once commercial tele-vision is on the horizon. Even though it was common knowledge that the BBC paid modest fees (with ITV offering up to three times more),[6] the idea of institutional "star wars" (Bourdon, 2004: 284) is apparent from the very start of competition. Just before ITV began, press reports explained how the BBC's competitive plans involved "stars signing exclu-sive contracts",[7] and there was also an emphasis on the BBC adopting a "Big-star policy" for its Light Entertainment shows. Behind the scenes at the BBC it was also noted that "unless [the Corporation] is able to decide which star personalities . . . it most desires and is prepared to invest con-siderable sums in long-term contracts",[8] talent would defect to commer-cial television. In many cases it did, although the BBC – perhaps rather optimistically – still felt that they had a trump card in so far as artists would prefer to "give a performance uninterrupted and undistorted by 'commercial breaks'".[9]

But at this point it is necessary to pause on issues of terminology. Turnock has suggested that "'celebrity' . . . might be a problematic term when thinking about television in the 1950s and 1960s" given that:

> Such a category is certainly useful when thinking about the paradigmatic hold "celebrity" has over the media landscape in the 1990s and early 2000s . . . . What characterises "celebrity" culture of the 1990s and 2000s is the expanding range of media outlets . . . which circulate an ever-increasing volume of "celebrity" traffic at an ever-increasing velocity. By contrast, the extent and speed of media circulation of "celebrity" discourses was more limited and much slower. (Turnock, forthcoming)

Turnock goes on to suggest that in order to differentiate the condition of television-generated fame in television's "era of scarcity" (Ellis, 2000) from "celebrity" in television's era of plenty, it indeed seems useful to adopt the term "television personality". On one level, this seems entirely fair. The concept of the TV personality clearly had a currency in the 1950s, and the term was variously used in relation to hosts, announcers or panel game faces (Sylvia Peters, Macdonald Hobley, Gilbert Harding, Isobel Barnett, Eamon Andrews), as well actors and actresses from popular fiction (*The Grove Family*, *Life with the Lyons*). But to end the discussion of terminology here too readily accepts the parameters set out by subsequent conceptual approaches in the field. The term "celebrity" *did* have a currency in relation to television in the 1950s, as did the term "star" – even while differences between television and film were being discussed. To accept the terminology of the "TV personality" neglects the range of terms in circulation, while it also misses how their use was shaped by discourses of cultural value. When the film fan magazine *Picturegoer* argues that it is better not to refer to TV names as "stars", it is because it wants to shore up the difference and superiority of the cinema: "TV is not a midget cinema . . . It's simply a developer of fireside friends".[10]

P. David Marshall has explored the longer historical genealogy of terms such as star and celebrity, and "celebrity" has long since carried a ring of disdain. As Marshall observes, it is in the nineteenth century use of the term that we see a shift from an affinity "with piety and religion to some modern sense of false value" (1997: 4). This ring of inauthenticity, as well as a more ubiquitous, and thus devalued, status, permeates David Wainwright's article, simply entitled "Celebrity", in a 1960 edition of the British newspaper *Weekly Post*. Reflecting on television's wider role in cultivating the "insidious influence of 'entertainment' on our national life", Wainwright bemoans how figures such as scientists and politicians, "people who have done most to make life pleasanter and more purposeful for their fellow men", are rarely applauded because they are not seen as celebrities. Furthermore, someone is now not seen as a celebrity unless they also have "the 'public face' that television requires".[11] Television was clearly preceded by the media framework of the press and radio, but as early as 1952 concern was expressed about television's impact on the public perception of politicians, and how public opinion may be influenced, or undermined, by politicians' "television appeal".[12] Wainwright's article also indicates how the terms used to describe public faces shift as the people move across media domains. People categorised as film stars, pop stars, authors or TV personalities might be described as celebrities when appearing on a television talk show (and this is how the BBC used the term when describing the subjects on *This is Your Life*).

But Wainwright's use of the term "celebrity" is also clearly intended to pass judgement. He invokes it to bemoan how those of television fame now attract the most "orgiastic" applause of all, despite the fact that they rarely seem to warrant it. Wainwright is expressing a concern here about the decline of a merited-claim-to-fame, or what Chris Rojek has termed a shift from *achieved* to *attributed* celebrity, in which fame is the result of concentrated media representation (2001: 17). This shift has not been attributed solely to television, but the medium has certainly occupied centre stage in debates about the status of modern fame (we only need to look at the discussion which has surrounded Reality TV). According to Joshua Gamson:

Television, with its constant flow . . . and vast space-filling needs, has from its initial boom provided the most significant new outlet for image creation . . . [I]t has become increasingly possible *in a practical sense* to create familiarity with images without regard to content . . . [A]s the prime outlet for, disseminator of, and certifier of public images, television has made decontextualised fame a ubiquitous currency. (2001: 271; original emphasis)

Gamson's work (1994, 2001) represents one of few attempts to situate the emergence of television within a longer historical trajectory of fame, and he associates the medium with a shift toward a heightened emphasis on celebrity as a commercial discourse. According to Gamson, it is in the post-war period, with the increasing growth of media outlets, that we witness the increasing visibility of the manufacture narrative of fame, when it henceforth becomes a "serious contender" in explaining celebrity (Gamson, 1994: 44).

Gamson is dealing with the American context, and his argument is rooted in contexts such as the decline of the Hollywood studio system, the ubiquitous spread of television, and the overt commercialism of the television persona (which was enmeshed with sponsorship and product promotion). But on a smaller scale, his emphasis on the sudden expansion of faces is relevant to the British context. Even the most cursory glance at *Picturegoer* fan magazine from this time indicates a considerable shift from a world defined by film names in the early 1950s, to a more crowded landscape later in the decade, with film, television and pop music stars all jostling for attention in the same space. But just how television was finding a place for itself within this entertainment culture is complex. On one level, and particularly in relation to the cry that TV must build its own stars, there was an emphasis on more traditional mythologies of fame – the importance of *discovering* an "innate" natural talent, of unearthing presence or "charisma", and what the *Daily Express* called "TV Oomph": that indefinable mixture of "talent, exhibitionism and enormous self-confidence that TV demands".[13] At the same time, and as broached by Wainwright above, television could be seen as emblematic of a cultural decline where fame was concerned.

The visible focus for such debates was undoubtedly the phenomenon of "Sabrina". A teenager from Blackpool, "Sabrina" (real name Norma Sykes) achieved fame by appearing in the Arthur Askey vehicle *Before Your Very Eyes* (BBC, 1953–58) as the "bosomy blonde" who didn't talk. The press marvelled at how she had achieved fame "without professional experience or training", and they wondered if she was a "bosomy Frankenstein-style construction produced in the BBC workshops and stuffed with old scripts".[14] Even the Corporation were apparently concerned that her success was "out of control", and as "one BBC

official put it: 'She's a wonder of our time which makes us absolutely ter-
rified of the power of television. Whoever heard of anything being
a screaming success for doing nothing?'"[15] The nature of Sabrina's
celebrity is clearly shaped by discourses of gender and class,[16] and it is
certainly invoked to express the idea (or fear) that television will "create
familiarity with images without regard to content" (Gamson, 2001:
271). In other words, television is positioned as the harbinger of a culture
in which people will simply be known simply for their "well-knowness"
(Boorstin, 1971).

This foregrounds how conceptions of television fame, which emphasise a close identification between persona and role, and suggest that the
TV personality gives the impression of just being "themselves" (Langer,
1981, Ellis, 1992), are themselves shaped by perceptions of cultural
value. For example, as Medhurst has explored, the grouchy Gilbert
Harding, initially famous for his role as an outspoken panellist on *What's
My Line?*, could be seen as simply trading on an aspect of his "genuine
personality – it was who he *was*" (Medhurst, 1991: 62; original emphasis). Little wonder, then, that Medhurst comes to the conclusion that
Harding became the country's "first unequivocal media personality. He
was famous for being famous" (1991: 64). To put it another way, the perceived specificities of television fame, as Christine Becker also observes,
have simultaneously functioned to "denigrate the stature of television
stardom" (2005: 9). It thus becomes important to examine how the relationship between the on-screen and off-screen self is constructed at the
level of historical evidence, and the degree to which one particular paradigm is simply applicable to "all".

Paradigms of television fame

Well-known interventions by scholars such as Ellis ([1982] 1992) and
Langer (1981) theorised the specificities of television fame at a time when
television studies was just beginning to expand. These interventions
invariably involved establishing the parameters of television fame by
invoking a comparison with the film star. Television fame seemed to be
constituted as much by what it was *not* (what it lacked) as by what it
was. Langer argues for example that:

> Whereas the star system operates from the realms of the spectacular, the
> inaccessible, the imaginary . . . [television's] personality system is culti-
> vated . . . as "part of life", whereas the star system always has the ability
> to place distance between itself and its audiences through its insistence on
> "the exceptional", the personality system works to foreground intimacy
> and immediacy; whereas contact with stars is . . . sporadic and uncertain,

contact with television personalities has regularity and predictability; whereas stars are always playing "parts" emphasising their identity as "stars" as much – perhaps even more than – the characters they play, television personalities "play" themselves. . . . [P]ersonalities are [also] distinguished for their "will to ordinariness", to be accepted, normalized, experienced as *familiar*. (1981: 355; original emphasis)

In drawing out these differences, both Langer and Ellis discuss the intertextual circulation of film and television fame. The construction of the film star is seen as encouraging a play in which the "real" identity of the star is imagined to reside outside of the film text. The image of the film star is paradoxical and incoherent, beckoning the spectator to continually return to view the star's performance on screen. In comparison, the construction of the TV personality involves a drastic reduction of distance between the circulated image and the performance, in so far as the "two become very much entangled, so that the performer's image is equated with that of the on-screen role" (Ellis, 1992: 106). As Ellis expands, subsidiary material is more concerned with "discovering if there is a personality separate from that of the television role, than it is with the paradox of the ordinary-but-extraordinary" (1992: 107).

Susan Murray's (2005) historical study can be seen as complementing the paradigms offered by Ellis and Langer. Murray focuses on 1950s American television, and examines television fame through variety and comedy stars such as Jackie Gleeson, Milton Berle, Arthur Godfrey and Lucille Ball. She argues that while the authentic identity of the film star is seen to be held back from the spectator:

[W]ithin the context of the discourses that constructed television's aesthetic, television viewers were encouraged to believe that they could actually locate the true personality of a television performer somewhere within his or her performance. . . . [T]his belief might have been stimulated by the popular rhetoric on television's intrinsic aesthetics . . . [B]ecause television was said to produce intimacy, immediacy, and spontaneity, it also generated authentic identities. (2005: 129–130)

Yet Murray's work differs by also aiming to provide more concrete historical and economic explanations for the emphasis on the "ordinary" "authenticity" of television fame. The concealment/revelation discourse which works to structure cinematic stardom represents an economic strategy intended to encourage repeat trips to the cinema. But the regular flow of television culture demands a different economy of viewing. As Murray outlines, the goal may have been to naturalise the performers in the domestic setting so as to make them appear less "aberrant in the context of the everyday, yet simultaneously make them engaging enough to capture the audience . . . and to draw positive attention to the sponsor's product" (ibid).

This immediately raises the question of national differences, not only in relation to television, but also with regard to the cinema. As Bruce Babington observes, dominant strands of star theory are almost wholly "Hollywood-orientated" (2001: 3), and it is questionable whether the contrast between cinematic and television fame looks so sharp once British cinema is brought into view. For example, we might consider the different currency of distance or "aura" where British film stars are concerned, and as Babington describes, British stars often operated as reflections "of the known and the close at hand . . . intimate dramatisations of local myths and realities" (2001: 10). More crucially, Murray's study of American television finds no easy application to British broadcasting. As acknowledged below, in the British context, television names could certainly appear *in* adverts to promote products, and with regard to ITV, the value of a programme in terms of advertising rates was clearly shaped by its star(s) or talent. But there is not the same economic enmeshment of star persona and advertising discourse which characterised sponsorship in 1950s American television (see Murray, 2005). This raises questions about how to account for the specificities of television fame in early British television. Are there ways in which the history of British television fame, particularly with regard to public service television, might have its own institutional and cultural inflections?

Circulating television fame

In examining coverage from fan magazines and the popular press, it is possible to get a sense of the types of knowledge, or discursive conventions, which shaped the circulation of television stars. In the early 1950s, BBC announcers such as Sylvia Peters, Macdonald Hobley and Mary Malcolm feature quite prominently in the fan publication *TV Mirror*. In the years 1953–54, this material is certainly almost exclusively focused on their professional roles (much like deCordova's (1990) emphasis on the "picture personality" in the earlier years of cinema). In a series of *TV Mirror* articles on Sylvia Peters, the announcer reflects on "What It's Like Being a TV Announcer", providing detailed information about training, rehearsals, clothes and timetables, while also discussing the experience of being recognised in public.[17] The reference to clothes is quite important here, as the often strikingly glamorous image of women on television at this time, from Sylvia Peters to the *What's My Line?* panellist Isobel Barnett, undermines the idea that television fame was simply constituted through discourses of an "ordinary" mundanity, or that proximity and familiarity were somehow antithetical to glamour. Female television announcers, hosts and actresses appeared in a regular spot in *TV Mirror* called "Star Choice", and this held them up as *desirable* and fashionable models of femininity. "Star Choice" explored the women's fashion tastes and conveyed fashion advice, while also giving details of how "the dress can be made from . . . pattern D.2,483 . . . order it from the *TV Mirror* Pattern Department".[18] In this respect, female television celebrities followed in the footsteps of Hollywood, and to a lesser degree British, female film stars, who had long since offered desirable models of femininity.

But in the case of Sylvia Peters, this emphasis on fashion is seen as part of her professional identity, and the concept of the announcer, a role which is perhaps less explicitly conceived as giving a "performance", may have doubly encouraged the idea that Peters's "real" self was on display. In other examples, such as the popular press coverage of BBC presenters Joan Gilbert or Jeanne Heale, or the *What's My Line?* panellist Elizabeth Allan, there is more of a deliberate bid to reflect on the existence of both a television self and a personal self, as often cued by the phrase "In her private life" or "at home . . . ". For example, with regard to Elizabeth Allan: "In private life she's Mrs Bill O'Bryen – and has been, perfectly happily, since 1933. She lives in a tall London house just off Knightsbridge, cooks . . . and is devoted to her . . . sentimental Bull terrier. . . . called Emmy".[19]

But as the discussion of *This is Your Life* makes clear, conceptions of what is private change over time, and from a contemporary perspective, this makes the interpretation of these discourses surrounding television fame complex. The articles *do* perceive that they are giving the audience access to the "private" self, and the regulated nature of this sphere simply reflects the cultural climate of the time. In the British context at least, nor can this apparently careful regulation of the private be invoked as clear evidence of the difference of television fame. When compared to Hollywood, the construction of British stars had always dramatised different conceptions of public/private, with a more limited emphasis on romance, marriage and sexual identity (Babington, 2001: 20). But it is nevertheless possible to suggest that the image of a limited margin of difference between public and private self may at least have reinforced the sense that the people on television *are* who they *appear* to be. This is at least the case with roles such as announcers, hosts and panellists, as fiction demanded slightly more reflection on the relationship between the "real" and the role. In this regard, the following section examines television-produced fame, and expanding on the analysis offered in Chapter 2, it focuses on the cast of *The Grove Family* (hereafter *TGF*).

The Groves – a "real genuine family": on screen and off

The actors and actresses who played the Groves enjoyed something of a ubiquitous intertextual circulation while *TGF* was on air. But the extent to which this circulation was actively courted by the BBC (we have noted the somewhat ambivalent attitude toward publicity) is more ambiguous. In the early stages of *TGF*, the Producer, John Warrington, complains about the billing of the programme in the *Radio Times*:

> From the beginning [the Head of Light Entertainment, Ronald Waldman] has had . . . the idea to play down the actors' names and authors' names and merely display the characters so that the viewers would not think in terms of actors and written scripts, but of a real genuine family. This idea was first-rate. Now we have a billing describing the family that Michael Pertwee [the chief writer] *has created*, putting us right back to any ordinary domestic drama.[20]

As discussed in detail in Chapter 2, in the initial conception of *TGF* as a family serial, the BBC placed an acute emphasis on the issue of class background, with the apparent aim of "reflecting" back an image of the families buying television sets. The fidelity of the programme's class representation was praised by critics and viewers, yet *TGF* clearly offered a very particular image of lower-middle-class family life, the power of which resided precisely in its claim to the "homely" and the "natural" (see also Thumim, 2004). What is significant in the context of this chapter is how this power intersected with, and impacted upon, the construction of the Grove family's fame.

The Producer's emphasis on a "real-life" rather than a fictitious family may have involved an implicit nod toward the real-life families in American sitcoms such as *I Love Lucy* (1951–57) or *The Burns and Allen Show* (1950–58), as well the BBC's own radio/television comedy, *Life with the Lyons*.[21] But while the American shows also claimed to be holding up a reflecting "mirror" to the audience (Murray, 2005: 173), they constantly *played* with the boundaries between theatricality and everyday life, constructing what Spigel calls an "intensely self-referential world where the distinction between fiction and reality was . . . thrown into question" (1992: 162–163). *TGF* drew upon comedy, but it did not understand itself to be a sitcom, and from the BBC's point of view, the use of comedy could sometimes threaten its realist aspirations. The bid to play down the "creation" of the family was surely in part undermined by their self-reflexive surname (which linked the Groves to Lime Grove Studios). But these realist aspirations nevertheless shaped the feeling that the presence of "actors and scripts" should be played down. This mapped out a rather ambiguous role for the intertextual circulation of the cast, and indeed the programme itself on a wider scale. In comparison, the main scriptwriters, Michael and Roland Pertwee, were rather more interested in the possibilities of circulating the Groves beyond the boundaries of the television screen.

The Pertwees would write to the BBC with suggestions for a range of intertextual ventures, and by 1956 a BBC memo noted the existence of:

a) The Grove Family novel [*Meet the Groves*]
b) The Grove Family Picture [*It's a Great Day*, directed by Michael Pertwee in 1956][22]
c) Cartoons
d) Mrs Grove's Diary [*TV Mirror*]
e) Many sundry articles, *Good Housekeeping* and other kindred magazines.[23]

Although not featured in the list, Ruth Dunning (Mrs Grove) also appears in a series of Persil adverts in 1955 on ITV. While this testifies to her status as the "nation's favourite housewife",[24] and clearly trades on her familiarity and identity *as* Mrs Grove, the actress introduces herself in the advert as "Ruth Dunning". Whether the BBC prevented the explicit use of "Mrs Grove" is unclear, but they were certainly not widely enthusiastic about any of these intertextual ventures. On one level, there is a pragmatic reason for this, given that the BBC's intention, as the memo states, is "not to make profits, but to hold protective rights".[25] But given the Producer's initial intention that the Groves should enjoy little or no intertextual circulation at all, there seems to be more at stake in terms of what is being "protected" here.

When the BBC initially objected to a Grove strip cartoon, the Producer complained that it would "wrongly suggest that there was something funny about being a Grove – the characters would become the Groves with 'quotation marks' around them" when viewers saw them again on screen.[26] The investment in realism is again evident here, but the Producer's comment also recognises that intertexts can expand the semiotic base of a text, providing multiple points of entry for spectators/viewers (Klinger, 1991). This framework includes celebrity circulation – something which exists at the often unstable intersection of the producing institution, the media, the celebrity and their audience (Turner, 2004). The importance of regulating the ideological contours of celebrity circulation is also acknowledged by the Producer of *TGF* when he claims: "We've got to be careful with the Groves. The television family is supposed to be so full of virtues that the actors and actresses are expected to carry them into their private lives".[27] Given the very regulated parameters of the press coverage already discussed, it might seem that the BBC had little to worry about here. But as the Producer's nod to how the TV family is *"supposed to be* so full of virtues [my emphasis]" implies, this relationship between on/off screen selves still required careful management and construction.

The Lyons family in the radio/television comedy *Life with the Lyons* were a family in real life, so is it is not surprising that popular discourse foregrounded a tight fit between their on- and off-air selves. After spending time with the Lyons, a *TV Mirror* reporter confirms how "true to their lives" the programme is (it was at this time only on radio), and Bebe Daniels Lyon ("Mum") explains that they just "exaggerate" their everyday lives for the fiction on screen.[28] A little more work had to be done to present a similar image of *TGF*. In 1955, for example, the BBC material in the *Radio Times Annual* devotes a four-page spread to the Groves, and the title "The Groves – Home and Away" announces the intention to explore the relationship between on- and off-screen identities. The article sets out extensive character biographies, detailing the background of the characters before they appeared on screen, and then positions these in relation to the actor or actress who plays the role. It quickly becomes apparent that there is an element of class disjuncture here, with the cast enjoying rather more privileged lifestyles than their on-screen counterparts. While eldest son Jack Grove professes to dislike "any occupation which demands persistent concentration" and attends technical college as he "failed to get into grammar school", actor Peter Bryant was "educated at grammar school" and is "the son of a secretary of a large London commercial company".[29] While Mr Grove was a "Sergeant in the Army Tank Corps" and "enjoys sea-angling and filling in football coupons", actor Edward Evans was a Captain, and he has two daughters, Gwenda, who is at RADA, and Carole, who is "pre-RADA".

Similar differences between actor/actress and role recur throughout the article, but there is nevertheless a clear attempt to negotiate this relationship. As little can be done with the more immovable facts of birthplace, upbringing and educational background, this negotiation takes place at the level of cultural capital, what Bourdieu (1986) defines as the markers of "taste" (class), as articulated by lifestyle, hobbies, commodities and food. As discussed in Chapter 2, these markers were central to how *TGF* shaped its image of lower-middle-class life, and the concept of "taste" seems particularly apt in relation to the *Radio Times* article given that one of the categories used to compare the "real" and the role is "favourite meal" (they are also asked about their hobbies and their "pet aversion"). For example, with respect to Ruth Dunning (Mrs Grove), her favourite meal "varies with [her] . . . mood, but it can be anything from chicken with truffles to steak and kidney pud". Similarly, Peter Bryant enjoys a wide range of food – "Italian pasta, steak tartare, and fish and chips out of a newspaper" – and he actively dislikes "people who are hypocrites, tea parties and eating prunes". Nancy Roberts (Granny Grove) does her own cooking, housework, washing and even motor repairs, and she especially dislikes "Stage-folk who act *off* the stage".

A similar structure shapes the mention of musical tastes and hobbies, and the reader is generally given the impression that the people who play the Groves may be a bit different to the characters on screen, but they are not so removed from the likes and dislikes of the homely, *lower*-middle class, nor the millions of people who the BBC imagined made up the mass audience for television. This supports Langer's wider argument that part of the ideological function of the TV personality is to reduce the "*social* distance between those who appear and those who watch" (1981: 363; original emphasis). The TV personality functions to suggest that everyone exists within a "common universe" of experience (a rhetoric which is of course also central to the construction of a television community). Indeed, a series of look-alike competitions in the *Daily Herald* in 1955 asked viewers to *see themselves* in the Groves, asking "Isn't Grandma Grove always like Auntie Thelma?" and "Maybe little brother Willie looks more than a little like Lennie Grove?" The newspaper offered £5 for photos bearing the best likeness, and the ultimate prize was an invitation for the whole "duplicate cast" to spend a day with the Groves.[30]

As this example suggests, the majority of the press coverage supported the image set out by the BBC, even if the bid to negotiate class differences is slightly less explicit. In 1954 the *Evening News* features an article on Ruth Dunning, who plays Mrs Grove:

> Viewers know all about the domestic trials and tribulations of the contemporary Serial Queen, Mrs Grove . . . But so far they know very little about the woman who plays Mrs Grove – actress Ruth Dunning. So I asked Mrs Dunning in what respect her home life differed from that of the Groves. [They clearly] have a good deal in common. Although . . . Mrs Dunning and her actor husband Jack Allen have no children, they are a good deal at home. Four weeks ago they bought their first TV set, which is now another inducement to stay in . . . Being a busy actress, Mrs Dunning does not do the housework alone . . . But [she] . . . and her mother do all the cooking, and she could hardly be more practical – much like the unflappable and tolerant Gladys Grove.[31]

It is notable that any interest in "explanations of fame" (Gamson, 2001) ("How did this person get here?") remains absent here, as it does in similar articles on the rest of the cast. There is no mythic emphasis on discovery, "star quality" or charisma (or "TV Oomph" for that matter), and no real attempt to construct a merited-claim-to-fame. At the same time, nor is there any anxious suggestion (as with Sabrina) of manufacture. Indeed, such evaluative discourses appear to be rendered redundant by the suggestion that there is simply a "natural" fit between persona and role.

In approaching television fame, Turnock (forthcoming) explores the significance of authenticity in broadcasting, which Scannell (1996) relates to the concept of sincerity. For Scannell, Turnock says, "performance implies insincerity, whereas sincerity presupposes a lack of performance. For persons perceived to be 'real' . . . they must be seen to eschew performance" (Turnock, forthcoming). But as Turnock observes, this simultaneously demands that the concept of work, and thus skill, is played down (ibid). The BBC profiles emphasise the training of the actors and actresses who play the Groves, as well as their often extensive experience in theatre acting. But the emphasis on skill and talent is not a dominant discourse in their construction. This reflects the extent to which the programme is discussed not as a form of *drama* but as a form of light entertainment. However, it also makes clear how the idea of "performance" – on any level – is downplayed.

This returns us to the suggestion that the perceived specificities of television fame are always also evaluative (being "oneself" is unlikely to be praised as a skill), and we notably still see this discourse circulating around Reality TV fame today. Winning contestants are often validated for appearing to "be themselves", but the cultural status of Reality TV fame is simultaneously denigrated (Holmes, 2004a). The wider press coverage of *TGF* cast took these constructions still further. For example, if the Ruth Dunning article promises to reveal her "real" self, to offer us a peep "behind the scenes", only to admit that there is little to see which cannot be gleaned from her on-screen role (Langer, 1981, Ellis, 1992), this was further consolidated by reports of confusions between actors and characters. After explaining how, "As a home-loving man himself, fond of doing jobs around the house, Ted [Evans] couldn't be happier in his role as [builder and decorator] Mr Grove",[32] the *Evening Telegraph and Post* displays an image of Mr Evans with his wife at home, and the caption exclaims: "No, it's not Mr Grove with the wrong wife! It's Edward Evans enjoying a cup of tea with his real-life wife Pauline!" Other articles were entirely built around this apparent confusion, such as the 1955 *Daily Sketch* piece which announces how "Bob Grove is a real Dad to the TV Kids", then details how "scores of children across the country have adopted Bob Grove as a kind of honorary Dad", writing to "Bob" to ask advice on homework, bicycle punctures or football skills.[33]

From this perspective, the question of the generic identity of *TGF* (Chapter 2) also raises questions about how to conceptualise its relations with celebrity. While the programme's textual relations with soap opera are complex, the circulation of its cast certainly resonates with discussions of soap opera celebrity. The changing boundaries of what is seen as "private" may have gradually opened up a larger gap between soap actors and actresses and their on-screen roles (see McNicholas, 2005), but Geraghty explores how the basis for interviews is often the similarities and differences between actor and character (1991: 21). These articles often appear to be reflecting on the newness, and thus specificity, of television fame, but this is not clear-cut. Similar discourses circulated around the cast of the BBC's radio serials, *Mrs Dale's Diary* and *The Archers*. The press frequently reported how listeners wrote to the radio characters as "real people", and in the case of *Mrs Dale's Diary* in particular (the correlation between female fans and a "duped" audience is notable here), there were frequent reports of confusions between actors and roles. In 1951 it is reported that "Mrs Dale will Stop Dieting" because too many women have written in to request her diet sheets for themselves,[34] and when the famous Dale cat was lost, "a woman telephoned to say that her little boy had found it in Portsmouth Road".[35] Nor is it necessarily the case that this blurring was more pronounced with television, simply because it visually identified the actor/actress with the role. In terms of radio, the BBC understood listeners to have their own "definite picture" of the characters in their minds, so in the programmes themselves "it was never wise to state the colour of their eyes or their hair".[36] But this idea was confounded by the circulation of the actors and actresses in the press. In fact, this material dwelt more self-consciously on aspects of physical appearance, precisely because it could not be accessed in the programme itself. As the *Evening Standard* explains, Alvys Maben who plays Sally Lane in *Mrs Dale's Diary* is a "28-year-old blonde with blue eyes and a poodle haircut", and the image confirms what is described.[37]

This may suggest that the emphasis on a close correlation between person and role is shaped by the regularity and (in the case of the radio programmes) the dailiness of serial forms, as much as it reflected something specific to television. It may be that part of investigating the historical relationship between 1950s television and conceptual paradigms of television fame is *also* to recognise the aesthetic and cultural continuities with radio. Based on the evidence considered here, it seems just as important to consider how the aesthetic, generic and ideological specificities of a particular *programme* shape its construction of fame. For example, while *TGF* has in common with *Mrs Dale's Diary* or *Life with the Lyons* the insistence on "ordinary" and familiar characters which pivot on a close fit between actor/actress and role, these other programmes lacked the quite deliberate bid to mediate this through discourses of class. As discussed in Chapter 2, if the BBC spoke of a mimetic relationship between the Groves and their audience, this was explicitly understood in terms of class, and at the level of the programme itself, class verisimilitude. These aspects combined to create the need for "more careful observation of the income groups around whom the series is based, and to whom we wish to appeal".[38]

Serialitis and Sheila Sweet: "I am *not* Pat Grove!"

This section began by acknowledging that the wider circulation of the programme was not entirely under the BBC's control. Furthermore, as Graeme Turner points out, celebrity is built upon a "web of conflicting interests" (2004: 35), as mapped across the producing institution, the media, the audience and the celebrity themselves. From this perspective, it is important to stress that the blurring between the "real" and the role was *not* simply played out homogenously across the Groves, nor was it always articulated through discourses of a "cosy" familiarity. While contemporary television actors and actresses, especially in soap operas, may articulate concerns about being type-cast, in the 1950s this was discussed with a self-conscious note of alarm, expressed as an irreversible obliteration of the person by the role.

In January 1955 the *Daily Sketch* runs the headline "Is Sheila just a dead-end star?", and explains:[39]

> The beauty of the family [Pat Grove] is suffering from Serialitis. Sheila Sweet . . . is catching one of the oddest ailments that radio and TV can threaten . . . [This] complaint has hit a few other people in their time. . . . But Ellis Powell, who is radio's Mrs Dale, has long ago given up the struggle. She IS Mrs Dale. The cast of the Dales and their rivals, *The Archers*, have also given in. Sheila Sweet, however, means to fight.

This offers its own playful perspective on the apparently low cultural value of broadcast fame. Not only might Sheila's fame be "dead-end", but it is imagined in terms of an irritating, if not fatal, disease. But it is precisely Sweet's bid to "fight" the curse of serialitis which makes the example interesting. In *TGF* itself, Pat expresses an ambivalence about settling down and occupying a domestic role, particularly when Mrs Grove appears to be firmly "sunk in domesticity"[40] (see Chapter 2). This anxiety is then amplified by the intertextual circulation of Pat Grove/Sheila Sweet, as the actress had been seeking to forge a discursive gap between Sheila and Pat for some time, particularly at the level of class and gender.

This is especially apparent in a *Picture Post* article, "The Dream Girls Next Door" which, as part of its new series of "Teleprofiles", featured an interview with Sweet and Patricia Dainton, an actress from ITV's rival serial, *Sixpenny Corner* (ATV, 1955–57).[41] Much of the article is organised around the women "arguing" about which serial is more true to life and "real" ("Now nobody *ever* dusts in yours, do they Sheila?"), and while Dainton is only too happy to affirm how true to life her character is, Sweet is less so. After being asked the now ritual question whether she is similar to Pat Grove, she exclaims "'Good gracious no' with a scornful laugh":

> [S]he isn't like anyone in the world – at least nobody I've ever met, anyway. All that sweetness – she's so sweet it makes you sick. And *so* unsophisticated. For instance, I wish she would occasionally read a book, instead of endless magazines. And it wouldn't kill her to go to a concert, instead of to the pictures for a change. [Also] look at the way she treats her boyfriends. She leads them on and flirts like mad and then, when they try and make a pass at her, she is Not That Sort of Girl.[42]

When asked why her character is so popular with the audience, the actress replies:

> Well I suppose because she is what every mother would like her daughter to be like . . . so when their own girl gets out of hand, they can sigh and tell them to behave like Pat Grove. Personally, I would *loathe* to be like her, or have a daughter like her . . . I am not Pat Grove! (ibid; original emphasis)

In dismissing Pat's (class) "taste", Sweet disrupts the BBC's bid to collapse the identities of actor and role in a strategy of class realism. But her discussion of femininity does rather more. On one level, it implicitly critiques the parameters in which Pat must negotiate her sexual identity. The programme itself presented Pat as a popular girl with a string of boyfriends, but there was a clear bid to suggest that she was – in the words of the early press constructions – "proper".[43] Pat has little choice but to insist that she is ultimately "Not That Sort of Girl". But Sweet pointedly goes on to question whether Pat is "real" at all.

The suggestion of a disjuncture between actress and role takes on further implications in 1955 when the press bring news of Sweet's real-life divorce. Still insisting on a conflation between actress and role, the *Daily Mail* ran the headline "Pat Grove to seek divorce".[44] This returns us to the BBC's concern about regulating the moral contours of the cast, and it also indicates why the bid to collapse on/off-screen selves could backfire. If viewers had been reading the BBC's publicity on Sweet, which detailed how she lives "in London with [her] parents, and spends most of her spare time dress-making",[45] they must have been rather surprised to hear that she had been married and living with her American actor husband, William Sylvester, since 1949. The idea of a married and then *divorced* actress hardly supported the verisimilitude of Pat's "girl-next-door" image, nor the programme's bid to promote the "family as the key to social life".[46] Under Lord Reith's reign, BBC employees (in all fields) could find themselves sacked if cited in a divorce case (Crisell, 2001: 44), and while the institutional and cultural climate had changed, the editorial policy for *Mrs Dale's Diary* at least states that *characters* "cannot be divorced".[47] Evidence of divorce could be discussed openly in designated spaces such as the BBC's problem show, *Is This Your Problem?*, but when it came to the parameters of family fiction, it was clearly a different matter.

Sweet leaves the programme in 1956, claiming in the press that she will go off on holiday in her car and wear snazzy clothes (courtesy of her earnings from *TGF*). It appears that she chose to go, as there is a year between her divorce announcement and her exit from the cast. In 1956 Sweet is replaced by the new Pat, played by Carole Mowlam, and Mowlam more often represents Pat in extant footage, stills and BBC documentary coverage of the programme. But in the text of stale press clippings held in the BBC archives, Sweet will not be silenced, and she draws attention to the fact that the programme's claim to the "real" had different implications for different characters. This in turn questions the prevailing, and ideologically coherent, emphasis on the sense that people on television are simply who they *appear* to be. Furthermore, while this example is no less intellectually valuable for being a micro-discourse, it seems unlikely that *TGF* included the *only* television character who did not comfortably reflect a homology between on- and off-screen selves.

"Public service fame?"

TGF, then, raises complex questions about the relationship between television history and conceptual approaches to television fame. Attempts by American scholars to provide historically specific inflections find no easy application to the British context, so issues of difference are important, although I would hesitate to extrapolate general conclusions from the case study offered here. It can tentatively be suggested, however, that one characteristic of "public service" television fame, in the 1950s at least, is that it has little interest in stars occupying "multifarious identities", which Murray describes in relation to the American context (2005: 131). While the American persona was intended to appear (ideologically) coherent, stars were not simply characters, personalities, and public/ private individuals: they were also representatives of networks, spokespersons for the sponsors' products, and were expected to extend and expand their persona across a range of commercial intertexts (ibid). In comparison, public service television fame is marked by the desire for a unified or even singular identity: recall the Producer's initial suggestion that the cast of *TGF* should remain unknown. It is also marked by an element of disinterest in capitalising on the commercial possibilities of celebrity (which nevertheless take on a life of their own). But as a case study, *TGF* also raises wider questions about the relationship between the conceptual and the historical here. The paradigms offered by Ellis and Langer do capture some of the discursive structures which brought television fame into being in the 1950s, particularly given the self-conscious bid to dwell on the perceived specificities of the medium. But there is undoubtedly a need to look more specifically at the contours of the case study, as well as the relationship with radio, to tease out how discourses of "ordinariness" and familiarity are being deployed. Finally, examples which don't seem to fit these paradigms might be seen as just as revealing as those that do, if not more so.

Even if the *prevailing* media constructions here encouraged the audience to "see themselves" in the Groves, beckoned by a reassuring unity between character and role, this was not the only way in which television's relations with fame were understood. Television was also seen as making a tasteless, cheeky or downright impertinent bid to snatch away the public "face", exposing an undesirable disjuncture between on- and off-screen identities. As it did so, the subject would hear the booming words: "This is Your Life!"

"How embarrassing . . . but how popular!":[48] *This is Your Life*

Growing up in the 1980s, I remember *This is Your Life* (hereafter *TIYL*) (BBC, 1955–69, ITV, 1969–93, BBC1, 1993–2003) for its reverential treatment of celebrities and ceremonious presentation of the "Big Red Book". The well-known format saw the subject surprised by the presenter, with the narrative of their life retold through the testimonies of friends, family and colleagues. It was something my parents might watch, and it certainly didn't seem exciting to me. In 2003 *TIYL* was axed by the BBC in the belief that it was outdated (Otzen, 2003) (although during the writing of this chapter, plans have been announced for its return). The *Guardian* reported that in the years leading up to 2003, "younger celebrities have been non-plussed at the thought of taking part", and rock star Noel Gallagher snubbed an invitation to appear "with a gruff

Figure 4 Eamon Andrews with the Big Red Book as the host of *This is Your Life* (1957)

'stuff your red book'" (ibid). Sentimental, nostalgic and respectful, when it began *TIYL* did not anticipate a culture which hungered for the drama-tisation of unseemly sexual scandal, which delighted in "papping" celebrities sporting scruffy clothes or spots, and in which celebrity was the primary marker of the dissolution of the boundary between public and private. Or *did* it?

TIYL was originally an American format, devised by its American host Ralph Edwards. It began on US radio in 1948, and transferred to network television in 1952. In 1955, the BBC agreed to take out a two-year option on the format, with Eamon Andrews as the host (see Figure 4). The amiable Irishman was already well known to the audience from his role as sports anchor on BBC radio, and as the chairman of the BBC's popular television panel game, *What's My Line?* Produced by the Light Entertainment department, *TIYL* began on British television on 29 July 1955. Before the series began the BBC were anticipating "the con-siderable impact of this important programme",[49] and it came to be guarded as something of a jewel in the BBC's schedule. According to BBC Audience Research, the programme regularly attracted audiences of 13 million, and "no other programme in the history of British television has anything like this combination of large audiences and high reaction indices".[50] For this reason, it was understood to be "one of the BBC's most valuable properties which ITA [could not] . . . touch".[51] (It did transfer to ITV, although not until 1969.)

The BBC would insist that *TIYL* had worthy credentials which reflected public service ideals. This ethos was yoked to the programme's use of ordinary people, as for a good many years the show alternated between celebrities and members of the public as its main subjects. As Stuart Hood, then Deputy Editor of News and Current Affairs, explained:

> A great deal of our output . . . is concerned with international tensions, racial antagonism, political intrigue and industrial strife. It is not often that we demonstrate that . . . people are doing good deeds in a naughty world. This . . . is the function and justification of *This is Your Life*.[52]

The programme was broadcast live between 1955 and 1961, and the main guest would be revealed in the studio itself, believing they were there for some other reason, or they would be surprised by Andrews in a public, work or leisure space (during the shooting of a film, in the middle of a theatre performance, or at a première). With friends and family emerging to animate the subject's journey from childhood to the present day, the succession of witnesses to the Life story were introduced in gradual succession, linked by the narration of the host.

In the opening of the programme, the camera roamed around the theatre and across the studio audience, and Andrews aimed to foster the possibility that "anyone" could be elected to appear on stage. In reality, the selection criteria were specific. Aside from celebrities (which was the programme's favoured term to cover the famous guests who appeared), those Andrews introduced as having experienced "adventures worth telling" included doctors and nurses who had won medals of bravery during the war, heroic military personnel, charity fundraisers, and people who had contributed to their community in other ways, for example by setting up youth clubs for the underprivileged. As this implies, there was a strong attachment to national pride and honour, particularly as related to the not so distant context of the Second World War. Apparently ordinary people were to be honoured as "special", and the aim was to transform them from do-gooders known to their local communities, to "celebrities" on a wider, national scale (Desjardins, 2002: 120). While members of the public were to be honoured as celebrities, so celebrities were to be honoured as "ordinary" people, as well as gifted talents and stars. The common criteria here were that *TIYL* celebrated "people who have made definite . . . contributions to society".[53]

The clear investment in meritocratic ideologies of fame is explored later in the chapter, but the celebrities largely emerged from cinema, theatre, sport, literature, music and dance. Actors and actresses, often from British cinema, represented by far the most frequent subjects, and guests appearing between 1955 and 1963 included Jessie Matthews, Gracie Fields, Richard Attenborough, Richard Todd, Harry Seacombe, John Mills, Anna Neagle, Kenneth More, Dora Bryan, Noel Purcell, Ronald Shiner and Hattie Jacques. Names from British theatre included Dame Sybil Thorndike and Louie Ramsay, while Bella Burge, the British music hall star, was the focus of an edition in 1958. Sportsmen included racing driver Stirling Moss, boxer Freddie Mills and footballer Matt Busby, while those variously associated with music ranged across the rock pianist Russ Conway, the "forces' sweetheart" Vera Lynn, the British jazz singer Humphrey Lyttleton, and the younger rock and roll star, Tommy Steele. People who did not fit into any of these categories included T.E.B. Clarke (screenwriter for British films, including some of the Ealing comedies), the war heroines Anne Brusslemans and Freddy Bloom, holiday camp entrepreneur Billy Butlin, the editor of the *Daily Express*, Arthur Christianson, and the television inventor, John Logie Baird. In a self-reflexive move, the host Eamon Andrews found himself the subject of the first British edition of *TIYL* (after the plan to focus on Stanley Matthews was leaked), and the television comic and then film star, Norman Wisdom, experienced the Life treatment in 1956. Victor Sylvester, known to viewers as the famous ballroom dancer from radio's *BBC Dancing Club* (from 1941) and *BBC Television Dancing Club* (from 1948), was the subject of a 1957 edition, and later in 1963, one programme focused on the *Z Cars* (BBC, 1961–78) actor, Stratford Johns. Despite these examples, names from television appeared infrequently, although this can in part be explained by the relative newness of the medium, particularly with regard to the earlier editions of the mid-1950s.

"The revolting emetic": courting controversy

Press discourse offers a crucial insight into the meanings and values which attended the circulation of *TIYL* – meanings which cannot simply be retrieved from existing editions of the show itself. The chapter now summarises the main themes of the press reception, which remained remarkably stable into the 1960s, before exploring the implications of particular strands in detail.

It is now difficult to convey the sheer volume of press coverage this programme received, as well as the negative nature of its tone. *TIYL* was not simply a programme that critics claim to dislike: they wanted it banned.

First, and in ways which overlap with the discussion of the quiz/game show in Chapter 3 and the problem show in Chapter 4, there were vehement objections to the ethics of the programme. In relation to *TIYL*, discussion circled around two key features: a concern over the ambushing and tricking of the subject, and its subsequent invasion of their privacy. These issues were seen to be inextricably linked given that the person had not consented to appear. The following comment is typical:

> [This programme] now heavily underlines a problem to which I . . . urge the BBC to give immediate and critical attention . . . To what extent is television justified in poking into the private life of a person who has not given his or her permission to appear in a "live" programme to be transmitted into millions of homes throughout the country? Is this entertainment? Or is it an unpardonable intrusion into personal privacy?[54]

The BBC's problem show has already made clear that "intrusions" into personal privacy could function *as* entertainment, and that these concepts were thus far from separate or opposed. Despite the differences in the intentions of the programmes (one celebrates the "great", the other deals with the less fortunate), *TIYL* and *Is This Your Problem?* were occasionally grouped together as indicative of television's new intrusions into the "private" sphere.[55] *TIYL* was also routinely described as a "weekly peepshow" or a "Cruel Keyhole",[56] echoing the criticism levelled at the problem show. With headlines such as "This is Torture by TV",[57] the reception of *TIYL* also had aspects in common with the public discussion of the quiz/game show: critics worried over the power dynamics which circulated between television, subject and viewing audience. According to many critics, *TIYL* was akin to torture and victimisation, and the popular parlance used to describe the subject was always that of the "victim" (even within the BBC).

Intertwined with each of these concerns was urgent discussion about the relationship fostered between programme and viewer. Some critics expressed outrage on behalf of the public, who were imagined as being unwillingly turned into "embarrassed onlookers" or "impertinent snoopers".[58] In other reviews, there was an emphasis on the complicity of the audience, and *TIYL* was variously described as "gobbled up and gloated over", catering to an "insatiable addiction to shockers and shocks", and as "the best-devised show yet for the mass exploitation of morbid curiosity".[59] A key strand of debate also circled around the tone of the programme. There were few reviews that failed to complain about its "unbearable sentimentality", and many critics claimed to experience physical symptoms of nausea while viewing. *TIYL* was "a revolting emetic",[60] a "great gooey meringue",[61] a slice of "stomach-heaving pie",[62] and a "saccharine encrusted process of personal exposure".[63] Finally, something which pervaded *all* of these concerns was the suggestion that *TIYL* was "utterly UnBritish".[64] Various assertions regarding the national character were advanced here, as encapsulated by the suggestion that Britain is a "private, self-derogatory, shy, modest and honest nation . . . [comprising] people of the grunt and understatement".[65]

Taking in all of these complaints, *TIYL* could be seen as a "high-smelling brew of torture, treacle, tears and trickery",[66] and in drawing on a heady mixture of tropes ranging from witchcraft to addiction to voyeurism, this quotation indicates the heated nature of the programme's reception. The idea of popular culture sparking controversy is clearly far from new, but it seems that *TIYL* became embroiled in concerns about the development of British television at this particular time. Critics undoubtedly perceived, for example, that *TIYL* had emerged as "part of the BBC's battle to beat commercial TV".[67] Perhaps even more strongly than the "give-away" show, it was invoked as the epitome of commercial fare and what the era of competition might mean for British television – particularly at the level of "taste". The fact that *TIYL* came from the apparently more respectable institution of the BBC only exacerbated these fears.

A range of discursive relations between class and culture are expressed through the guise of Americanisation (Strinati, 1992: 47), and it is thus no surprise that the emphasis on the American origins of the format was key. The BBC had known about *TIYL* for some time, and it was only after viewing US editions that they agreed that "with the necessary precautions [it] . . . could be made a 'BBC' programme".[68] As with the quiz/game show and the problem show, this again places emphasis on the question of adaptation or "textual translation" (Camporesi, 1993, 1994). Formats are attractive to broadcasters because they offer a framework which has been tested elsewhere, while they also leave scope for national inflections and variations (Moran, 1998). But the Corporation's emphasis on the need to make *TIYL* a "BBC programme" also nodded toward its controversial status in America, and this is something conveniently overlooked by the British reception. Mary Desjardins (2002) has considered the American version of *TIYL* in the 1950s as part of her study of the film star Maureen O'Hara. Prominent television critics such as Jack Gould and Gilbert Seldes complained about its invasion of privacy and its appeal to the "craven curiosity of the mob" (Desjardins, 2002: 127), although it does seem that the controversy was more prolonged and hysterical in the British context. But while the process of translating formats contains "clues about national identities" (Moran, 1998: 67), it is also important to recognise that this process operates at the level of public discourse, as much as it is reflected by the text itself. The British discussion of the programme is in every sense refracted through a "mythical America" (Hebdige, 1988: 74): after all, most of the British critics had never seen the American version. The responses have more to do with British attitudes toward American culture, and American television, than they speak to any real contrasts between the British and American versions of *TIYL*.

"Triumph over adversity, long slog to fame": mediating myths of stardom

In view of the vehement press criticism of the show, the overriding question which might be posed is: "Just what was the problem with *TIYL*?" Given the claim that it was a gross intrusion into the person's *life*, a key place to start is with the narrative material which animated the subject's life on screen. The Controller of Television Programmes, Kenneth Adam, explains in 1955 how the BBC:

> came to the conclusion that provided the people, the type of story (success not failure) and the incidents (not sordid or embarrassing in any way) were carefully selected, we could avoid the obvious dangers, except the criticism of intruding into the life of a private individual . . . If after four weeks of intensive research, matters are disclosed which might prove embarrassing to the subject, they are either eliminated from the life story or . . . the whole project is dropped.[69]

The emphasis on the "sordid or embarrassing", and thus the danger of being intrusive, clearly referred to the BBC's perception of the American version. The perception that the US programme was "naturally" more intrusive may have been shaped by the fact that there had always been more emphasis on the private life of the star in America, at least where the cinema was concerned. Historically, this had still been regulated by the moral boundaries of the star system, but with the decline of the studio system in the 1950s, this protective barrier was gradually eroded. The tabloid scandal magazine, for example, steps in to exploit precisely this shift. *Confidential* was the most high-profile example here, and when *TIYL* began, a number of American stars were embroiled in high-profile legal cases which aimed to prove that the magazine had invaded their privacy (see Desjardins, 2002). With respect to the cinema, there were no real British equivalents to the American scandal magazine, although *Confidential* could be purchased in London (for a relatively hefty 8–10 shillings) (Davis, 2002). But it is more problematic to map these contrasts in star construction onto television.

Desjardins hints that the American *TIYL* could be more confessional in tone: the American host, Ralph Edwards, for example, was dubbed a "spiritual prosecutor" after quizzing the former film star, Frances Farmer, about the nature of the "problem" that landed her in a sanatorium "('Was it drugs? Was it alcohol?')" (2002: 121). Yet this example does not appear to have been typical. In terms of their approach to the biographical material, many of the American editions are very similar to the BBC's.

As an illustration of the British version, it is useful to examine the edition featuring the variety, television and film star Norman Wisdom. Although certainly shaped by the specific inflections of Wisdom's star persona, this edition is typical of the narrative structure of *TIYL*. It begins with Andrews hiding in the wings of the stage, and Wisdom thinks he has been invited to the studio to perform. Andrews then springs out with the cry "Norman Wisdom – this is your life!" as the stage is illuminated and the studio audience is revealed. Andrews then introduces the story thus:

> This is the story of a poor cockney boy who drew on the hard, struggling experiences of life and turned them to his advantage, and who today stands at the top of his profession. And to his credit he still takes the same size in hats . . . [T]here are millions who love him . . . But how many of them know what a fight it has been? Your story, Norman Wisdom, starts in the dark, grimy streets of Paddington. Frail and small . . . for your years, you're still pugnacious and always trying to emulate your big brother Fred.[70]

Unlike the American version, which swung into view elaborate sets that literally recreated scenes from the past (Roy Rogers's family emerge situated in a huge ranch set, Lou Costello's mother appears on her "front porch"), the British version, which cost £950 per edition against the American budget of £30,000, relied solely on testimonies, photographs and film clips.[71] With Wisdom positioned in the main chair, the guests emerge one by one through the curtains at the back of the set – each announced with a brief trumpet fanfare. As Andrews's opening speech suggests, the narratives were always told in the present tense ("It is 1941", "You are 11 years old"). This was possibly intended to a create anticipation and drama given that – for the subject and the audience – the outcome of the story was already known. But it also contributed to the *presentism* of the programme itself: the biography may be past, but the witnesses to the Life narrative are constructing the story in live, television, time.

Wisdom's mother, the first guest, speaks of his "determination to succeed", before his school friend, Tom King, tells stories of a shy Wisdom, bullied and vulnerable at school. We then hear about his job in a grocer's and the difficulties he experienced in riding the grocer's tricy-cle, but how, according to his old boss, he was a "wonderful worker, on the go from 8 every morning to 7 at night . . . although he did pinch the cheese from the shop next door". We cut back to Andrews's narration as we move closer to Wisdom's performing aspirations. At first he finds that the "streets of London are not paved with gold". We are told how his first act "dies the death" at a music hall in Islington, but how "fate and the kindness of a fellow-artiste . . . takes a hand, as well as, of course, [his] irrepressible talent" when Wisdom gives a well-received perform-ance in a Brighton variety show. The "fellow artiste" is Vera Lynn, and after a filmed message from Lynn on the television monitor (and the mention of further setbacks), we hear testimonies from theatre, television and film colleagues which enable Andrews to stress how Norman "is clearly still the same kid from Paddington". The programme ends on contributions from Norman's children, who are so proud of "his journey to success".

As this example makes clear, the story structure of the programme was paradigmatic of the "success myth" (Dyer, 1998), in which a combin-ation of talent, "ordinariness", hard work, setbacks and lucky breaks function to catapult the subject to celebrity status. When an "ordinary" (extraordinary) person represented the subject of the show, as with Dr Philip Byard Clayton, "companion of Honour, holder of the Military Cross, and Doctor of Divinity", the emphasis was on personal achieve-ments, with testimonies revealing the subject's selflessness and the impact of their actions on the lives of others. Although there was arguably rather a difference between "rescuing the dying and injured from a train acci-dent" (Edith Powell), saving people in Africa "from the ravages of leprosy" (Dr Philip Byard Clayton) and the success of a "glittering film career" (Anna Neagle), the emphasis on hard work and determination prevailed. This was in every respect intended to be a valorisation of "achieved celebrity" (Rojek, 2001) at a time when, as suggested earlier in the chapter, such traditional explanations of fame were arguably subject to challenge.

The *News Chronicle* observed how *TIYL* recognises "no story more subtle than Triumph over Adversity, Long Slog to Fame, Hardship Endured, or Good Works Performed",[72] which suggests how the pro-gramme was seen as recycling old-fashioned and hackneyed tropes of star construction. This seems further interesting when we consider Babington's suggestion that, due to the more class-bound structure of society and the closer relations between cinema and theatre, the idea of the success myth had less currency in Britain, at least in relation to British film stars (2001: 18). This complements the analysis of quiz/game shows offered in Chapter 3 of this book: compared to America, the "egalitarian" emphasis on class mobility was less visible where the British contestants were concerned. Yet the success myth was boomed out on a weekly basis by *TIYL*.

On one level, this might be explained by the American roots of the format, as the basic structure of the Life narrative was adopted with little change. But it may also point to television's bid to negotiate the modalities of star identity within its own aesthetic form. The success myth is one site upon which the ordinary/extraordinary dialectic of film stardom is played out (Dyer, 1998). In this respect, it may have been seen as an ideal verbal basis for a programme that wanted to exploit the glamour, aura and unattainability of show business, while simultaneously using television apparatus to reveal the subject's "ordinary" self. Furthermore, such mythic tropes of stardom have long since functioned to construct the mass audience for stars. In relation to *TIYL*, these stories were seen as having a particular relationship with the newly competitive television environment and the expanding (class) audience for television. This is captured by a memo outlining the BBC's plans for the first few editions:

> Programme 1: Big Sporting celebrity (to hold audience with "names" against Palladium opposition on [ITV] . . .)
> Programme 2: Courage theme. Woman war-time parachutist.
> Programme 3: Internationally-known artiste almost at retiring age . . . with immense following with all classes of the public.
> Programme 4: Unknown man. Varied and exciting life – with appeal to all?
> Programme 5: Triumph over hardship theme. Woman, working class – must have . . . mass appeal.
> Programme 6: Stage star – with . . . feature such as humble beginnings or "come-back" after adversity etc.[73]

The memo shows how these mythic tropes are being used, at least from the BBC's point of view, to construct a mass audience for the programme. While the Producer, T. Leslie Jackson, emphasised how *TIYL* aimed to take "its stories from all strata of society",[74] it undoubtedly displayed a penchant for working-class narratives – rags to riches tales in which the subject is delivered from the jaws of poverty to bask in the sparkling lights of the stage or screen. But in terms of the celebrity editions, what united all the narratives was the extent to which subjects were presented as remaining essentially *unchanged* by their fame, a long-standing trope in star construction which pivots on what Dyer calls bearing "witness to the continuousness of the self" (1998: 21). British film star Ronald Shiner is praised because his "cockney ordinariness" stayed with him throughout his life, while Vera Lynn is introduced as "the international star, now at the peak of her profession, [but who] . . . is still the same unspoiled girl who sang around the house at number three, Thackeray Road, East Ham".[75] Crucially, this laid the context for a seamless intertwining of the personal/professional self which could not have been more coherent.

When compared to the celebrity editions, the shows focusing on ordinary people could legitimately be viewed in a different light. The identities of these people were not circulating in the public domain, so any facet of their biography could essentially be conceived as private. Some critics saw these editions as the programme's ultimate intrusion, adding that celebrities at least worked in a profession where the aim "was to publicise their private lives".[76] Yet this was a minority response. For most critics, *TIYL* was shamefully intrusive whoever the guest happened to be.

But it has been established that the Life narratives were only slightly more detailed than fan magazine or press material, and they were in many ways comparable to biographies. The controversy surrounding the show certainly speaks to the shifting and historical nature of how the private is perceived: what might be seen as unproblematic now could be viewed as a gross intrusion in the 1950s. But the reviews from the time also undermine the need for such a qualification. While complaining profusely about the intrusive nature of *TIYL*, a critic commenting on the Eamon Andrews edition complains that "hardly any one of the witnesses had anything very novel to tell us",[77] while an article on the edition featuring the cricketer David Sheppard observes that it told "us little we didn't already know about the man".[78] So how was it an "intrusion" into the private sphere?

Caught unready, off-guard: the appeal to "the real"

The recurrent complaint that *TIYL* exposes the subject's private *life* now seems to imply the exposition of an off-screen existence. Yet the controversy really circles around the *visual* – the imaging of the subject by the television apparatus, and the articulation of their identity through the formal and aesthetic codes of the medium. This is suggested by the fact that while the BBC may not have wished to intrude into the subject's life on a discursive level, they nevertheless wanted *TIYL* to display another side to the person. In discussion of the edition featuring the comedian Ted Ray, the Controller of Television Programmes complained that "this was so unemotional as to be dull. [A]fter the first few moments of surprise, [he] used his considerable stage experience . . . and simply 'gagged' . . . his way through the programme".[79] Disappointment emerges from the fact that Ray's performance was too similar to his professional persona. This example may also reflect back on the relative paucity of stars *from* television (or indeed radio, for that matter), even as the programme progressed into the 1960s. To return to the example of the Groves, if the prevailing media construction suggested that they were who they appeared to be, would there be anything else to "reveal"? This argument, however, only works so far: the non-celebrity participants had little or no pre-existing public persona, but BBC Audience Research revealed that both types of programmes were enjoyed by viewers. A "good" (visual) performance within the format was usually enjoyed in itself – as suggested by the viewers' criticism of the second edition, featuring the wartime resistance worker Yvonne Bailey. According to the BBC, "Mrs Bailey's unresponsive personality [was] . . . a severe blight to the proceedings. [Viewers] . . . felt the main attraction of this programme must lie in watching the reactions of the 'victim' and on this occasion they felt considerably cheated".[80] The BBC may have foregrounded the inspirational narratives when questioned about the programme's function and appeal, but they were clearly well aware of where the *real* attraction lay.

When it first began Kenneth Adam emphasised how "the success of *This is Your Life* is due to its 'shock' and 'stunt value'",[81] and although subjects responded to the surprise in different ways, the promise of this moment always pivoted on liveness. Whether viewed in real time or not, television's capacity to capture a "true authentic moment as it unfolds" (Desjardins, 2002: 121) is now seen as part of its *capacity* for "liveness". In the 1950s, and in relation to *TIYL*, this is doubly invoked, as the programme is literally live. The fact that this compelling spontaneity was the product of risk is acknowledged by the fact that the BBC always had the Eamon Andrews edition loaded on the Telecine in case something should go wrong – namely an adverse reaction by the subject. In this regard, *TIYL* was an extensively planned and crafted arena, but with an appeal to the unscripted and the unpredictable at its core. Not dissimilar to Reality TV today, it deliberately orchestrated a space to both *produce and then capture* "the real". This is implicit in the BBC's description of the programme which notes that "as a *documentary method* it is strikingly dramatic . . . [and] compulsive . . . [T]he question of taste apart, [it is] one of the most . . . original ideas produced by American television".[82]

When it came to film stars appearing on TV cinema programmes, television's liveness had already been discussed as potentially undermining the image a star wished to project. Stars could appear nervous and flustered in the new, live, performative context of television, even while the interviews were highly genteel and polite affairs (Holmes, 2005a). In comparison, *TIYL* specifically aimed to capture its subjects off-guard, offering its own particular spin on the bid to negotiate authenticity in the star image. This of course now has a staunch place in the tabloid rhetoric of paparazzi photographs: *heat* magazine literally promises to capture celebrities "off-guard, unkempt, unready, unsanitized" (Llewellyn-Smith: 2001: 120, cited in Holmes, 2005b: 23). The ethos of *TIYL* was evidently less boisterously "democratic" in its treatment of its guests, but the fact that the surprise moment was later called the "sting"[83] suggests a sharp sadistic intent in an otherwise apparently benign forum. As Desjardins notes, despite their apparently oppositional relationship, the scandal magazine and *TIYL* both trade on "candid reactions to constructed surprises" (2002: 128), and both share the visual desire to penetrate the polished nature of the public façade. As each new media form develops, it has to negotiate its own claim to access the authenticity of the celebrity image in an increasingly crowded media landscape. While in *TIYL* television is circulating very traditional explanations of fame, it is also keen to provide its own "fresh markers" of authenticity (Desjardins, 2002: 128) as the basis for its appeal.

From a contemporary perspective, the key difference between then and now is less the aesthetic construction of authenticity than the fact that it is not questioned or challenged – as the strength of the controversy surrounding *TIYL* itself makes clear. The dominant emphasis on the subject as the "victim" evacuated any suggestion of agency or complicity, and thus any hint of a staged performance. In over sixty reviews and press articles on the programme, there was only one which questioned the authenticity of the surprise.[84] Given that debate surrounding the quiz/game show in Britain and America at this time acknowledged that television emotion could be the product of a choreographed performance (the scandals), the largely unquestioning reception of *TIYL* is all the more intriguing. This is particularly so given that, in contrast to the "ordinary" contestants on quiz/game shows, the concept of putting *on* a performance is recognised as part of the skill of the celebrity persona.

The compulsive close-up: uncomfortable aesthetics

This response to *TIYL* may reflect a culture less cynical about the "performative aspects of the private" where celebrity is concerned (Macdonald, 2003: 93). But the responses also speak to the then contemporary discourses which structured the meanings of the television close-up. As Jacobs has explored in relation to television drama, while the close-up was routinely discussed in terms of intimacy, this was not simply equated with familiarity, closeness and proximity. Intimacy here had an epistemological dimension, with the close-up imagined as a penetrating "microscope". As one reviewer comments:

> The camera is ruthless in its exposure of those facial forgeries of emotion which get by in the auditorium; the proximity of the actor to his audience imposes upon him a severe discipline of integrity in all he does with a smile or an eyebrow. (cited in Jacobs, 2000: 119)

The televisual close-up was not primarily discussed in terms of identification or seduction (as in the cinema), but in terms of observation. It aims to observe how "motives and emotions" are interpreted – up close (Jacobs, 2000: 120). What comes across strongly here is the insistence on the penetrating realism and thus the truth claim of the television close-up (forgeries will be detected). But once non-fiction programming is brought into view, it seems that this epistemological promise was not always welcome. In fact, a key problem with *TIYL* is that its images were seen as only *too real*.

As with the problem show (Chapter 4), the BBC's conception of *TIYL* suggests a competing struggle between what they perceived would make "good TV", and questions of taste, ethics and integrity which are seen to be consistent with public service ideals. As discussed in Chapter 1, the Head of Light Entertainment, Eric Maschwitz, emphasises in 1960 how BBC Light Entertainment producers should now follow certain rules of production. If a programme was to be an "audience getter" and an "audience holder", it was crucial to consider:

> [T]the impact of [the] . . . opening moments. These, if compulsive, will hold the audience beyond what is known in U.S. television as the "nuts point" – i.e. the moment at which the viewer might mutter the fatal words "Aw, nuts!" and switch over to an alternative channel.[85]

Here defined as a ratings "getter", the suggestion of a commercial or "popular" aesthetic could not be more pointed, and *TIYL* seems to offer an early example of this approach. In addition to the BBC's acknowledgement of the compulsive appeal of the opening surprise, the introduction of each witness by voice ("Hello Kenneth . . . do you remember me?") was designed to enable the camera to linger on the participant's face as it captured a mixture of confusion, anticipation and emotion. Yet the BBC also claimed that one of their precautions in adapting it from America concerned the more restrained use of the close-up. As the Producer explains, the British *TIYL* is more "tactful and sober . . . I never use a close-up on a face that is obviously overcome with emotion if I can avoid it. Sensationalism doesn't pay".[86] But there were critics and viewers who strongly disagreed that the BBC avoided sensational and exploitative aesthetics, and the most controversial edition in this respect featured the British film star Anna Neagle.

Neagle's roles in films such as *Victoria the Great* (1937, Herbert Wilcox), *Odette* (1950, Herbert Wilcox) and *The Lady with the Lamp* (1951, Herbert Wilcox) contributed to her status as a privileged cinematic signifier of Britishness. Neagle also epitomised the values of "stoicism and feminine modesty", playing strong, but unthreatening, female roles (Street, 1997: 126–127). But with headlines such as "Anna Neagle Weeps Before TV Millions",[87] this was not the image viewers saw on television. Rather, they were greeted by the "unecessary spectacle of an adult, mature woman being moved to tears, trying to hide her face from the relentless cameras which . . . would not spare her the discomfort of being exposed . . . and us the sensation of being made into impertinent snoopers".[88]

In the existing footage of this edition, Neagle seems to be having a wonderful time until she is shown a clip of the actor Jack Buchanan, who had died the previous year. When the clip ends and the camera cuts back to the studio, Neagle begins to cry, and is seen dabbing her eyes with a white handkerchief (see Figure 5.1). Eamon Andrews notices her reaction, but decides to march on with the Life narrative, while intermittently sneaking nervous glances at the distressed star and patting her on the head. *TIYL* was shot with three cameras, and with the programme caught "off-guard" by Neagle's reaction, there seems to be an uncertainty about *what* the cameras should do, and what they should show. At first, the image remains fixed on Neagle and Andrews in a medium shot, and the next guest to emerge from behind the curtain is Neagle's husband, the producer/director Herbert Wilcox. As Wilcox stands next to Neagle, she turns her head and hides her face from the cameras, and then begins to nudge her face behind his arm (see Figure 5.2). With the subject literally trying to escape television's gaze, the camera suddenly takes its cue and cuts to focus on Wilcox, as he proceeds to tell his story about "finding" Anna (see Figure 5.3). Rather than alternating between witness and subject as the anecdote is told, the camera remains fixed on Wilcox so that Neagle can compose herself off-screen. This takes some time, and as Wilcox tries to string out his narrative, we are made acutely aware of Neagle's trembling figure below the margins of the frame. To put it another way, what dominates this image is not what it contains, but what it withholds. Despite this apparent reticence, BBC Audience Research recorded how there were some "complaints [about] . . . the number of close-ups", while others appreciated "the 'tactful' way in which the cameras were taken off Miss Neagle when she was crying".[89] Even if we acknowledge that judgements of proximity and distance are both subjective and historical, it is difficult to locate any "close-ups" of Anna Neagle's face in this scene.

Figure 5.1

Figure 5.2

Figure 5.3

The BBC had been careful to regulate the verbal narrative of the programme, but this sequence, or rather the anxiety which surrounds it,
seems to support Thumim's wider point that:

> images could not always be contained by the narrative structures within
> which they were located . . . Effectively this was a recognition that the
> nuanced meanings conveyed in the visual image – especially in the close-up
> view of facial expression – could not be adequately controlled. (2004: 20)

Recognition of the power of the close-up, and thus the need for it to be
(in Thumim's words) "adequately controlled", pervaded the imagery of
the BBC's *Is This Your Problem?*, in so far as the identity of participants
was often withheld from the viewer's gaze. In comparison, the more celebratory arena of *TIYL* gleefully sets a trap to capture the "nuanced
meanings conveyed in the visual image" (ibid), but it is then less bold
about showcasing these for public view.

According to Thumim, the suggestion that the visual capacities of television might rampage out of control implied a passive viewer. This in turn
was displaced onto fears surrounding the "American" and/or the "feminine", and was articulated as a concern about the "debasement" of British
culture. In examining the press reception of *TIYL*, it is clear that in a programme seen as transgressing the boundary between public and private,
discourses of gender are once more apparent (see also Chapter 4). The
suggestion of feminisation is barely even a subtext here, with the domestic, intimate medium of television indiscriminately causing men and
women, celebrities and ordinary people, to weep before the public gaze.
In this regard, *TIYL* challenged what critics self-reflexively understood to
be the British script of personhood, as based on notions of "stoicism,
understatement, the stiff upper lip" (Furedi, 2004: 21). The cultural
reception of *TIYL* reflects on the changing status of emotions being displayed in public life, as well as television's role in producing and mediating individual subjectivities. We now live in an era which validates the self
through the display of emotion, and celebrity culture has been a key site
upon which this transformation of public discourse has occurred
(Macdonald, 2003). From a wider perspective, it is also worth recalling
that the spectacle of *male* emotion on television has only recently become
more acceptable in British culture, whether we point to the outpouring of
public grief following the death of Princess Diana, the changing construction of masculinity in soap operas, or the wider advent of talk shows
and Reality TV.

The persistent emphasis on *TIYL* as a "peepshow" speaks of a society
in which feeling and emotion still retain much of their private character.
Critics and viewers alike made such comments as *TIYL* "is like looking

through a window at something we had no business to see", or "I find it so often uncomfortable that . . . while I am watching . . . I feel a little guilty I switched on".[90] Here, imagining the home as what Spigel elsewhere calls a "private pleasure dome" (1992: 109) takes on more ambiguous and anxious connotations. As Spigel explores, the "threatricalisation of the home" was intended to draw a line between public and private – the space where the spectacle took place and the reception context of the viewer. Unlike theatre or cinema:

> The spectator was now physically isolated from the crowd, and the fantasy was . . . one of imaginary unity with "absent" others. This inversion entailed a set of contradictions that weren't easily solved. . . . [T]elevision had to recreate [a] . . . sense of social proximity . . . [making] . . . the viewer feel as if he or she was taking part in a public event. At the same time . . . it had to retain the necessary distance between the public sphere and private individual upon which middle-class ideals of reception were based. (1992: 116–117)

In relation to *TIYL*, this is not so much a "window" that takes the viewer *out* to a public event, nor one through which they can enjoy the "fantasy of imaginary unity with absent others" while remaining in the domestic comfort of the home. In fact, the descriptions of watching the programme suggest that people feel as though they are experiencing an entirely private viewing. This may have been heightened by the newly privatised experience of spectatorship, but in relation to *TIYL*, this worked in tandem with the feeling that television was offering access to events which the camera, and thus the viewer, should not see. From this perspective, the programme wilfully transgressed the distance between "the public sphere and private individual upon which middle-class ideals of reception were based" (ibid), precisely because it was not seen as mediating "the public" in the first place.

But in the descriptions of *TIYL* as a voyeur's paradise, somewhat guiltily enjoyed inside "private pleasure domes", it would be hard to miss the subtext of the sexual. Indeed, the suggestion that the subjects are compelled to "expose themselves" implicitly conflates the private with the sexual (Desjardins, 2002: 127, Foucault, 1990). Desjardins notes in relation to the American context that as forms of "new" media in the 1950s, television and the scandal magazines appeared to diverge in their mediation of stars' sexual identity. But she goes on to argue that it is possible to map a more "fluid discursivity" here (Desjardins, 2002: 128) (and in Britain, it is certainly notable that both media forms were explicitly referred to as catering to "gutter-like" curiosities). Descriptions of the guests on *TIYL* being ambushed, "pushed unsuspectingly into the glare of the studio lights",[91] often sound as though they are describing someone who has been "caught" in the nude. Sexual undertones also pervade suggestive visual recollections, such as how "last week's edition . . . ended with a huge close-up of a wet-eyed, quivering lipped A.E. Matthews",[92] while other critics observed how a common reaction "is . . . a gasp of surprise".[93] But the subtext of the sexual is most clearly linked to the viewer's curiosity and pleasure: while Peeping Toms are imagined as indulging "base and reprehensible desire[s]",[94] critics insisted that "one of the sensations enjoyed by connoisseurs of this programme . . . is the titillating disclosure".[95] The ambushing of the subject is referred to by the BBC as the "pick up", and while this "climactic" moment comes at the start of the programme, *TIYL* can be interpreted as a sophisticated format in its continual play with its exposure and revelation. Indeed, *TIYL* offered what Eric Maschwitz described as the "big confrontation, and then the . . . succession of surprises which keeps the momentum going".[96]

Richard deCordova describes the "sexual scandal as the primal scene of all star discourse, the only scenario that offers the promise of a full and satisfying disclosure of the star's identity" (1990: 141). *TIYL* did *not* offer this "satisfying disclosure", far from it, yet it still beckoned the viewer with the promise of a privileged access to the person's self, which ultimately pivots on the sexual (Foucault, 1990). This suggests that in examining how television participated in the circulation of knowledge about the famous, matters can be more complex than they first appear. Indeed, it is only the press reception that questions the more predictable emphasis on a safe, conservative and familial construction of the star.

And finally . . . the "refusal": is this the end of *This is Your Life*?

On a weekly basis, critics had talked of the day when (not if) someone would refuse the dubious honour of the Life treatment. The refusal finally came in 1961, as vividly dramatised by the recollection of one celebrity "being chased down the passages of Broadcasting House by BBC employees. [He was] . . . running in the hope that his . . . dignity and privacy might be saved".[97] The celebrity in question was the footballer Danny Blanchflower, and his actions received a great deal of media coverage, as well as a large measure of public support (despite the still considerable popularity of the programme). The *Daily Mail* featured a cartoon in which the footballer kicked "a television cameraman out of his house", with the camera sporting the label "TV intrusion".[98] The fact that the camera is imagined as having strayed from the BBC studios into *his home* is notable here. It suggests a fear that television's "social eye"

(Scannell, 1979) knows no bounds, or that with a propensity for "nosey sociability" (Corner, 2000) it will gatecrash spaces that are not seen as "social" at all. If Anna Neagle's appearance provided an occasion to worry about television peering *into* scenes which should not be available for public view, the Blanchflower incident dramatised how television's gaze might be omnipresent and unstoppable, rampaging *out* into the public sphere and into the domestic sphere of the home.

Celebrities can be understood to function as the most visible figures for dramatising discourses on privacy, individualism and selfhood at any one time, and their existence within a highly mediated framework provides the hyperbolic context for this to take place (Dyer, 1986). But the fact that *TIYL* did not discriminate between celebrities and ordinary people as the main subjects of the show made it doubly disturbing (and functional) where debates about the regulation of privacy were concerned. Rather than the ultimate form of symbolic validation, the debate surrounding *TIYL* approaches public visibility on television with great trepidation. The Danny Blanchflower incident sparked such comments as: "We've now reached a highly dangerous position where it is possible to haul anyone – be he butcher, baker or candlestick maker – before the cameras",[99] or "You're almost bound to be on television at least once in the next ten years. The whole country is. So I'll be seeing you . . . on my screen".[100]

TIYL had just shifted from live transmission, so Blanchflower's refusal was never transmitted (and it is unclear if it actually still exists). But the incident was significant in effecting changes to programme policy where *TIYL* was concerned. As the BBC's Board of Directors enquired: "Would it not be possible to consider informing the victim in advance, while keeping secret what will actually happen in the programme?"[101] While some objected that this would be "Hamlet without any prince at all!", or asked "are we not going to emasculate the programme entirely?",[102] it was ultimately agreed that the opening confrontation would be filmed at an earlier date. If all went to plan, this would include the subject consenting to participate, and the main programme would then be filmed in the studio, with everyone secure in the knowledge that the person was willing to appear. One viewer seemed to express the views of many when they complained: "Now it has been made clear that we shan't see a 'victim' refuse to appear . . . there is no point in even viewing the first five minutes".[103] This confirms that the controversy over *TIYL*, as well as its frisson of excitement, was intrinsically related to the temporality of *live* television, and its claim to spontaneity and authenticity. As this era of television was now passing, the decision to alter the format seemed to happen after the fact.

"The face behind the public face": *Face to Face* (1959–62)

From a contemporary perspective, this chapter has positioned *TIYL*, as well as its cultural reception, as at once strange *and* familiar. The outrage surrounding the programme points to a different set of attitudes toward celebrity culture, its relations with public/private, and television's role in mediating these spheres. At the same time, with the desire to capture the self "off-guard", to peep behind the masquerade of public performance (particularly as signified through the intimacy of emotional response), *TIYL* seems to be marching toward the present.

The BBC's interview-in-depth programme, *Face to Face*, beginning in 1959, already gestured toward this development. The first section of this chapter referred to David Wainwright's comment in 1960 that people were now only "'celebrities', [if they] . . . have the 'public face' that television requires".[104] But *TIYL* might suggest that television was one step ahead of Wainwright's commentary, aiming, from an early stage, to probe "behind" this face as much as promote it. From this perspective, *Face to Face* is significant for suggesting a strengthening of this claim where television was concerned. According to its Producer, Hugh Burnett, *Face to Face* aimed to reveal "the face behind the public face of anybody prepared to . . . show themselves",[105] and its interviewer, John Freeman, proudly explained how he didn't want to know "what a member of the cabinet thinks about the cabinet, but rather to find out about the nightmare he had last night".[106] The programme interviewed a wide range of people with vastly different backgrounds and careers, moving across cabinet ministers, royalty, philosophers, literary geniuses, sportsmen, artists, film directors, film stars, singers and television entertainers. Some of the many guests included King Hussein of Jordan, Nubar Gulbenkian, Martin Luther King, Aristotle Onassis, Carl Jung, milords Birkett, Boothby and Shawcross, Stirling Moss, Evelyn Waugh, Augustus John, Noel Coward, Lord Reith, John Osborne, John Houston, Albert Finney, Simone Signoret, Sir Laurence Olivier, Adam Faith, Gilbert Harding and Tony Hancock. There was some overlap between *TIYL* and *Face to Face* where names from the arts were concerned, but *Face to Face*, which was produced by Talks rather than Light Entertainment, saw itself as adopting a more serious remit.

Particularly when compared to the distaste for *TIYL*, that "sentimental slush" and "great gooey meringue", it is not coincidental that this seriousness emerged from a more masculinised framework. The interviewer was required to display the qualities of an aggressive "tenacity [and] . . . obstinacy",[107] and in terms of the guests themselves, women appeared infrequently (the original working title was actually *Men of the Moment*).[108] In ways which distinguished it from *TIYL*, Freeman's background also lent the programme a certain political legitimacy. He had been a Socialist MP, had previously worked on the BBC's *Panorama*, and was to become the editor of the *New Statesman* while *Face to Face* was still on air. *Face to Face* seemed keen to associate itself with the spheres of current affairs, and through the rhetoric of current affairs, television could claim it was getting close to its subject in order to offer a "public look" (Jacobs, 2000: 159). Yet in relation to *Face to Face*, the subject matter was clearly more autobiographical than "current". Furthermore, and as Freeman's comment about the cabinet minister makes clear, it was far more interested in the "private" self than the public role.

The programme's intention of probing the "off-stage" self influenced its verbal, as well as its visual rhetoric. Freeman asked questions which probed more deeply into the person's private life than was common in the television interview (and Gilbert Harding is quizzed mercilessly on everything from his dreams, disappointments, to his attitude toward punishment or physical pain). But it is clear that the premise of *Face to Face* rested on two assumptions: first, that public selves were the products of constructed personae, and second, that television had the capacity to uncover the "real", authentic self before the viewer's eyes. This epistemological claim sat at the core of *TIYL*, but it did so more tentatively and nervously when compared to *Face to Face*. Further foregrounding the gendered inflections at work here, *Face to Face* is bolder and more aggressive in its intentions, and television now seems sure that it wants to showcase what it can do.

Face to Face was influenced by the American interview series *Person to Person* (1953–61) which was hosted by the distinguished journalist, Ed Murrow.[109] In both Britain and America, the interview-in-depth technique had been part of radio journalism, and Burnett had previously worked on the BBC's *Personal Call* in the 1940s. But the idea of revealing the "face behind the public face" took on quite literal connotations in the context of television. In Burnett's original conception of the programme, he explains how he intends to:

> [hide] the interviewer and concentrate the cameras exclusively on the subject under scrutiny. This is a new departure for television, producing extremely interesting results. The viewer at home can concentrate and indulge his curiosity in an interrupted scrutiny of the face of the public figure under pressure.[110]

Commercial television (TWW) offered a rival programme called *Two's Company* (1961), but it lacked the distinctive visual style of *Face to Face*.

Freeman was either off-camera, or he was glimpsed partially from behind – silhouetted in the dark. In contrast, the subject was picked out under a harsh white light, framed in an *extraordinarily* tight and unwavering close-up. While in the *TIYL* edition featuring Anna Neagle, it was hard to locate the much criticised close-up, in *Face to Face* it takes centre stage, and the proximity between subject and camera is far closer than is customary in the television interview today. As Medhurst observes in his discussion of Gilbert Harding's appearance, the lighting and staging of the programme prefigured the quiz show *Mastermind*, while the "specialist subject" was always the person's own self (1991: 64). Although *Face to Face* also received considerable praise, with Freeman heralded as introducing the interviewing "style of the future",[111] it was certainly criticised as intrusive. Comparisons with interrogation were frequently noted, and BBC Audience Research recorded complaints about the subjects "sweating under police interrogation" or "positively frying under the lamps".[112] The moment in 1960 when Gilbert Harding "cracks", wobbling on the brink of tears when asked about the subject of death (which reminds him of his late mother), still retains its extraordinary, and uncomfortable, power. This edition in particular gave rise to a broader debate about the social encounter of the television interview, and its ethical, political and social implications (see also Bell and van Leuwen, 1994).

Face to Face seems exemplary of what Gamson (2001) describes as key trends in celebrity construction from the post-war period onwards. With a greater supply of celebrities, a heightened awareness of media construction,[113] and a gradual destabilisation of more traditional explanations of fame, there is an increased emphasis on a "behind-the-scenes" rhetoric. In aiming to protect the authenticity of the celebrity enterprise, this instructs "the [audience] . . . further in reading performances, finding the 'real' behind the 'image' . . . If there is a problem in peeling away the veneer, viewers need simply be given better viewing tools" (Gamson, 2001: 274).

Harding was perpetually plagued by the sense that his work in Light Entertainment had sold short what Freeman calls his "first-class mind" (Medhurst, 1991: 66). In comparison, *Hancock's Half Hour* (BBC, 1956–60) on television was a critical and popular success, and Hancock was acknowledged as a clear comic talent. But there was nevertheless the suggestion – from viewers and critics – that people *from* television would not provide sufficient "depth" for the programme's probing approach. Hancock's uniquely "expressive face" was pivotal to the visual comedy of *Hancock's Half Hour* (Goddard, 1991: 82), but on *Face to Face* it was seen in a different light. Hancock was seen "drawing feverishly" on a cigarette stub, and offering "the outpourings of a confused mind".[114] Viewers referred to him as a "fish out of water" who seemed "unable to cope with the stringent demands of the programme", and there was an expression of "surprise at the lack of fluency and wit (bearing in mind his amusing series)".[115] Although many viewers sympathised with Harding's "tortuous ordeal", responses to his interview similarly skirted around the sense that he was not a legitimate subject for the programme in the first place.

These reservations reflect on the cultural value of fame in what one critic called the "peculiarly ephemeral world of television".[116] But they also indicate how these judgements are *shaped by* television's perceived relations with familiarity and intimacy. They lead us back to the argument that the medium appears to collapse the distance between the "real" and the role (Langer, 1981, Ellis, 1992). Despite the differences in their public, television roles, there was a greater level of shock at how *Face to Face* revealed an apparent disjuncture between "brilliant comic"/confused Tony, and "Old Crust"/tearful Harding. Was this because, in comparison with the other guests, viewers had been encouraged to locate the "real" self somewhere within the on-screen role? Perhaps. But this chapter has also aimed to question whether this argument captures the range of meanings, and discursive structures, which structure television fame, and which television history can help to bring into view.

Gilbert Harding's appearance on *Face to Face* represents television cannibalising its own creation (and by 1959, Harding, along with Sylvia Peters, Mary Malcolm, Joan Gilbert, Jeanne Heale and Philip Harben, had already been described as "TV beachcombers, picking up whatever crumbs they can get from the tables of a whole bunch of new stars"[117]). But it also represents the fusion of the two spheres explored in this chapter. Television constructs its own personalities, while it circulates, and reframes, famous faces from other domains. This distinction has never been clear cut, and it has certainly become progressively blurred since the 1950s: the majority of people appearing on television chat, talk and magazine shows are now celebrities *from* television itself. But in examining this earlier period, this chapter has argued that there is value in returning to such distinctions in aiming to capture the range of meanings which structured television's relations with fame, while simultaneously retaining the depth and insight offered by the case study.

TGF, *TIYL* and *Face to Face* do not necessarily offer oppositional discourses on television fame, and they all pivot on television's search for intimacy and familiarity. As Langer observes, television's "talk shows, interviews, [and] talking heads" are bids to incorporate the guest into "television's personality system by disclosing for the purposes of television, one's 'personality'" (Langer, 1981: 360). In relation to film, this search for intimacy takes place on an extratextual level, but television incorporates it "as a routine part of its discourse" (ibid). The conventions of television were not necessarily "routine" in the 1950s, however, and Langer's perspective reinforces the idea that television's relations with fame are safe, conservative and reassuring, when cultural commentators of the time saw them as anything *but*. Given that the argument that television does not "produce stars of . . . complexity, depth and cultural value", especially when compared to film, is often yoked to its "essential familiarity and intimacy" (Becker, 2005: 9), this seems important. It is clear that more needs to be done to examine the relationship between longer, macro narratives (such as Gamson's, 1994, 2001), and the inflections of particular historical and national case studies. In the examples offered here, discourses of "ordinariness" or "authenticity" do not emerge as innate qualities of the medium. In relation to *TGF*, these discourses were intimately linked to the programme's particular audience address, and its relations with class verisimilitude. In relation to *TIYL*, and through a range of registers specific to television's aesthetic and technological capacities in the mid- to late 1950s, discourses of authenticity and ordinariness were associated with the televisual apparatus itself.

But *TIYL* does not just offer a snapshot of cultural attitudes toward fame: it also represents a highly visible cultural site for the expression of anxieties surrounding popular television in Britain in the mid to late 1950s. In relation to this, and within the context of this book, it is worth reiterating that it was a programme absolutely identified with the BBC. The BBC took on the format well aware of its controversial American reputation, and despite all the bids to "tame" the unruly nature of its popular appeal, the BBC *wanted it*, and weathered a barrage of criticism which makes the initial reaction to Reality TV look tame.

Given the current surge of interest in celebrity culture, it seems more important than ever to recover neglected debates, moments and junctures from the past. Critics exclaiming in the 1950s that "celebrities crying in close-up is surely not the future of television!"[118] may have been interested to witness the later development of celebrity Reality TV. In *TIYL* we can locate the germ of the desire to capture the self off-guard, to probe into the interior, "private" space that resides behind public performance, particularly as mediated through emotional response. It seems that far from belonging to an earlier era, part of the problem with this programme was that it appeared before its time.

Notes

1 Huw Wheldon to Alan Lawson, 22 July 1955. T32/1,777/1.
2 Audience Research report, *Is This Your Problem?*, 10 November 1955 and 29 September 1955.
3 Nest Bradley to Head of Publicity, 29 September 1958. T16/168/2.
4 *The Star*, 24 April 1955.
5 *Radio Times*, 22 February 1957, p. 22.
6 *The People*, 10 May 1959.
7 *The Star*, 24 July 1955.
8 Undated memo, "Future attitude toward sponsored television organisations", T16/48.
9 Ronald Waldman to Director of Television Broadcasting, "Notes on BBC Light Entertainment (Television)", 18 January 1960. T16/91/2.
10 "You see – TV's only got six stars . . .", *Picturegoer*, 18 June 1955, p. 26.
11 "Celebrity", *Weekly Post*, 26 November 1960.
12 "Petty Politics", *News Chronicle*, 12 June 1952.
13 "TV Oomph", *Daily Express*, 22 January 1951.
14 "The Sabrina Phenomenon", *Sunday Express*, 20 March 1956.
15 "Sabrina Scare", *Sunday Graphic and Sunday News*, 16 September 1955.
16 Valued for their looks rather than their work, female celebrities are more likely to be invoked as emblematic of the decline of a merited-claim-to-fame (Geraghty, 2000: 187). Modern examples in Britain would be Jordan (Katie Price) or Jodie Marsh. The construction of Sabrina can be situated in relation to the circulation of other "blonde bombshells" in the 1950s (such as Marilyn Monroe, Jayne Mansfield and Diana Dors), although it is important to recognise that she is invoked to express anxieties about the cultural status and possibilities of television fame.
17 *TV Mirror*, 9 January 1954, p. 12.
18 *TV Mirror*, 24 April 1954, p. 11.
19 *News Chronicle*, 5 November 1951.
20 John Warrington, 2 April 1954. T12/137/20; original emphasis.
21 Both the American series were imported in Britain: *I Love Lucy* was screened on ITV1, and *The Burns and Allen Show* on the BBC.
22 Given the perceived differences between cinematic and televisual fame, it is interesting to note that *It's a Great Day* had a cinema release in 1956.
23 John Warrington to Head of Light Entertainment, 8 October 1956. T12/137/4.
24 Andy Medhurst, *The Lime Grove Story* (BBC1, 26 July 1991).
25 As above.
26 John Warrington to Head of Light Entertainment, 9 September 1954. T12/137/1.
27 *Evening Standard*, 14 September 1955.
28 *TV Mirror*, 14 November 1953, p. 19.
29 "The Groves – Home and Away", *Radio Times Annual*, 1955. T12/137/20.

30 "Know Anyone Like Granny?", *Daily Herald*, 1 October 1955.

31 *Evening News*, 27 August 1954.

32 *Evening Telegraph and Post*, 9 January 1956.

33 *Daily Sketch*, 17 October 1955.

34 *Daily Herald*, 19 June 1951.

35 *Answers*, 13 January 1951.

36 *Good Housekeeping*, 11 March 1952.

37 *Evening Standard*, 28 November 1951.

38 John Warrington to Head of Light Entertainment, 31 May 1954. T12/137/1.

39 *Daily Sketch*, 5 January 1955.

40 Elizabeth Wilson, *The Lime Grove Story*.

41 The emphasis on the "Girls Next Door" might productively be considered in relation to the argument that stars represent social types in television as well as film (Dyer, 1998).

42 Venetia Murray, "The Dream Girls Next Door," *Picture Post*, 12 November 1955; original emphasis.

43 *Daily Mail*, 17 March 1954.

44 *Daily Mail*, 28 April 1955.

45 *Radio Times*, 25 April 1955.

46 Undated memo, c. 1953. T12/137/20.

47 "Mrs Dale's Diary", undated editorial policy, R19/779/2.

48 *Yorkshire Evening Post*, 31 May 1961.

49 T. Leslie Jackson to Head of Light Entertainment, 12 July 1955. T12/522/1.

50 "The Future of This is Your Life", 27 February 1961. Controller of Television Programmes to Director of Television Broadcasting. T16/590.

51 As above.

52 "Policy", Stuart Hood to Director of Television Broadcasting, 9 March 1961. T16/590.

53 "TV Policy, This is Your Life", 8 February 1961. T16/590.

54 *Daily Herald*, 18 November 1958.

55 See for example *Manchester Guardian*, 25 January 1957.

56 *Daily Express*, 19 February 1958.

57 *Western Mail*, 25 March 1958.

58 *Manchester City News*, 4 April 1958.

59 *Stage*, 4 December 1958.

60 *Daily Mirror*, 6 January 1959.

61 *Daily Mirror*, 18 February 1960.

62 *Daily Mirror*, undated, cited in "General Press Comment on 'This is Your Life'", undated. T16/590.

63 *Daily Mirror*, 7 January 1959.

64 *Daily Mail*, 30 July 1955.

65 *Sunday Telegraph*, 14 May 1961.

66 Untitled press clipping, 15 October 1958.

67 *Daily Express*, 19 February 1958.

68 Controller of Television Programmes to Director of Television Broadcasting, 21 November 1955. T12/522/1.
69 Kenneth Adam to Director of Television Broadcasting, 21 November 1955. T12/522/1.
70 *This is Your Life* script, Norman Wisdom.
71 Ronald Waldman to Head of Purchasing, Television, 29 June 1955. T12/522/1.
72 *News Chronicle*, 2 February 1959.
73 Undated memo, but c. 1955. T12/522/1.
74 T. Leslie Jackson to Mrs A. F. Oliver, 22 May 1958. T12/503/2.
75 Transmitted 14 October 1957.
76 *Yorkshire Evening Post*, 22 January 1958.
77 *Observer*, 31 July 1955.
78 *Daily Herald*, 4 October 1960.
79 Controller of Television Programmes to Director of Television Broadcasting, 21 November 1955. T12/522/1.
80 Viewer Research Report, *This is Your Life*, 25 September 1955.
81 Controller of Television Programmes to Head of Light Entertainment, 29 November 1955. T12/522/1.
82 Controller of Television Programmes to Director of Television Broadcasting, 21 November 1955. T12/522/1; my emphasis.
83 It did not appear to have this name in its very early years.
84 *Evening Standard*, 15 January 1958.
85 "Notes on the Future of Light Entertainment", 1960. T16/91/2.
86 *Sunday Dispatch*, 11 May 1958.
87 *Daily Express*, 18 February 1958.
88 *Manchester City News*, 4 April 1958.
89 Audience Research Report, *This is Your Life*, 17 February 1958.
90 *Daily Express*, 19 February 1958.
91 *Daily Telegraph*, 18 January 1957.
92 *Sunday Dispatch*, 5 November 1958.
93 *Daily Sketch*, 30 July 1955.
94 *Manchester City News*, 4 April 1956.
95 *Manchester Guardian*, 22 January 1957.
96 Assistant Head of Light Entertainment to Director of Television Broadcasting, "Policy", 12 June 1960. T16/590.
97 Untitled press report, 9 February 1961.
98 "General Press Comment on This is Your Life", T16/590.
99 *Yorkshire Evening Post*, 3 March 1961.
100 *Everybody's*, 1 November 1961.
101 "TV Policy, This is Your Life", undated memo, T16/590.
102 Michael Mills to Head of Light Entertainment, 20 January 1965. T12/1,302/1.
103 *Daily Mail*, 8 February 1961.
104 "Celebrity", *Weekly Post*, 26 November 1960.

105 *The Unknown Hancock* (BBC2, 26 December 2005).
106 *Good Housekeeping*, 4 July 1960.
107 As above.
108 Head of Talks, Television to Hugh Burnett, 9 December 1958. T32/640/1.
109 Hugh Burnett to Assistant Head of Television, 27 February 1958. T32/640/1.
110 Undated memo, Hugh Burnett. T32/640/2.
111 *Birmingham Evening Mail*, 1 February 1959.
112 BBC Audience Research Report, *Face to Face*, 28 September 1960.
113 In this respect it would be interesting to consider the relationship between the construction of celebrity culture and the satire boom in the 1960s, from magazines such as *Private Eye* to television's *That Was the Week That Was*.
114 Audience Research Report, *Face to Face*, 7 February 1960.
115 Audience Research Report, 7 February 1960.
116 *Guardian*, 19 September 1960.
117 *The People*, 10 May 1959.
118 *Evening News*, 20 December 1959.

Conclusion: "There's nothing *really* better than what you're *used* to, is there?"

In discussing "The Television Archive: Past, Present and Future", Jacobs describes the need to be "alive to the possibility of contingent opportunities that the archive may hide" (2006: 18). This involves:

> [r]epeated periods of blind searching, rogue searching, or "chancing it" in the hope that something relevant will turn up, or what seemed irrelevant takes on a new significance in the light of additional findings: one gradually discovers a sharper grasp of history or *even discovers a history one had not anticipated* (Jacobs, 2000: 17; my italics).

To some extent, this book is the product of "chancing it". My first foray into the television archives was when undertaking doctoral research into the 1950s British cinema programme, and I repeatedly found that my *own* expectations of BBC television from this time (elitist, dismissive of popular film culture?) were reshaped and challenged. Having read about the institutional background to the early co-existence of BBC and ITV, ranging across institutional attitudes, ratings discourse and audience address, I was surprised to find a good many similarities in their cinema programmes. In fact, I discovered a BBC which positively celebrated popular film culture, aggressively pursued access to the film stars (it got the big Hollywood names more often than ITV), and previewed some of the more risqué "Continentals" that were finding an increasing circulation in Britain at this time (Holmes, 2005a). In moving away from this particular genre, I wanted to tell a broader story about what I had encountered, and I hoped that I would find the programmes, and the evidence, to do this. Yet while the quote from Jacobs suggests the value of a research experience which is open and contingent, pleasurably uncertain of its own direction, any project progressively takes on the characteristics of a firmer agenda. So what of my agenda here?

In *The History of Broadcasting in the United Kingdom' Volume V: Competition*, Briggs details the vehement criticism levelled at ITV's programming by the *Manchester Guardian* critic Bernard Levin. After six months of viewing the new channel, Levin:

> [a]llotted 160 minutes of ITV programming to category X – neutral, 320 to category A ("programmes which people of taste and intelligence might be able to watch for two hours a week without actually feeling ill"), 345 minutes to category B ("ordinary trash") and 1,195 minutes to category C ("not fit to be fed to the cat"). (Briggs, 1995: 13)

There is a sense in which an overriding aim of this book, perhaps somewhat unusually, has been to try and convince the reader that this description could just as easily have been of the BBC. As discussed in Chapter 1, while a key intention has been to rehabilitate the historical value of popular programming often dismissed by critics at the time (and then subsequently ignored or marginalised by television historiography), the book also wanted to demonstrate that BBC television in the 1950s was more derided, "trashy", controversial and populist than existing historical accounts would have us believe.

But there is of course a wider question as to why this (ultimately modest agenda) matters at all, and I think it matters for a number of reasons which relate to the project of television historiography, as well as to the specific contours of television history in the British context. At a time when the archival study of particular programmes and genres is continuing to expand, there is a need to perpetually reassess the relationship between wider macro – and often institutional – narratives and the knowledge emerging from case studies or texts. The increasing shift toward studies of historical programme cultures is not only contributing, with the "qualities of depth and sustained scrutiny" (Corner, 2003: 275), to an existing body of knowledge, but it is making knowledge about television available in new ways. This history also matters in terms of approaching the relations between public service television and the popular – a relationship which continues, perhaps more so than ever, to represent a pressing topic of debate (see van Zoonen, 2004). If the topics and genres covered in this book can be characterised, in Bourdon's (2004) terms, as "ghosts" which have haunted the confrontations between public service television and the popular, then their significance lingers on in new forms and guises. In terms of the particular context of *British* television (and broadcasting) history, this narrative matters in terms of how we think about the institutional identity of the BBC, how we conceptualise television's relationship with the emerging mass audience in the 1950s, how we think about the historical emergence of particular genres, and how we understand the aesthetic development of television at this time.

But in adopting a self-reflexive attitude to the process of constructing history, the "new historian" also lays claim to a "subjective and 'intimate relation' with their historical project" (Sobchack, 2000: 301, in Johnson, 2006), and this is also related to why the contents of this book matter (to me). In undertaking archival research, it is possible to feel what Jacobs aptly describes as "the sheer palpability of history in the texture, colour and smell of written files" (Jacobs, 2006: 17), and there is also the privileged feeling of opening up what they might hold. As part of this experience I repeatedly encountered sincere and enthusiastic attempts to conceptualise, produce and explore television programming which would speak to popular pleasures and desires. Thus, to read the polarised constructions of BBC and ITV, in which the "stuffy" and "paternalistic" Corporation is variously accused of "ignoring" the viewer, or of failing to address the interests of the expanding mass viewership for television, is to deny that this history – and my journey through its fragments – ever existed. But in foregrounding a more active intervention (we do not, of course, just piece together fragments), I am no doubt drawn to this material, and to arguing for its significance for television historiography, because my own viewing pleasures are resolutely populist (as my colleagues and students will quickly confirm). Much of what I have "seen" in this history, and the connections made between now and then, has been inflected by the fact that I keep up with more than one soap, adore *Big Brother*, purchase celebrity magazines and am regularly entertained by quiz or talk shows.

Each chapter has offered its own conclusion, and the differences between the programmes should be allowed to breathe. But across the case studies, it often seemed from the BBC's perspective that the popular, somehow perceived as dangerously fluid and powerful, was to be netted like a shoal of fishes, harnessed and contained. The story told in this book is certainly best characterised as less an active *pursuit* of the popular than a qualified engagement with it. But it is an engagement which is no less significant for sometimes being tentative and contradictory. Indeed, it is precisely this movement back and forth which seems dynamic and exciting, and which keeps the historian on their toes. Without a doubt, case studies could confirm and challenge existing perceptions of the BBC simultaneously, refusing to lie still for reconstruction and analysis.

But there are two key points to make here. First, although internal written material on ITV programmes from the 1950s does exist, including, for example, that contained in the Sidney Bernstein Collection (Granada) and the ITC Collection (now held by the BFI), it is far less

extensive than that relating to the BBC. It would not have been possible
to produce a similar narrative of the internal struggles and tensions surrounding these genres on ITV – even if such a narrative existed. But it
seems to be precisely the point that we don't *know* if it did. Certainly,
there were likely to have been differences, and it is perhaps easy to
assume that some of the debates were "uniquely BBC". But the available
evidence limits the scope for a parallel narrative and comparison to
emerge here. Second, this project has drawn attention to the different
traces left by archival evidence, not simply in terms of a contrast between
audiovisual and written sources, but the layering of discourses *within*
and across written material. The significance of American television in
this book is a case in point. Far from the BBC simply taking "occasional
glimpses, not always in envy, across the Atlantic" (Briggs, 1979: 279), it
is clear in looking at entertainment programming that the interaction was
extensive, not only in terms of format adaptation, but as regards the circulation of ideas and concepts. Camporesi is right that within this
process, American radio/television was often held up as the "imperfect
model", but she also observes the presence of a double articulation in
which, while the "*official emphasis* was always . . . on the conflicting
aims of two diverging systems of broadcasting" (1994: 626; my emphasis), the BBC was simultaneously scoping out American formats for
British use. Similarly, at Programme Boards or meetings with the BBC's
Board of Governors, a series such as *This is Your Life* is understood to
be about celebrating the commendable deeds of ordinary people. But in
the more routine rhythms of programme production, there is little doubt
that it was recognised as a "compulsive" format, the pleasure of which
pivoted on its "shock and stunt value".[1] This framework is part of the
sophisticated, although that is not to imply conspiratorial, way in which
the BBC weaves stories around its own programmes – stories which we
encounter and then rearticulate as television historians.

In this respect, television history emerges in many forms, academic,
popular, biographical, personal, and it is also self-consciously made by
television itself. It is often interesting to note the circulation of what
Bignell refers to as the medium's own "retelling of its history" (2005b:
60). Documentaries on the history of BBC radio and television positively
revel in perceptions of the Corporation's class elitism – its stringent
patrolling of moral boundaries, or its suppression of popular taste. In
The Lime Grove Story: The Grove Family (26 August 1991), the programme gathers together academics, BBC personnel and ex-cast
members to construct an overall image of the serial which fixes its status
as an instrument of education. This is bolstered by a keen emphasis on
the programme's conservative representation of gender roles, class, youth

and family values, as consolidated by an image of Mrs Grove (played in a reconstructed sequence by the then *Brookside* actress Sue Johnston), in which she addresses the viewer with the rhetorical question: "There's nothing *really* better than what you're *used* to, is there?" Similarly, in *The Story of Light Entertainment* (BBC2, 3 September 2006), *Face to Face* is positioned as distinctly "unshowbiz" in its bid to insert political leaders, royalty or geniuses alongside film, television or sport stars. This description in itself is less problematic, but it is then used as evidence of how "the BBC avoided celebrity *again*" (again?). Little wonder, then, that in this narrative, *This is Your Life* hardly receives a mention, a programme which kept the terms celebrity, controversy and BBC in constant company from the mid 1950s to the mid 1960s. Finally, this image of good old "Auntie" BBC is also functional at an institutional level. Public service broadcasters point to the unique nature of their institutional histories when under threat, and the constructions above might be seen as part of a process in which the BBC shores up its status as a quality "brand".

Across the case studies examined here, it is not difficult to see an ultimate bid to promote highly normative family values (*The Grove Family*, *Is This Your Problem?*), to observe distaste for the "gambling" working-class (the quiz/game show) or to witness attempts to discipline the wayward visual possibilities of television (*Is This Your Problem?*, *This is Your Life*). But it is also difficult to avoid the presence of those "criminal lunatics" brandishing a meat-axe in the Grove family kitchen, Pat Grove eyeing marriage and domesticity with a wary eye, the twisting and turning hands of that "Unmarried Mother", or the BBC's decision to exploit a format which had already outraged American critics. While critics in the 1950s worried over viewers of *This is Your Life* developing an "insatiable addiction to shockers [and] shocks",[2] it is in fact possible to become "desensitised" to these research surprises. They become looked for, expected and anticipated, and it then becomes necessary to start "blind searching, rogue searching, or 'chancing it'" (Jacobs, 2006: 17) – all over again.

Notes

1 Controller of Television Programmes to Head of Light Entertainment, 29 November 1955. T12/522/1.
2 *Stage*, 4 December 1958.

Bibliography

Addison, Paul (1985) *Now the War is Over: A Social History of Britain 1945–51*, London: BBC/Jonathan Cape.

Allen, Robert (1988) *Speaking of Soap Operas*, Chapel Hill and London: University of North Carolina Press.

Altman, Rick (1999) *Film/Genre*, London: BFI.

Anant, Victor (1955) "The 'Give-Away' Shows – Who is Really Paying?", *Picture Post*, 10 December, p. 27.

Anderson, Kent (1978) *Television Fraud: The History and Implications of the Quiz Show Scandals*, Westport, CT: Greenwood Press.

Ang, Ien (1985) *Watching Dallas: Soap Opera and the Melodramatic Imagination*, London: Methuen.

—— (1991) *Desperately Seeking the Audience*, London: Routledge.

Arnheim, Rudolph (1944) "The World of the Daytime Radio Serial", in Paul F. Lazarsfeld and Frank M. Stanton, *Radio Research 1942–43*, New York: Hawthorne Books (repr. Arno, 1979), pp. 83–84.

Aslama, Minna and Mervi Pantti (2006) "Talking Alone: Reality TV, Emotions and Authenticity", *European Journal of Cultural Studies*, 9 (2), pp. 167–184.

Babington, Bruce (2001) "Introduction: British Stars and Stardom", in Babington (ed.), *British Stars and Stardom: From Alma Taylor to Sean Connery*, Manchester: Manchester University Press, pp. 1–28.

Barnard, Stephen (1989) *On the Radio: Music Radio in Britain*, Milton Keynes: Open University Press.

Becker, Christine (2005) "Televising Film Stardom in the 1950s", *Framework*, 26 (2), pp. 5–21.

Bell, Philip and Theo van Leuwen (1994) *The Media Interview: Confession, Contest and Conversation*, Sydney: NSW Press.

Benjamin, Walter (1973) *Illuminations*, London: Collins.

Bennett, James (2006) "Review of Janet Thumim, *Inventing Television Culture: Men, Women and the Box* and William Boddy, *New Media and Popular Imagination: Launching Radio, Television and Digital Media in the United States*", *Screen*, 47 (1), pp. 119–124.

Bennett, Tony (1980) "Popular Culture: A Teaching Object", *Screen Education*, 34 (Spring), pp. 17–30.

—— (1998) "Popular Culture and the Turn to Gramsci", in John Storey (ed.), *Cultural Theory and Popular Culture: A Reader* (2nd edn), London: Prentice Hall, pp. 217–224.

Bernbaum, Gerald (1967) *Social Change and the Schools*, London: Routledge and Kegan Paul.

Bignell, Jonathan (2005a) "Exemplarity, Pedagogy and Television History", *New Review of Film and Television*, 3 (1), pp. 15–32.

—— (2005b) "And the Rest is History: Lew Grade, Creation Narratives and Television Historiography", in Catherine Johnson and Rob Turnock (eds.), *ITV Cultures: Independent Television Over Fifty Years*, Buckingham: Open University Press, pp. 57–70.

Bird, S. Elizabeth (2003) *The Audience in Everyday Life: Living in a Media World*, London: Routledge.

Biressi, Anita and Heather Nunn (2005) *Reality TV: Realism and Revelation*, London: Wallflower.

Black, Peter (1972) *The Mirror in the Corner: People"s Television*, London: Hutchinson.

Boddy, William (1990) *Fifties Television: The Industry and its Critics*, Urbana: University of Illinois Press.

—— (2004) *New Media and Popular Imagination: Launching Radio, Television and Digital Media in the United States*, Oxford: Oxford University Press.

Bonner, Frances (2003) *Ordinary Television*, London: Sage.

Boorstin, Daniel (1971) *The Image: A Guide to Pseudo-Events in America*, New York: Atheneum.

Bourdieu, Pierre (1986) *Distinction: A Social Critique of the Judgement of Taste*, London: Routledge.

Bourdon, Jerome (2004) "Old and New Ghosts: Public Service Television and the Popular – a History", *European Journal of Cultural Studies*, 7 (3), pp. 283–304.

Branston, Gill (1998) "Histories of British Television", in Christine Geraghty and David Lusted (eds.), *The Television Studies Book*, London: Arnold, pp. 51–62.

Braudy, Leo (1986) *The Frenzy of Renown: Fame and its History*, Oxford: Oxford University Press.

Briggs, Asa (1961) *The History of Broadcasting in the United Kingdom, volume 1: The Birth of Broadcasting*, Oxford: Oxford University Press.

—— (1965) *The History of Broadcasting in the United Kingdom, volume 2: The Golden Age of Wireless*, Oxford: Oxford University Press.

—— (1979) *The History of Broadcasting in the United Kingdom, volume 3: The War of Words*, Oxford: Oxford University Press.

—— (1979) *The History of Broadcasting in the United Kingdom, volume 4: Sound and Vision*, Oxford: Oxford University Press.

—— (1995) *The History of Broadcasting in the United Kingdom, volume 5: Competition*, Oxford: Oxford University Press.

Brunsdon, Charlotte (1997) *Screen Tastes: Soap Opera to Satellite Dishes*, London: Routledge.

Brunvatne, Raina and Andrew Tolson (2001) " 'It Makes it Okay to Cry': Two Types of 'Therapy Talk' in TV Talk Shows", in Tolson (ed.), *Television Talk Shows: Discourse, Performance, Spectacle*, London: Lawrence Erlbaum, pp. 139–154.

Buscombe, Ed (1980) "Broadcasting from Above", *Screen Education*, 81 (47), pp. 73–78.

Butler, Jeremy (2002) *Television: Critical Methods and Applications*, London: Lawrence Erlbaum.

Camporesi, Valeria (1993) *Mass Culture and the Defence of National Traditions: The BBC and American Broadcasting, 1922–54*, Florence: European University Institute.

—— (1994) "The BBC and American Broadcasting, 1922–55", *Media, Culture and Society*, 16, pp. 625–639.

Cannadine, David (1998) *Class in Britain*, London: Penguin.

Cassidy, Marsha F. (2005) *What Women Watched: Daytime Television in the 1950s*, Austin: University of Texas Press.

Chaney, David (1993) *Fictions of Collective Life: Public Drama in Late Modern Culture*, London: Routledge.

Clarke, Michael (1987) "Quiz and Game Shows", in Clarke, *Teaching Popular Television*, London: Methuen, pp. 49–61.

Conrad, Peter (1982) *Television: The Medium and its Manners*, London: Routledge and Kegan Paul.

Cooke, Lez (2003) *British Television Drama: A History*, London: BFI.

Corner, John (1991) (ed.) *Popular Television in Britain: Studies in Cultural History*, London: BFI.

—— (1996) *The Art of Record*, Manchester: Manchester University Press.

—— (2000) "What Can We Say about Documentary?", *Media, Culture and Society*, 22, pp. 681–688.

—— (2003) "Finding Data, Reading Patterns, Telling Stories: Issues in the Historiography of Television", *Media, Culture and Society*, 25, pp. 273–280.

Couldry, Nick (2000) *The Place of Media Power: Pilgrims and Witnesses of the Media Age*, London: Routledge.

Crisell, Andrew (2001) *An Introductory History of British Broadcasting* (2nd edn), London: Routledge.

Dahlgren, Peter (1995) *Television and the Public Sphere: Citizenship, Democracy and the Media*, London: Sage.

—— (2000) "Key Trends in European Television", in Jan Wieten, Peter Dahlgren and Graham Murdock (eds.), *Television Across Europe: A Comparative Introduction*, London: Sage, pp. 25–34.

Davie, Grace (1994) "Religion in Post-war Britain: a Sociological View", in James Obelkevich and Peter Catterall (eds.), *Understanding Post-war British Society*, London: Routledge, pp. 165–177.

Davis, Victor (2002) "The Father of Scandal", *British Journalism Review*, 13 (4), pp. 74–80.

deCordova, Richard (1990) *Picture Personalities: The Emergence of the Star System in America*, Urbana and Chicago: University of Illinois Press.

Dent, C. (1949) *Secondary Education for All*, London: Routledge and Kegan Paul.

DeLong, Thomas A. (1991) *Quiz Craze: America's Infatuation with Game Shows*, New York: Praeger.

Desjardins, Mary (2002) "Maureen O'Hara's "'Confidential'" Life: Recycling Stars Through Gossip and Moral Biography", in Janet Thumim (ed.), *Small Screen, Big Ideas: Television in the 1950s*, London: I.B. Tauris, pp. 118–130.

Dovey, Jon (2000) *Freakshow: First Person Media and Factual Television*, London: Pluto.

Dyer, Richard (1973) *Light Entertainment*, London: BFI.
—— (1986) *Heavenly Bodies: Film Stars and Society*, London: Routledge.
—— (1998) (2nd edn) *Stars*, London: BFI.
Ellis, John ([1982] 1992) (2nd edn) *Visible Fictions: Cinema, Television, Video*, London: Routledge.
—— (2000) *Seeing Things: Television in the Age of Uncertainty*, London: I.B. Tauris.
Evans, Jeff (1995) *The Guinness Television Encyclopaedia*, London: Guinness World Records Ltd.
Fiske, John (1987) *Television Culture*, London: Routledge.
—— (1992) "Popularity and the Politics of Information", in Peter Dahlgren and Colin Sparks (eds.), *Journalism and Popular Culture*, London: Sage, pp. 45–63.
Fiske, John and John Hartley (1978) *Reading Television*, London: Methuen.
Foucault, Michel (1970) *The Order of Things: An Archaeology of the Human Sciences*, London: Tavistock.
—— (1990) *The Will to Knowledge: The History of Sexuality*, vol. 1, London: Vintage.
Friedan, Betty (1963) *The Feminine Mystique*, New York: W.W. Norton.
Furedi, Frank (2004) *Therapy Culture: Cultivating Uncertainty in an Uncertain Age*, London: Routledge.
Gamson, Joshua (1994) *Claims to Fame: Celebrity in Contemporary America*, Berkeley: University of California Press.
—— (1999) "Taking the Talk Show Challenge: Television, Emotion and Public Spheres", *Constellations*, 6 (2), pp. 190–205.
—— (2001) "The Assembly Line of Greatness: Celebrity in Twentieth-Century America", in C. Lee Harrington and Denise D. Bielby (eds.), *Popular Culture: Production and Consumption*, Oxford: Blackwell, pp. 259–282.
Gavron, Hannah ([1966] 1983) *The Captive Wife: Conflicts of Housebound Mothers*, London: Routledge and Kegan Paul.
Geraghty, Christine (1981) "The Continuous Serial – a Definition", in Richard Dyer, Christine Geraghty, Marion Jordan and John Stewart (eds.), *Coronation Street*, London: BFI, pp. 9–26.
—— (1991) *Women and Soap Opera*, Oxford: Polity.
—— (2000) "Re-examining Stardom: Questions of Texts, Bodies and Performance", in Christine Gledhill and Linda Williams (eds.), *Reinventing Films Studies*, London: Arnold, pp. 183–201.
—— (2003) "Aesthetics and Quality in Popular Television Drama", *International Journal of Cultural Studies*, 6 (1), pp. 25–45.
—— (2005) "The Study of Soap Opera", in Janet Wasko (ed.), *A Companion to Television*, London: Blackwell, pp. 308–323.
—— (2006) "Discussing Quality: Critical Vocabularies and Popular Television Drama", in James Curran and David Morley (eds.), *Media and Cultural Theory*, London: Routledge, pp. 221–232.
Giddens, Anthony (1991) *Modernity and Self-Identity: Self and Society in the Late Modern Age*, Cambridge: Polity Press.
Gledhill, Christine (1987) "The Melodramatic Field: An Investigation", in Gledhill (ed.), *Home is Where the Heart is: Studies in Melodrama and the Woman's Film*, London: BFI, pp. 1–44.

—— (1992) "Speculations on the Relationship between Soap Opera and Melodrama", *Quarterly Review of Film & Video*, 14 (1–2), pp. 103–124.

Glynn, Kevin (2000) *Tabloid Culture: Trash Taste, Popular Power, and the Transformation of American Television*, Durham, NC: Duke University Press.

Goddard, Peter (1991) "Hancock's Half Hour: A Watershed in British Comedy", in John Corner (ed.), *Popular Television in Britain: Studies in Cultural History*, London: BFI, pp. 75–89.

Goffman, Erving (1972) *The Presentation of the Self in Everyday Life*, London: Pelican.

—— (1981) *Forms of Talk*, Oxford: Blackwell.

Gramsci, Antonio (1998) "Hegemony, Intellectuals, and the State", in John Storey (ed.), *Cultural Theory and Popular Culture*, Hemel Hempstead: Prentice Hall, pp. 206–219.

Haarman, Louann (2001) "Performing Talk", in Tolson (ed.), *Television Talk Shows: Discourse, Performance, Spectacle*, London: Lawrence Erlbaum, pp. 31–65.

Habermas, Jürgen (1984) "The Public Sphere: An Encyclopaedia Article" (1964), *New German Critique*, 3, pp. 49–55.

Hall, Stuart (1998) "Notes on Deconstructing 'The Popular' ", in John Storey (ed.), *Cultural Theory and Popular Culture: A Reader* (2nd edn), London: Prentice Hall, pp. 442–453.

Hand, Chris (2003) "The Advent of ITV and Television Ownership in Lower Income Households: Correlation or Causation?", www.rhul.ac.uk/media-arts/staff/TV%20in%20lower%20income%20households%5B1%5D.pdf (accessed 16 May 2006).

Heath, Stephen and Gillian Skirrow (1977) "Television: A World in Action", *Screen*, 18 (2), pp. 7–59.

Hebdige, Dick (1988) *Hiding in the Light*, London: Comedia.

Hestroni, Amir (2004) "The Millionaire Project: A Cross-Cultural Analysis of Quiz Shows from the United States, Russia, Poland, Norway, Finland, Israel, and Saudi Arabia", *Mass Communication and Society* 7 (2), pp. 133–156.

Hill, Annette (2005) *Reality TV: Audiences and Popular Factual Television*, London: Routledge.

Hill, John (1986) *Sex, Class and Realism: British Cinema 1956–63*, London: BFI.

Hills, Matt (2005) "Who Wants to be a Fan of *Who Wants to be a Millionaire?*: Scholarly Television Criticism, 'Popular Aesthetics' and Academic Tastes", in Catherine Johnson and Rob Turnock (eds.), *ITV Cultures: Independent Television Over Fifty Years*, Buckingham: Open University Press, pp. 177–195.

Hilmes, Michele (2007) "*Front Line Family*: 'Women's Culture' Comes to the BBC", *Media, Culture and Society*, 29 (1), pp. 1–25.

Hobson, Dorothy (2003) *Soap Opera*, Oxford: Polity.

Hoerschelmann, Olaf (2000) "Beyond the Tailfin: Education and the Politics of Knowledge on Big Money Quiz Shows", *Journal of Communication Inquiry*, 24 (2), pp. 177–194.

—— (2006) *Rules of the Game: Quiz Shows and American Culture*, New York: State University of New York Press.

Hoggart, Richard (1958) *The Uses of Literacy*, London: Penguin.

Holbrook, Morris B. (1993) *Daytime Television Gameshows and the Celebration of Merchandise*, Bowling Green, OH: Bowling Green State University Popular Press.

Holland, Pat (2006) *The Angry Buzz: This Week and Current Affairs Television*, London: I.B. Tauris.

Holmes, Su (2004a) " 'All you've got to worry about is the task, having a cup of tea, and what you're going to eat for dinner': Approaching Celebrity in *Big Brother*", in Su Holmes and Deborah Jermyn (eds.), *Understanding Reality Television*, London: Routledge, pp. 111–135.

—— (2004b) " 'Reality Goes Pop!': Reality TV, Popular Music and Narratives of Stardom in *Pop Idol* (UK)", *Television and New Media*, 5 (2), pp. 147–172.

—— (2005a) *British Television and Film Culture in the 1950s: Coming to a TV Near You!*, Bristol: Intellect Books.

—— (2005b) " 'Off Guard, Unkempt, Unready?': Deconstructing Contemporary Celebrity in *heat* Magazine", *Continuum: Journal of Media and Cultural Studies*, 19 (1), pp. 21–38.

—— (2005c) " 'Not the Final Answer': *Who Wants to be a Millionaire* and Revisiting Critical Approaches to the Quiz Show", *European Journal of Cultural Studies*, 8 (4), pp. 483–503.

—— (2005d) " 'It's a Woman!': The Question of Gender in *Who Wants to be a Millionaire*", *Screen*, 46 (2), pp. 155–173.

—— (2006) "It's a Jungle Out There!: The Game of Fame in Celebrity Reality TV", in Su Holmes and Sean Redmond (eds.), *Framing Celebrity: New Directions in Celebrity Culture*, London: Routledge, pp. 45–66.

—— (2007) "Torture, Treacle, Tears and Trickery: Celebrities, 'Ordinary' People, and *This is Your Life* (1955–65)", in Sean Redmond and Su Holmes (eds.), *A Reader in Stardom and Celebrity*, London: Sage.

Hopkins, Harry (1963) *The New Look: A Social History of the Fifties and Forties*, London: Secker and Warburg.

Horton, Donald and R. Richard Wohl (1956) "Mass Communication and Para-Social Interaction: Observations on Intimacy at a Distance", repr. in *Participations*, 3 (1), May 2006, www.participations.org/volume%203/issue%201/2-01-hotonwohl.htm (accessed 26 May 2006).

Huyssen, Andreas (1986) *After the Great Divide: Modernism, Mass Culture and Postmodernism*, Bloomington: Indiana University Press.

Jacobs, Jason (2000) *The Intimate Screen: Early British Television Drama*, Oxford: Clarendon Press.

—— (2001) "Issues of Judgement and Value in Television Studies", *International Journal of Cultural Studies*, 4 (4), pp. 427–444.

—— (2006) "The Television Archive: Past, Present, Future", *Critical Studies in Television*, 1 (1), pp. 13–20.

Jermyn, Deborah (2006) " 'Bringing out the Star in You': SJP, Carrie Bradshaw and the Evolution of Television Stardom", in Su Holmes and Sean Redmond (eds.), *Framing Celebrity: New Directions in Celebrity Culture*, London: Routledge, pp. 67–86.

Johnson, Catherine (2006) "Aesthetic Evaluation and Television History", plenary paper delivered at *Screen* conference, 30 June–2 July 2006.

Johnson, Catherine and Rob Turnock (eds.) (2005) *ITV Cultures: Independent Television Over Fifty Years*, Buckingham: Open University Press.

Jordan, Marion (1981) "Realism and Convention", in Richard Dyer, Christine Geraghty, Marion Jordan and John Stewart (eds.), *Coronation Street*, London: BFI, pp. 27–39.

Klinger, Barbara (1991) "Digressions at the Cinema: Reception and Mass Culture", in Patrick Bratlinger and James Naremore (eds.), *Modernity and Mass Culture*, Bloomington and Indianapolis: Indiana University Press, pp. 80–103.

Kress, Gunther (1986) "Language in the Media: The Construction of the Domains of Public and Private", *Media, Culture and Society*, 8, pp. 395–419.

Kumar, Krishan (1986) "Public Service Broadcasting and the Public Interest", in Colin MacCabe and Olivia Stewart (eds.), *The BBC and Public Service Broadcasting*, Manchester: Manchester University Press, pp. 46–61.

Laing, Stuart (1986) *Representations of Working-class Life, 1957–64*, Basingstoke: Macmillan.

Langer, John (1981) "Television's Personality System", *Media, Culture and Society*, 4, pp. 351–365.

—— (1998) *Tabloid Television: Popular Journalism and Other News*, London: Routledge.

Leman, Joy (1987) "Programmes for Women on 1950s British Television", in Gillian Dyer and Helen Baehr (eds.), *Boxed In: Women and Television*, London: Pandora Press, pp. 73–88.

Littler, Jo (2004) "Making Fame Ordinary: Intimacy, Reflexivity and 'Keeping it Real' ", *Mediactive*, 2, pp. 8–25.

Livingstone, Sonia (2005) "On the Relation between Audiences and Publics", in Livingstone (ed.), *Audiences and Publics: When Cultural Engagement Matters for the Public Sphere*, Bristol: Intellect Books, pp. 17–41.

Livingstone, Sonia and Peter Lunt (1994) *Talk on Television: TV Talk Shows and Public Debate*, London: Routledge.

Llewellyn-Smith, Caspar (2001) *Poplife: A Journey by Sofa*, London: Sceptre.

Lunt, Peter and Paul Stenner (2005) "*The Jerry Springer Show* as an Emotional Public Sphere", *Media, Culture and Society*, 27 (1), pp. 59–81.

Lury, Karen (1995) "Television Performance: Being, Acting and 'Corpsing' ", *New Formations*, 26, pp. 114–127.

MacCabe, Colin (1986) "Preface", in Colin MacCabe and Olivia Stewart (eds.), *The BBC and Public Service Broadcasting*, Manchester: Manchester University Press, pp. vii–viii.

Macdonald, Myra (2003) *Exploring Media Discourse*, London: Arnold.

Macnab, Geoffrey (2000) *Searching for Stars: Stardom and Screen Acting in British Cinema*, London: Continuum.

Mann, Denise (1992) "The Spectacularisation of Everyday Life", in Lynn Spigel and Denise Mann (eds.), *Private Screenings*, Minneapolis: University of Minnesota Press, pp. 41–69.

Marshall, P. David (1997) *Celebrity and Power: Fame in Contemporary Culture*, Minnesota: University of Minnesota Press.

McNicholas, Anthony (2005) "*EastEnders* and the Manufacture of Celebrity", *Westminster Papers in Communication and Culture*, 2 (2), pp. 22–36.

Medhurst, Andy (1991) "Every Wart and Pustule: Gilbert Harding and Television Stardom", in John Corner (ed.), *Popular Television in Britain: Studies in Cultural History*, London: BFI, pp. 60–74.

Mittell, Jason (2002) "Before the Scandals: The Radio Precedents of the Quiz Show Genre", in Michele Hilmes and Jason Loviglio (eds.), *Radio Reader: Essays in the Cultural History of Radio*, London: Routledge, pp. 319–342.

—— (2003) "Quiz and Audience Participation Programs", in Christopher Sterling and Michael Keith (eds.), *The Encyclopaedia of Radio*, New York: Fitzroy Dearborn, pp. 34–36.

—— (2004a) *Television and Genre: From Cop Shows to Cartoons*, London: Routledge.

—— (2004b) "A Cultural Approach to Television Genre Theory", in Robert C. Allen and Annette Hill (eds.), *The Television Studies Reader*, London: Routledge, pp. 171–181.

Modleski, Tania (1987) *Loving with a Vengeance: Mass Produced Fantasies for Women*, North Haven, CT: Shoestring Press.

Moran, Albert (1998) *Copycat TV: Globalisation, Program Formats and Cultural Identity*, Luton: University of Luton Press.

Moseley, Rachel (2000) "Makeover Takeover on British Television", *Screen*, 41 (3), pp. 299–314.

—— (2006) "Reconstructing Early Television for Women in Britain: Marguerite Patten, Television Cookery and the Production of Domestic Femininity", paper delivered at *Screen* conference, 30 June–2 July 2006.

Murray, Susan (2005) *Hitch Your Antenna to the Stars: Early Television and Broadcast Stardom*, London: Routledge.

Neale, Steve (1986) "Melodrama and Tears", *Screen*, 27 (6), pp. 2–22.

—— (1990) "Questions of Genre", *Screen*, 31 (1), pp. 45–66.

Newsom, John (1948) *The Education of Girls*, London: Faber and Faber.

O'Sullivan, Sara (2005) " 'The whole nation is listening to you': The Presentation of the Self on a Tabloid Talk Radio Show", *Media, Culture and Society*, 27 (5), pp. 719–738.

Oakley, Ann (1983) "New Introduction", in Hannah Gavron, *The Captive Wife: Conflicts of Housebound Mothers*, London: Routledge and Kegan Paul, pp. vii–xvi.

Obelkevich, James (1994) "Consumption" in James Obelkevich and Peter Catterall (eds), *Understanding Post-war British Society*, London: Routledge, pp. 141–154.

Otzen, Ellen (2003) "This is Your Life", *Guardian*, 15 May, www.guardian.co.uk (accessed 3 June 2005).

Petro, Patrice (1986) "Mass Culture and the Feminine: The 'Place' of Television in Film Studies", *Cinema Journal*, 25 (3), pp. 5–21.

Pilkington Report (1962) *Report of the Committee on Broadcasting, 1960*, Cmnd paper 1753. London: HMSO.

Rojek, Chris (2001) *Celebrity*, London: Reaktion Books.

Root, Jane (1986) *Open the Box: About Television*, London: Comedia.

Rose, Nikolas (1990) *Governing the Soul: The Shaping of the Private Self*, London: Routledge.

Scannell, Paddy (1979) "The Social Eye of Television, 1946–1955", *Media, Culture and Society*, 1, pp. 97–106.

—— (1990) "Public Service Broadcasting: The History of a Concept", in Andrew Goodwin and Garry Whannel (eds.), *Understanding Television*, London: Routledge, pp. 11–29.

—— (1991) (ed.) "Introduction: The Relevance of Talk", in Scannell (ed.), *Broadcast Talk*, London: Sage, pp. 1–13.

Scannell, Paddy (1996) *Radio, Television and Modern Life: A Phenomenological Approach*, Oxford: Blackwell.

Scannell, Paddy and David Cardiff (1981) "Radio in World War II", in *The Historical Development of Popular Culture in Britain 2*, Buckingham: Open University Press, pp. 32–77.

—— (1991) *A Social History of British Broadcasting*, Oxford: Basil Blackwell.

Sendall, Bernard (1982) *Independent Television in Britain: Origin and Foundation: 1946–62*, London: Macmillan.

Shattuc, Jane (1997) *The Talking Cure: TV Talk Shows and Women*, London: Routledge.

—— (1998) " 'Go Rikki': Politics, Perversion and Pleasure in the 1990s", in Christine Geraghty and David Lusted (eds.), *The Television Studies Book*, London: Arnold, pp. 212–227.

Silvey, Robert (1974) *Who's Listening? The Story of BBC Audience Research*, London: Allen and Unwin.

Sinfield, Alan (1989) *Literature, Politics and Culture in Post-war Britain*, Oxford: Blackwell.

Singer, Ben (2001) *Melodrama and Modernity: Early Sensational Cinema and its Contexts*, New York: Columbia University Press.

Skovmand, Michael (2000) "Barbarous TV: Syndicated Wheels of Fortune", in Horace Newcomb (ed.), *Television: The Critical View* (6th edn), Oxford: Oxford University Press, pp. 367–382.

Smith, W.O. Lester (1957) *Education*, Harmondsworth: Penguin.

Sobchack, Vivian (2000) "What is Film History? or, the Riddle of the Sphinxes", in Christine Gledhill and Linda Williams (eds.), *Reinventing Film Studies*, London: Arnold, pp. 300–315.

Sparks, Richard and John Tulloch (eds.) (2000) *Tabloid Tales: Global Debates over Media Standards*, Oxford: Rowman and Littlefield.

Spigel, Lynn (1992) *Make Room for TV: Television and the Family Ideal in Post-war America*, Chicago: University of Chicago Press.

Stokes, Jane (1999) *On Screen Rivals: Cinema and Television in the United States and Britain*, London: Macmillan.

Storey, John (2001) *Culture Theory and Popular Culture: An Introduction*, London: Prentice Hall.

Street, Sarah (1997) *British National Cinema*, London: Routledge.

Strinati, Dominic (1992) " 'The Taste of America': Americanisation and Popular Culture in Britain", in Dominic Strinati and Stephen Wagg (eds.), *Come On Down: Popular Culture in Post-War Britain*, London: Routledge, pp. 46–81.

Sutcliffe, Thomas (2000) "The Year the Quiz Show Addiction Became Something More Obsessive", *Independent*, 29 December, p. 12.

Sydney-Smith, Susan (2002) *Beyond Dixon of Dock Green: Early British Police Series*, London: I.B. Tauris.

Teurlings, Jan (2001) "Producing the Ordinary: Institutions, Discourses and Practices in Love Game Shows", *Continuum: Journal of Media & Cultural Studies*, 15 (2) pp. 249–263.

Thomas, Howard (1977) *With an Independent Air*, London: Weidenfeld and Nicholson.

Thompson, J.P. (1990) *Ideology and Modern Culture*, Cambridge: Polity Press.

Thumim, Janet (2002a) "Introduction: Small Screens, Big Ideas", in Thumin (ed.), *Small Screen, Big Ideas: Television in the 1950s*, London: I.B. Tauris, pp. 1–18.

—— (2002b) "Women at Work: Popular Drama on British Television c1955–60", in Thumim (ed.), *Small Screen, Big Ideas: Television in the 1950s*, London: I.B. Tauris, pp. 207–222.

—— (2004) *Inventing Television Culture: Men, Women and the "Box"*, Oxford: Oxford University Press.

Tolson, Andrew (2001) "Introduction: The Talk Show Phenomenon", in Tolson (ed.), *Television Talk Shows: Discourse, Performance, Spectacle*, pp. 1–30.

Tulloch, John (1976) "Gradgrind's Heirs: The Presentation of 'Knowledge' in British Quiz Shows", *Screen Education*, Summer, pp. 3–13.

Turner, Graeme (1996) *British Cultural Studies: An Introduction*, London: Routledge.

—— (2004) *Understanding Celebrity*, London: Sage.

Turnock, Rob (forthcoming) *Television and Consumer Culture: Britain and the Transformation of Modernity*, London: I.B. Tauris.

van Zoonen, Liesbet (2001) "Desire and Resistance: *Big Brother* and the Recognition of Everyday Life", *Media, Culture and Society*, 23 (5), pp. 299–677.

—— (2004) "Popular Qualities in Public Broadcasting", *European Journal of Cultural Studies*, 7 (3), pp. 275–282.

van Zoonen, Liesbet, Joke Hermes and Kees Brants (1998) "Introduction: of Public and Popular Interests", in Liesbet van Zoonen, Joke Hermes and Kees Brants (eds.), *The Media in Question: Popular Cultures and Public Interests*, London: Sage, pp. 1–13.

Walker, Janet (1991) "Interventions in Families", in David Clarke (ed.), *Marriage, Domestic Life and Social Change*, London: Routledge, pp. 188–213.

Wayne, Mike (2000) "*Who Wants To Be a Millionaire?*: Contextual Analysis and the Endgame of Public Service Television", in Dan Fleming (ed.), *Formations: A 21st Century Media Studies Textbook*, Manchester: Manchester University Press, pp. 196–216.

Whannel, Garry (1992) "The Price is Right but the Moments are Sticky: Television, Quiz and Games Shows and Popular Culture", in Dominic Strinati and Stephen Wagg (eds.), *Come On Down: Popular Culture in Post-War Britain*, London: Routledge, pp. 179–201.

Wheatley, Helen (2002) "*Mystery and Imagination*: Anatomy of a Gothic Anthology Series", in J. Thumim (ed.), *Small Screens, Big Ideas: Television in the 1950s*, London: I.B. Tauris.

—— (2004) "The Limits of Television? Natural History Programming and the Transformation of Public Service Broadcasting", *European Journal of Cultural Studies*, 7 (3), pp. 325–339.

—— (2006) "Colonial Spectacle, Domestic Space: Natural History Television in the 1950s", paper delivered at *Screen* conference, 30 June–2 July 2006.

White, Mimi (2002) "Television, Therapy and the Social Subject; or the TV Therapy Machine", in James Friedman (ed.), *Reality Squared: Televisual Discourse on the Real*, New Brunswick, NJ: Rutgers University Press.

Wieten, Jan, Graham Murdock and Peter Dahlgren (eds.) (2000) *Television Across Europe: A Comparative Introduction*, London: Sage.

Williams, Melanie (2003) "Housewife's Choice: *Woman in a Dressing Gown*", in Ian Mackillop and Neil Sinyard (eds.), *British Cinema of the 1950s: A Celebration*, Manchester: Manchester University Press, pp. 143–156.

Williams, Raymond (1983) *Keywords: A Vocabulary of Culture and Society*, London: Fontana.

Wilson, Elizabeth (1980) *Only Halfway to Paradise: Women in Post-war Britain, 1945–68*, London and NY: Tavistock.

Wilson, Sherryl (2005) "Real People with Real Problems? Public Service Broadcasting, Commercialism and *Trisha*", in Catherine Johnson and Rob Turnock (eds.), *ITV Cultures: Independent Television Over Fifty Years*, Buckingham: Open University Press, pp. 159–176.

Wood, Helen (2001) " 'No, YOU Rioted!': The Pursuit of Conflict in the Management of 'Lay' and 'Expert' Discourses on *Kilroy*", in Tolson (ed.), Television Talk Shows: Discourse, Performance, Spectacle, pp. 65–88.

Wyndham-Goldie, Grace (1977) *Facing the Nation: Television and Politics 1936–76*, London: Bodley Head.

Index